Cinemas and Cinema-Going in the United Kingdom

Decades of Decline, 1945–65

Cinemas and Cinema-Going in the United Kingdom

Decades of Decline, 1945–65

Sam Manning

LONDON
ROYAL HISTORICAL SOCIETY
INSTITUTE OF HISTORICAL RESEARCH
UNIVERSITY OF LONDON PRESS

Published by

UNIVERSITY OF LONDON PRESS
SCHOOL OF ADVANCED STUDY
INSTITUTE OF HISTORICAL RESEARCH
Senate House, Malet Street, London WC1E 7HU

Available to download free or to purchase the hard copy edition at
https://www.sas.ac.uk/publications.

ISBNs
978-1-912702-34-3 (hardback edition)
978-1-912702-35-0 (paperback edition)
978-1-912702-36-7 (PDF edition)
978-1-912702-38-1 (ePub edition)
978-1-912702-37-4 (.mobi edition)

DOI 10.14296/320.9781912702367

New Historical
PERSPECTIVES

Cover image: Interior of Odeon, Sheffield, July 1956 (Picture Sheffield,
Sheffield City Council Archives and Local Studies Service).

Contents

List of illustrations		vii
Acknowledgements		ix
List of abbreviations		xi
Introduction		1
1.	Cinema-going experiences	17
2.	The decline of cinema-going	51
3.	Cinema-going and the built environment	91
4.	Cinema exhibition, programming and audience preferences in Belfast	129
5.	Film exhibition in post-war Sheffield	163
	Conclusion	193
	Appendices	201
	Bibliography	209
	Index	225

List of illustrations

Figure

1.1   Children in Botanic Gardens, Belfast, 1950s.   26

2.1   Ritz stage show, Belfast, June 1953.   57

2.2   Recorded admissions in Northern Ireland cinemas,
      1948–57.   62

3.1   Lido, Shore Road, Belfast, 1955.   97

3.2   Rathcoole, 1936 and 1960–1 (Alpha circled).   99

3.3   Interior of Odeon, Sheffield, July 1956.   113

5.1   Rex Cinema (centre) and surrounding area, Intake,
      Sheffield, 1951.   165

5.2   Rex Cinema, Sheffield, c.1943–5.   165

5.3   Gross revenue of ancillary items at the Rex Cinema,
      Sheffield, 1945–65.   169

5.4   Cartoon Cinema, Fitzalan Square, Sheffield, c.1959–60.   180

5.5   Classic Cinema, Fitzalan Square, Sheffield, 1963.   181

5.6   Percentage of total admissions sold by day of week at
      the Cartoon Cinema, April 1961–January 1962 and the
      Classic Cinema, January 1962–November 1964.   181

5.7   Annual attendance of film screenings at the Library
      Theatre, Sheffield.   187

5.8   Film screening at the Library Theatre, Sheffield,
      November 1950.   187

Table

2.1   Introduction of UK television services.   53

2.2   Belfast cinema admissions at six-monthly intervals,
      March 1952–September 1954.   60

2.3   Number of cinema licences granted in Belfast and
      Sheffield, 1945–64.   61

2.4   Percentage of families owning television licences, 1957–65.   63

4.1	Entertainments Duty receipts in Northern Ireland, 1949–60.	130
4.2	Revenue, taxation and admissions in selected Belfast cinemas, 1948–61.	133
4.3	Ten highest-grossing films at the Ritz, 7 April 1952 to 28 March 1953.	144
4.4	Exhibition of *The Quiet Man* in Belfast.	146
4.5	Dutiable admissions at Belfast cinemas, 1952–3 and 1956–7.	152
4.6	Dutiable admissions at the Broadway and the Regent, 1952–61.	154
5.1	Selected revenue and expenditure at the Rex Cinema, Sheffield, 1945–64.	167
5.2	Ten highest-grossing main features at the Rex Cinema, August 1945–July 1960.	175
5.3	Most successful programmes at the Rex Cinema by year (August to July), 1945–6 to 1959–60.	175
5.4	Gross box-office revenue and admissions at the Sheffield Cartoon/Classic Cinema, 1961–4.	183
5.5	Ten highest weekly attendances, Classic Cinema, January 1962–November 1964.	184

Acknowledgements

This book has been a long time in the making and many people helped to make it possible. My interest in cinema history began as an undergraduate student at the University of Sheffield and was then developed during an MA at Queen's University Belfast. I then furthered this interest in the doctoral thesis from which this book emerged. I am grateful to all the students and staff who encouraged (or at least tolerated) my enthusiasm for historical cinemas.

I wish to thank the late Keith Jeffery for his help during my MA and for his encouragement in the PhD application process. My PhD supervisor Sean O'Connell has been very generous with his advice, guidance and support. Since completing my PhD, I have received support from many academic colleagues both at Queen's University Belfast and on the *European Cinema Audiences* project.

I have been extremely fortunate that many intelligent people have read part or all the manuscript. I would like to thank Kieran Connell, Ida Milne, Tim Somers, Conor Campbell, Stuart Irwin, Ryan Mallon and Jack Crangle for kindly reading parts of my PhD thesis. My examiners, Melvyn Stokes and Fearghal McGarry, offered positive feedback and encouraged me to convert the thesis into a monograph. One of the great benefits of publishing in the *New Historical Perspectives* series has been the guidance, mentoring and support of several talented historians. John Sedgwick, Penny Summerfield, Heather Shore and Robert James all read a draft of my monograph and offered suggestions for improvement. Their advice and editorial guidance has undoubtedly made this a far better book than it might have been. I am also indebted to everyone at the Royal Historical Society, the Institute of Historical Research and University of London Press who helped to create this book, particularly Jane Winters, Emily Morrell, Philip Carter and Kerry Whitston.

The work was carried out in a number of archives and libraries. I would like to thank archivists and staff at Belfast Central Library, the Cinema Museum, the Cinema Theatre Association Archive, PRONI, Sheffield City Archives, Sheffield Local Studies Library and Sheffield University. I am particularly grateful to my former colleagues at McClay Library Special Collections, who accommodated my employment alongside doctoral research. My extended research trips to Sheffield could not have happened without the kind hospitality of Chris Wood and the Dobson family. Thank you for tolerating me during two enjoyable summers.

I am privileged to have spent so much of my research speaking to people about their memories and experiences of cinema-going. Thank you to everyone I interviewed as part of this project and to the many people who helped organize these interviews.

I would like to thank all my friends and family members who offered support and guidance throughout this process. I am especially grateful to my two nieces, Daisy and Tilly, who always put a smile on my face when times are tough. My greatest debt is to Lauren Rose Browne, without whose love and support this book would never have seen the light of day. I dedicate this book to her.

List of abbreviations

ABC	Associated British Cinemas
BBC	British Broadcasting Corporation
BBFC	British Board of Film Censors
CEA	Cinematograph Exhibitors' Association
FIDO	Film Industry Defence Organisation
ITV	Independent Television
NATKE	National Association of Theatrical and Kinema Employees
PRONI	Public Record Office of Northern Ireland
UTV	Ulster Television

Introduction

Cinema-going was the most popular commercial leisure activity in the first half of the twentieth century. UK cinema attendance grew significantly in the Second World War and peaked in 1946 with 1.6 billion recorded admissions. Though 'going to the pictures' remained a popular pastime for the remainder of the 1940s, the transition from war to peacetime altered citizens' leisure habits. During the 1950s, a range of factors including increased affluence, the growth of television ownership, population shifts and the diversification of leisure activities led to rapid declines in attendance. By 1965, admissions had plummeted to 327 million and the cinema held a far more marginal existence in the nation's leisure habits. Many cinemas closed their doors and those that remained open increasingly competed with a range of venues including bingo halls, dance halls, bowling alleys, cafés and people's homes. Cinema attendances fell in all regions, but the speed, nature and extent of this decline varied widely across the United Kingdom. By linking broad national developments to regional case studies of two similarly-sized industrial cities, Belfast and Sheffield, this book adds nuance and detail to our understanding of regional variations in film exhibition, audience habits and cinema-going experiences during a period of profound social and cultural change.

Over the past thirty years, many cinema historians have shifted their focus away from the aesthetic and textual analysis of a small number of canonical films towards an understanding of cinema as a cultural institution and cinema-going as a historically situated leisure practice located in specific geographical and temporal contexts.[1] The historical literature on cinemas and cinema-going has expanded greatly and scholars have used diverse methodologies to address a wide range of topics such as censorship, exhibition, distribution, film popularity, programming and reception. Proponents of new cinema history conceive cinema-going as 'a social act performed by people of flesh and blood … situated within specific social,

---

[1] For further information on recent developments in audience studies see D. Biltereyst and P. Meers, 'Film, cinema and reception studies: revisiting research on audience's filmic and cinematic experiences', in *Reception Studies and Audiovisual Translation*, ed. E. Di Giovanni and Y. Gambier (Amsterdam, 2018), pp. 21–42.

cultural, historical and spatial confines'.[2] In these studies, the places where people watched films and their experiences of cinema-going are as important as the films that were shown. More recently, new cinema history has witnessed a spatial turn as scholars have increasingly asked how geography and topography impacted on audiences and exhibition.[3] In spite of this recent scholarship, further work is required to comprehensively understand the regional variations of UK cinema attendance, the heterogeneous nature of audiences and the ways that consumer tastes were shaped by local identities. In his 2003 article on the geography of cinema-going in Great Britain, Barry Doyle stated that while cinema historians had created a 'clearer picture of the class, age and gender elements in the changing cinema audience', the geography of cinema's decline had not been fully investigated.[4] This remains true, and the following analysis expands the geographical range of cinema-going studies, demonstrates the benefits of using detailed local case studies in cinema history research and shows that place was as significant a factor as age, class or gender in shaping the cinema-going experience.

Beginning at the end of the Second World War, this book builds upon Richard Farmer's study of wartime cinemas and cinema-going. He demonstrated the profound impact that government regulations, wartime conditions, enemy bombing campaigns and the conscription of staff had on cinemas. He charted the growth in admissions throughout the Second World War, arguing that wartime cinema-going can only be understood with reference to wartime experiences.[5] The upheaval of war also had an impact on the operation and profitability of post-war cinemas. On the same day that Germany offered its unconditional surrender to the Allies, the *Belfast Telegraph* commented that:

---

[2] D. Biltereyst, R. Maltby and P. Meers, 'Cinema, audiences and modernity: an introduction', in *Cinema, Audiences and Modernity: New Perspectives on European Cinema History*, ed. D. Biltereyst, R. Maltby and P. Meers (Abingdon, 2012), pp. 1–16, at p. 2. See also *Explorations in New Cinema History: Approaches and Case Studies*, ed. R. Maltby, D. Biltereyst and P. Meers (Chichester, 2011); *The Routledge Companion to New Cinema History*, ed. D. Biltereyst, R. Maltby and P. Meers (Abingdon, 2019).

[3] R. C. Allen, 'The place of space in film historiography', in *Tijdschrift voor Mediageschiedenis*, ix (2006), 15–27; J. Klenotic, 'Putting cinema history on the map: using GIS to explore the spatiality in cinema', in *Explorations in New Cinema History: Approaches and Case Studies*, ed. R. Maltby, D. Biltereyst and P. Meers (Chichester, 2011), pp. 58–84; P. Ercole, D. Treveri Gennari and C. O'Rawe, 'Mapping cinema memories: emotional geographies of cinemagoing in Rome in the 1950s', *Memory Studies*, x (2017), 63–77.

[4] B. Doyle, 'The geography of cinemagoing in Great Britain, 1934–1994: a comment', *Historical Journal of Film, Radio and Television*, xxiii (2003), 59–71, at p. 59.

[5] R Farmer, *Cinemas and Cinema-Going in Wartime Britain: the Utility Dream Palace* (Manchester, 2016).

[c]inemas must be coining money. I would like to build a cinema anywhere in Northern Ireland! How many times in the last six years has one heard that remark when either passing a cinema and seeing the crowds or while waiting in the queue to get in to a cinema. The average patron has not given a thought as to what it really costs to run a modern cinema.[6]

Payments for Entertainment Tax, film rentals, wages, utility bills, rates, advertising, rents and repairs all added to operating costs and cinemas had to generate large amounts of revenue to make ends meet.[7] In 1958, the same paper reported that '[r]unning costs and overheads have increased by anything from 200 to 400 per cent since before the war – yet cinema prices have gone up only a fraction of that figure'.[8] These reports offer a glimpse of the constraints that cinemas faced in the post-war years. How they adapted to these challenges to provide entertainment for their patrons is one of this book's key concerns.

The operation of cinemas, however, cannot be fully understood without consideration of the audiences who regularly paid to see their favourite stars projected on the silver screen. People chose to spend their time and money at the cinema in preference to other forms of commercial leisure. While these people increasingly opted to spend their disposable income on other activities and goods, cinema-going remained a profoundly important social activity and provided a great deal of pleasure for millions of UK citizens. The cinema was more than just a place to watch films; it provided a range of important social functions, such as a site for children to congregate on Saturday mornings or a darkened space for courting couples to meet free from parental supervision. Many of the routines of cinema attendance were similar in Belfast and Sheffield. But by contrasting the responses to certain customs, such as the playing of the British national anthem at the end of an evening's performance, this book puts geographical variations in attitudes and behaviour into sharp relief.

There was no single cinema-going experience and age, class, gender and location were all key determinants of cinema attendance. In 1949, Mark Abrams found that the most frequent cinema-goers were female, young and working class.[9] During the 1950s, cinema audiences were increasingly male and the proportion of sixteen- to twenty-four-year-olds increased dramatically. Sue Harper and Vincent Porter claimed that these changes

---

[6] *Belfast Telegraph*, 7 May 1945.

[7] Entertainment Tax (also referred to as Entertainments Duty by the Northern Ireland Government) was a sales tax on cinema tickets introduced in 1916 and abolished in 1961.

[8] *Belfast Telegraph*, 14 Feb. 1958.

[9] M. Abrams, 'The British cinema audience, 1949', *Hollywood Quarterly*, iv (1950), 251–5.

'were so extensive that they affected patterns of popularity' and that the film industry struggled to cope with variations in audience taste.[10] Audience habits and the nature of attendance changed as post-war austerity gave way to increased affluence and a burgeoning consumer society. During the 1950s, rising incomes, population shifts, the introduction of television, new forms of youth culture and a greater range of leisure activities were some of the myriad factors that contributed to the rapid decline in cinema attendance. By the mid 1960s, cinema-going was still popular, especially among the young working class, yet it was no longer the predominant leisure activity in the United Kingdom. Many of the first cinemas to close were smaller local neighbourhood venues and, while many people attended the cinema less frequently, greater amounts of disposable income meant that they were prepared to spend more on individual trips to larger, more luxurious city centre and suburban cinemas. Another key development was the shift towards home-oriented consumption. As Richard Farmer stated, 'the declining appeal of the cinema, both absolutely and relatively, needs to be assessed vis-à-vis the growing appeal of the home'.[11] Economic gains also led to increased car and television ownership and greater expenditure on consumer goods. These gains, however, were geographically uneven and it is clear that many people in working-class areas were unable to participate in the benefits of the affluent society.

Post-war social scientists and subsequent historians have debated the relative importance of the factors that led to cinema's decline. In the early 1960s, a group of exhibitors, distributors and producers asked economist John Spraos to examine the problems facing the industry. In 1962, he published a statistical report analysing cinema's demise, the industry's response and implications for future policy. He cited the growth in working-class television ownership, the closure of neighbourhood cinemas, increased travel distances, less frequent public transport and higher admission prices as key factors in cinema's decline.[12] The Broadcasting Research Unit's 1987 report downplayed a monocausal relationship between television and cinema, arguing that 'television was framed; the real culprits were Elvis Presley, expresso [sic] coffee, the Town and Country Planning Act of 1947 and the sclerosis of the British film industry'.[13] Stuart Hanson also de-emphasized the causal relationship between cinema and television, placing

[10] S. Harper and V. Porter, 'Cinema audience tastes in 1950s Britain', *Journal of Popular British Cinema*, ii (1999), 66–82, at p. 67.

[11] Farmer, *Cinemas and Cinema-going*, p. 241.

[12] J. Spraos, *The Decline of the Cinema: an Economist's Report* (London, 1962).

[13] D. Docherty, D. Morrison and M. Tracey, *The Last Picture Show? Britain's Changing Film Audiences* (London, 1987), p. 5.

greater emphasis on the changing nature of consumer capitalism and the emergence of the 'affluent society'. He acknowledged a wide range of factors and observed that television ownership, the growth of consumerism and the relocation of working-class communities all contributed to the decline in cinema attendance.[14] Only by digging deeper into the source material can we assess the relative impact of these factors at a regional level.

The findings presented here also make a broader contribution to the social and cultural history of post-war Britain and Ireland. Leisure historian Jeffrey Hill observed that the interwar years have received far more attention than the post-war period and this study builds on the work of social historians, such as Claire Langhamer and Adrian Horn, who have investigated post-war women's leisure and juke boxes respectively.[15] It follows Brett Bebber's assertion that 'in neglecting close attention to the political and social contexts from which forms of leisure emerged and developed, historians risk separating their analysis of leisure and how people enjoyed them from the structural and material circumstances in which people lived'.[16] Its chronology allows also for a reconsideration of social change in the 1950s in a broader context. In 2008, Nick Thomas asserted that the 1950s has 'often been dealt with as an interim period between the decades standing on either side, and in particular as a kind of antechamber of the social upheaval of the 1960s'.[17] In their authoritative account of 1950s British cinema, Harper and Porter reconsidered a misunderstood decade 'widely perceived as being a dull period – an interregnum sandwiched between the inventive 1940s and the exciting 1960s'.[18] Detailed regional case studies show that the 1950s was neither an antechamber nor an interregnum. The decade's social changes had a clear and profound impact on leisure patterns, consumer taste and people's engagement with popular culture, marking a momentous period of change for both cinemas and the cities that housed them. It is for this for this reason that this book investigates how changes to

---

[14] S. Hanson, *From Silent Screen to Multi-Screen: a History of Cinema Exhibition in Britain Since 1896* (Manchester, 2007).

[15] J. Hill, '"What shall we do with them when they're not working?": leisure and historians in Britain', in *Leisure and Cultural Conflict in Twentieth-Century Britain*, ed. B. Bebber (Manchester, 2012), pp. 11–40, at pp. 31–2; C. Langhamer, *Women's Leisure in England* (Manchester, 2000); A. Horn, *Juke Box Britain: Americanisation and Youth Culture, 1945–60* (Manchester, 2010).

[16] B. Bebber, 'Introduction: Contextualising leisure history', in *Leisure and Cultural Conflict in Twentieth-Century Britain*, ed. B. Bebber (Manchester, 2012), pp. 1–10, at p. 1.

[17] N. Thomas, 'Review essay: will the real 1950s please stand up? Views of a contradictory decade', *Cultural and Social History*, v (2008), 227–36, at p. 228.

[18] S. Harper and V. Porter, *British Cinema of the 1950s: the Decline of Deference* (Oxford, 2003), p. 1.

the built environment and the spaces of film exhibition shaped patterns of post-war cinema attendance.

A tale of two cities

The regional approach taken in this book allows us to go beyond the peculiarities and idiosyncrasies of a single location. It is a response to Richard Maltby's assertion that new cinema history 'requires its practitioners to work out how to undertake small-scale practicable projects that, whatever their local explanatory aims, also have the capacity for comparison, aggregation and scaling'.[19] It also addresses the suggestion of Kuhn et al.that a positive step towards understanding cinema-going habits is comparative work between cities and regions within a single country.[20] There are several excellent national studies, such as Trevor Griffiths's book on Scottish cinema-going in the first half of the twentieth century and Peter Miskell's social history of cinema in Wales. [21] The national scope of these studies, however, means that they are often unable to pay close attention to the local context required to compare particular communities. Meanwhile, local studies often fail to place their conclusions in a broader context and to connect their findings to those in other localities. The focus on two medium-sized industrial cities in different parts of the United Kingdom closes this lacuna. It follows the example of Robert James, who emphasized local sources to investigate cinema-going in interwar Portsmouth, Derby and South Wales. He then linked these examples to broader national trends and to other leisure activities to assess the geographical diversity of film consumption.[22]

In the period under review, Belfast and Sheffield relied on a small number of labour-intensive industries, were populated by large numbers of skilled labourers and displayed low levels of immigration. In both cities, slum clearance, new housing developments and employment changes resulted in centrifugal population shifts. Despite these surface similarities, Belfast and Sheffield faced different social pressures and developed along separate trajectories. These changes affected the everyday leisure habits of

[19] R. Maltby, 'New cinema histories', in *Explorations in New Cinema History: Approaches and Case Studies*, ed. R. Maltby, D. Biltereyst and P. Meers (Chichester, 2011), pp. 3–40, at p. 13.

[20] A. Kuhn, D. Biltereyst and P. Meers, 'Memories of cinema-going and film experience: an introduction', *Memory Studies*, x (2017), 3–16, at p. 11.

[21] T. Griffiths, *The Cinema and Cinema-Going in Scotland, 1896–1950* (Edinburgh, 2013); P. Miskell, *A Social History of the Cinema in Wales, 1918–1951* (Cardiff, 2006).

[22] R. James, *Popular Culture and Working-Class Taste in Britain 1930–1939: a Round of Cheap Diversions?* (Manchester, 2010).

their citizens in specific ways and this book examines how localized factors impacted on cinema exhibition and attendance. While cinema-going habits varied between neighbourhoods, communities and cities, the existence of separate local and national governments meant that cinemas operated in different regulatory frameworks. Cinemas in Belfast and Sheffield, for instance, were subject to different rates of taxation, film quota legislation and Sunday opening laws.

Belfast is the largest city in Northern Ireland, which comprises the six counties which remained part of the United Kingdom after the 1921 partition of Ireland. Though the city is infamous for the sectarian divisions between Protestants and Catholics, Sean O'Connell highlighted that it was subject to many of the same developments as other UK industrial cities. He characterizes the years from 1914 to 1968 in Belfast as a period of 'conservative modernity ... marked by a dichotomy between new forms of work, consumption and recreation and a regressive cultural politics'.[23] Belfast grew rapidly in the late nineteenth century and was the industrial heartland of the province of Ulster, noted for its shipbuilding industry and the large numbers of women employed in its tobacco factories and textile mills. In 1944, trade journal *Kinematograph Weekly* (hereafter *Kine Weekly*) claimed that it 'lives, eats, dreams and thinks in terms of the building of ships, of aircraft, of naval bases, of the American Army, of the German "blitz" that has left gaping wounds in its narrow, dirty streets and in its gaunt buildings'.[24] The war had a long-lasting effect on the built environment with slum areas and bomb-sites remaining well into the 1950s, when its population stood at 443,680.[25] Traditional industries declined after the war, though new jobs were created on greenfield sites and there was an increase in public sector and administrative roles.[26] While wages and living conditions improved dramatically during the period under review, Graham Brownlow noted that in Northern Ireland 'unemployment was considerably higher, and incomes per head generally much lower, than the UK average'.[27] Journalists often highlighted Belfast's geographical and cultural distance from its counterparts in England, Scotland and Wales. In 1954, for instance, *Picture Post* noted the city's cultural conservatism, describing it as a city 'as different from the rest of the United Kingdom as

---

[23] S. O'Connell, 'An age of conservative modernity, 1914–1968', in *Belfast 400: People, Place and History*, ed. S. Connolly (Liverpool, 2012), pp. 271–316, at p. 315.

[24] *Kinematograph Weekly*, 13 Jan. 1944.

[25] *The Ulster Year Book: the Official Year Book of Northern Ireland* (Belfast, 1953), p. 35.

[26] W. Maguire, *Belfast: a History* (Lancaster, 2009), pp. 213–17.

[27] G. Brownlow, 'Business and labour since 1945', in *Ulster since 1600: Politics and Society*, ed. L. Kennedy and P. Ollerenshaw (Oxford, 2012), pp. 291–307, at p. 292.

pickles from suet pudding: a city that builds great ships – and has grave unemployment; where religion is a fire – and the police carry guns; where loyalties battle – and jokes are cracked about it'.[28] However, a focus on these more conspicuous aspects of Belfast life obscures the fact that it was architecturally and economically similar to many industrial British cities. By looking beyond, but not ignoring, Belfast's sectarian divisions, we can assess how post-war changes affected everyday leisure habits.

The inclusion of Belfast is a response to Adrian Horn, who, in his study of post-war juke boxes, claimed that the 'regionality of American popular culture's reception by young people in Britain is one that could be pursued much further'. He suggested Northern Ireland as an area 'that should prove to be particularly fruitful for the cultural historian'.[29] Given the predominance of Hollywood films in the period under review, this study looks at the relative popularity and impact of American films and builds on the work of historians who have shown the various ways in which American popular culture was received in, and mediated by, communities in various localities.[30] The inclusion of Belfast expands the underdeveloped social history of Northern Ireland before the Troubles.[31] As Kevin Bean observed, scholars often view the post-war years through the prism of the later Troubles failing 'to situate the post-war development of the region in a broader context as a product of wider and more powerful external forces and ideologies'.[32] This book both places Belfast in the broader context of UK cinema-going and contributes to the historiography of cinema on the island of Ireland. While there are many studies that successfully address the experiences of post-war cinema-goers, they are related mostly to the British rather than the Irish context.[33]

---

[28] *Picture Post*, 20 Feb. 1954.

[29] Horn, *Juke Box Britain*, p. 193.

[30] P. Swann, *The Hollywood Feature Film in Postwar Britain* (London, 1987); M. Glancy, *Hollywood and the Americanization of Britain: From the 1920s to the Present* (London, 2014); *Hollywood Abroad: Audiences and Cultural Exchange*, ed. R. Maltby and M. Stokes (London, 2004); *Identifying Hollywood's Audiences: Cultural Identity and the Movies*, ed. R. Maltby and M. Stokes (London, 1999); *American Movie Audiences: from the Turn of the Century to the Early Sound Era*, ed. R. Maltby and M. Stokes (London, 1999); *Hollywood Spectatorship: Changing Perceptions of Cinemas Audiences*, ed. R. Maltby and M. Stokes (London, 2001).

[31] Notable exceptions include M. Elliott, *Hearthlands: a Memoir of the White City Housing Estate in Belfast* (Belfast, 2017) and J. Crangle, '"Left to fend for themselves": immigration, race relations and the state in twentieth century Northern Ireland', *Immigrants and Minorities*, xxxvi (2018), 20–44.

[32] K. Bean, 'Roads not taken', in Belfast Exposed Photography, *Portraits from a 50's Archive* (Belfast, 2005), pp. 8–19, at p. 8.

[33] Notable exceptions include S. McBride and R. Flynn, *Here's Looking at you, Kid! Ireland goes to the Pictures* (Dublin, 1996); H. Byrne, '"Going to the pictures": the female audience

In 1956, the Yorkshire city of Sheffield held a population of 526,000 and was known for its industrial workforce and steel industry, which provided its largest source of employment.[34] Despite the success of this industry, journalist Joan Skipsey painted a bleak picture of post-war Sheffield, warning that the 'casual visitor to the city is likely to go away without a clue as to the grounds for confidence. Whichever station he arrives at, a bleak expanse of roadway confronts him, unadorned by welcoming café or suggestion of metropolis'.[35] In 1954, *The Economist* observed that '[t]here is nothing showy about Sheffield. Unlike the typical mercantile city, it has no fine buildings, no great tradition in art or music'. It added, nonetheless, that an 'unexpected attraction of Sheffield is the indefinable air of romance that haunts the ugly, smoky streets'.[36] In the 1950s, the numbers employed in manufacturing declined and there was a considerable increase in those occupied in construction, distribution and professional services.[37] Despite this, in 1957, 650 of the UK's 700 cutlery firms were still located in Sheffield, and, in 1961, over 44 per cent of its working population were employed in engineering and metals.[38] In 1962, sociologist M. P. Carter observed that the city housed a large working-class population and that women were 'restricted to employment as clerks, shop assistants and factory workers'.[39] The perception of Sheffield as a solely industrial city persisted into the 1960s, when journalist Stan Gee stated that any claim 'that Sheffield can be classed as an entertainments centre is more than likely to be greeted with derision'.[40]

A regional analysis of Belfast and Sheffield contributes to the historiography of both cities. Belfast is served by many general historical surveys and edited collections that provide a wealth of information across

---

and the pleasures of cinema', in *Media Audiences in Ireland*, ed. M. Kelly and B. O'Connor (Dublin, 1997), pp 88–106; D. McGuinness, 'Media consumption and Dublin working class cultural identity' (unpublished Dublin City University PhD thesis, 1999); E. O'Leary, *Youth and Popular Culture in 1950s Ireland* (2018); G. Finlay, '"Celluloid menace", art or the "essential habit of the age"?', *History Ireland*, xv (2007), 34–40.

[34] S. Pollard, 'The growth of population', in *Sheffield and its Region: a Scientific and Historical Survey*, ed. D. L. Linton (Sheffield, 1956), pp. 172–80, at pp. 179–80.

[35] *Illustrated*, 31 May 1947, quoted in *Damned Bad Place, Sheffield: Anthology of Writing About Sheffield Through the Ages*, ed. S. Pybus (Sheffield, 1994), p. 217.

[36] *The Economist*, 16 Jan. 1954.

[37] W. Hampton, *Democracy and Community: a Study of Politics in Sheffield* (London, 1970), p. 47.

[38] D. Hey, *A History of Sheffield* (Lancaster, 2011), p. 280; Hampton, *Democracy and Community*, p. 40.

[39] M. P. Carter, *Home, School and Work: a Study of the Education and Employment of Young People in Britain* (Oxford, 1962), p. 18.

[40] *The Star*, 27 Feb. 1964.

a broad time period.[41] Details of Belfast's historical cinemas are well documented and studies by scholars such as John Hill and Kevin Rockett provide assessments of film production, exhibition and distribution in Northern Ireland.[42] While David Fowler has assessed Northern Ireland's youth culture, there has been little focused analysis of its citizen's everyday leisure and social habits.[43] There are few historical surveys of Sheffield and, in 2011, David Hey observed that his general survey was the first since the 1948 publication of Mary Walton's *Sheffield: its Story and its Achievements*.[44] Aside from several local publications documenting Sheffield's historical cinemas, the history of post-war Sheffield often excludes its leisure habits and focuses on its socialist politics, steel industry and public housing schemes, such as Park Hill.[45]

The growth and development of cinema was broadly similar in Belfast and Sheffield. From its emergence in the late nineteenth century, cinema's provision of affordable and accessible entertainment guaranteed its popularity, particularly among the urban working class. By the outbreak of the First World War, there were 3,500 British cinemas and weekly cinema admissions increased from 7 million in 1914 to over 20 million in 1917.[46] While a variety of Sheffield's halls and theatres exhibited films from 1896 onwards, its first purpose-built cinema, the Union Street Picture Palace, opened in August 1910. The construction of twenty-nine cinemas between 1910 and 1915 marked the city's first cinema building boom.[47] The development of Belfast's cinema exhibition industry mirrored many industrial British cities

---

[41] *Enduring City: Belfast in the Twentieth Century*, ed. F. W. Boal and S. A. Royle (Belfast, 2006); *Belfast 400: People, Place and History*, ed. S. Connolly (Liverpool, 2012); Maguire, *Belfast: a History*.

[42] M. Open, *Fading Lights, Silver Screen: a History of Belfast Cinemas* (Antrim, 1985); J. Doherty, *Standing Room Only: Memories of Belfast Cinemas* (Belfast, 1997); T. Hughes, *How Belfast Saw the Light: a Cinematic History* (Newtonards, 2014); Belfast Public Libraries, Irish and Local Studies Department, *Checklist of Belfast Cinemas* (Belfast, 1979); P. Larmour, 'Cinema paradiso', *Perspective*, iv (1996), 23–7; 'The big feature', *Perspective*, v (1997), 29–36; J. Hill, *Cinema and Northern Ireland: Film, Culture and Politics* (2006); K. Rockett with E. Rockett, *Film Exhibition and Distribution in Ireland, 1909–2010* (Dublin, 2011).

[43] D. Fowler, *Youth Culture in Modern Britain, c.1920–c.1970* (Basingstoke, 2008).

[44] Hey, *A History of Sheffield*, p. viii.

[45] Sheffield Cinema Society, *The A.B.C. of the Cinemas of Sheffield* (Sheffield, 1993); C. Shaw and S. Smith, *Sheffield Cinemas: Past and Present* (Sheffield, 1999); P. Tuffrey, *South Yorkshire's Cinemas and Theatres* (Stroud, 2011); R. Ward, *In Memory of Sheffield's Cinemas* (Sheffield, 1988).

[46] N. Hiley, '"Let's go to the pictures": the British cinema audience in the 1920s and 1930s', *Journal of Popular British Cinema*, ii (1999), 39–53, at p. 40.

[47] C. Shaw and C. Stacey, 'A century of cinema', in *Aspects of Sheffield 2: Discovering Local History*, ed. M. Jones (Barnsley, 1999), pp. 182–200, at pp. 197–200.

and the number of Belfast cinemas increased from sixteen at the outbreak of the First World War to twenty-six in 1920.[48]

The interwar years were characterized by the switch from silent to sound cinema, the introduction of legislation designed to protect the British film industry, the construction of larger suburban cinemas and the growth of the three major circuits: Associated British Cinemas (ABC), Gaumont and Odeon.[49] In the 1920s, fifteen new Sheffield cinemas opened and the 1927 *Kinematograph Year Book* lists forty-five operational venues.[50] The lack of new housing developments and the large British circuit's limited presence in Northern Ireland meant that only two Belfast cinemas opened in the 1920s and, by 1927, it had twenty-five cinemas.[51] However, seventeen new Belfast cinemas were constructed in the 1930s, the majority of which were located on the main arterial roads leading away from its city centre. Admissions rose in the 1930s and the cinema remained an inexpensive, exciting and pleasurable activity in a period of poverty and economic hardship for many working-class patrons. Cinema's social appeal widened and the middle-classes were drawn to the new upmarket city centre and suburban 'picture palaces'. Cinema-going was often habitual and many patrons went several times a week, irrespective of what was shown. By 1939, UK cinema admissions totalled 990 million and there were thirty-nine cinemas listed in Belfast. In Sheffield there were fifty-two venues listed, with an estimated seating capacity of 56,300.[52]

Higher wages, a greater need for relaxation and reduced competition from alternative leisure activities meant that cinema attendance increased dramatically during the Second World War. Towns and cities across the UK and Ireland housed a range of cinemas, which were a visible presence in, and central to the communal life of, city centres, suburbs and inner-city neighbourhoods. In 1948, Rachael Low estimated that there were 4,706 cinemas in Great Britain and the *Kinematograph Year Book* lists a further 120 cinemas in Northern Ireland.[53] *The Economist* noted that while approximately

---

[48] Rockett, *Film Exhibition*, p. 37.

[49] For further information on the major cinema circuits, see A. Eyles, *Odeon Cinemas: Oscar Deutsch Entertains our Nation* (London, 2001); *Odeon Cinemas 2: from J. Arthur Rank to the Multiplex* (London, 2005); *Gaumont British Cinemas* (London, 1996); *ABC: the First Name in Entertainment* (London, 1993). From 1941, the Rank Organisation operated both the Gaumont and Odeon circuits.

[50] *Kinematograph Year Book 1927* (1927), pp. 392–4.

[51] *Kinematograph Year Book 1927* (1927), pp. 445–6.

[52] *Kinematograph Year Book 1939* (1939), pp. 632–4, 710–1; C. Shaw, *Images of England: Sheffield Cinemas* (Stroud, 2001), p. 8.

[53] R. Low, 'Trade statistics', in *Kinematograph Year Book 1949* (1949), pp. 50–1; *Kinematograph Year Book 1948* (1948), pp. 445–9.

2,000 cinemas were 'of good modern standard', the rest were 'small, locality houses which deserve none of the superlatives of the industry and show old films of poor quality'.[54] There was a great contrast between local neighbourhood 'fleapits' and city centre 'picture palaces'; venues varied widely in terms of price, programming, seating capacity, décor, amenities, clientele and status.

As attendances fell dramatically during the 1950s many cinemas closed down. In April 1950, the Board of Trade estimated that there were 4,583 cinemas operating in Great Britain with a total seating capacity of 4,221,200.[55] By 1965, these figures fell to 1,971 and 2,012,600 respectively.[56] In Sheffield, while two new city centre first-run cinemas opened in 1956 and 1961, thirty-nine cinemas closed from 1957 to 1965. In 1956, Belfast was served by forty-four cinemas with a total seating capacity of 40,000.[57] While several new cinemas were built in Belfast suburbs in the mid 1950s, attendances fell precipitously and the number of Belfast cinemas declined to thirty-seven by 1961, and to thirty-one by 1963.[58] No further venues closed until 1966.

These developments should be understood in a broader geographical context. Cinema attendance fell elsewhere, though there were wide international variations in the nature of this decline. In the United States, where television penetrated homes earlier than in the UK, average weekly admissions fell from their peak of 90 million in 1946 to 60 million in 1950 and 40 million in 1960.[59] The 1946 peak in UK cinema attendances was earlier than in other European nations such as France (1947), Italy (1955) and West Germany (1956).[60] In the Republic of Ireland, cinema-going retained its popularity for longer than in Northern Ireland and cinema admissions fell from their peak of 54.1 million in 1954, to 43.8 million in 1959 and to 30 million in 1965.[61] Audiences also fell out of love with the cinema at

---

[54] *The Economist*, 27 Dec. 1947.

[55] Central Statistical Office, *Annual Abstract of Statistics 1951*, no. 88 (London, 1951), p. 83.

[56] Central Statistical Office, *Annual Abstract of Statistics 1966*, no. 103 (London, 1966), p. 81.

[57] *Kinematograph Year Book 1956* (1956), pp. 407–8; *Kinematograph Weekly*, 5 July 1956; F. W. Boal, 'Big processes and little people: the population of metropolitan Belfast 1901–2001', in *Enduring City: Belfast in the Twentieth Century*, ed. F. W. Boal and S. A. Royle (Belfast, 2006), pp. 57–83, at p. 82.

[58] *Kinematograph and Television Year Book 1961* (London, 1961), pp. 410–11; *Kinematograph and Television Year Book 1963* (London, 1963), pp. 353–4.

[59] United States Census Bureau, *The Statistical History of the United States, from Colonial Times to the Present* (New York, 1986), p. 400.

[60] P. Sorlin, *European Cinemas, European Societies 1939–1990* (1991), p. 89.

[61] UNESCO, *Basic Facts and Figures: International Statistics Relating to Education, Culture and Mass Communication* (Paris, 1960), pp. 159–64; Rockett, *Film Exhibition*, p. 461; E. O'Leary, 'Teenagers, everyday life and popular culture in 1950s Ireland' (unpublished National University of Ireland, Maynooth PhD thesis, 2013), pp. 92–3.

different rates, with Sedgwick et al. observing that the 'dramatic decline in attendance seen in the United States, United Kingdom, and elsewhere in the 1950s and 1960s did not occur in Italy until the 1970s'.[62]

Sources and methodology

How can historians access the everyday cinema experiences of individuals, communities and neighbourhoods? Richard Maltby advocated the use of localized oral history projects in new cinema history as they 'consistently tell us that the local rhythms of motion picture circulation and the qualities of the experience of cinema attendance were place-specific and shaped by the continuities of life in the family, the workplace, the neighbourhood and the community'.[63] This book follows scholars who use memory as a tool to investigate historical experiences of cinema attendance across the UK.[64] The most recent of these is the 'Cultural Memory and British Cinemagoing of the 1960s' project, led by Melvyn Stokes, which has gathered responses from 893 questionnaires and eighty interviews.[65] This book deploys oral history testimony gathered from fifty residents (nineteen female, thirty-one male) of Belfast and Sheffield born between 1925 and 1950, the majority of whom self-identified as working class.[66] Interviewees were recruited through interaction with local community groups, recommendations from colleagues and contacts from previous projects. They were drawn from a wide age range and from different geographical areas within Belfast and Sheffield. They displayed wide variation in their cinema-going habits, the venues they attended and their levels of film consumption. Participants were offered the option of anonymity, though only three interviewees requested the use of a pseudonym. While aliases protect the identity of participants and can encourage them to speak more candidly, they treat people as representatives rather than as individuals and clash with many

[62] J. Sedgwick, P. Miskell and M. Nicoli, 'The market for films in postwar Italy: evidence for both national and regional patterns of taste', *Enterprise & Society*, xx (2019), 199–228, at p. 204.

[63] Maltby, 'New cinema histories', p. 9.

[64] H. Richards, 'Memory reclamation of cinema going in Bridgend, South Wales, 1930–1960', *Historical Journal of Film, Radio and Television*, xxiii (2003), 341–55; J. Stacey, *Star Gazing: Hollywood Cinema and Female Spectatorship* (London, 1994), p. 236; A. Kuhn, *An Everyday Magic: Cinema and Cultural Memory* (London, 2002); *Enter the Dream-House: Memories of Cinemas in South London from the Twenties to the Sixties*, ed. M. O'Brien and A. Eyles (London, 1993); A. Martin, *Going to the Cinema: Scottish Memories of Cinema* (Edinburgh, 2000).

[65] For further information, see 'Cultural memory and British cinema-going' <https://www.ucl.ac.uk/library/digital-collections/collections/cinema/index> [accessed 5 June 2019].

[66] See Appendix 3 for further information on all the interviewees.

of social history's fundamental objectives. This research follows Donald Ritchie's statement that, '[h]aving sought to give "voice to the voiceless", it is inconsistent to render them nameless'.[67]

Given that details of historical cinemas in Belfast and Sheffield, such as location, opening date and seating capacity, are already well documented, the main purpose of the interviews was not to gather empirical information. Rather, it was to uncover emotional responses, to gather unique memories of cinema-going, to understand what the cinema *meant* to interviewees, and to reveal where they placed their memories in relation to their broader social and leisure lives. Rather than ask participants to narrate their life histories, the interviews followed a thematic approach and questions focused on the social background of the participants, memories of cinema-going, film preferences, leisure habits and the wider social history of post-war Belfast and Sheffield. While a questionnaire was used throughout the interviews, participants were free to discuss other subjects and digressions from the topic of cinema-going were often revealing in situating the place of cinema-going in participants' wider social lives. These sources are assessed critically by acknowledging that memory texts do not provide a transparent view of the past. As Matthew Jones observed, cinema memory is constructed rather than simply recalled, recollections are shaped by the context in which they are collected and there are problems of selective memory, misremembering and hindsight. He argued that memory itself should become the object of study and analysed as discourse rather than data.[68]

Oral history interviewees are not the only sources available to investigate the social and spatial elements of cinema attendance, and this is not an oral history of cinemas and cinema-going like Annette Kuhn's pioneering ethnography of 1930s film audiences.[69] Rather, it is a history of cinemas and cinema-going that uses a range of primary source material to complement oral history testimony. Memories provide personal, subjective and socially constructed accounts, and they both corroborate and challenge the evidence provided by box-office returns, cinema records, newspapers, council minutes and trade journals. This book uses a combination of qualitative and quantitative sources and emphasises the use of box-office statistics, business records and financial data. This broad range of sources allows us to drill down into the specific institutional arrangements in the two cities and then link these to audience experiences and the operation of cinemas. Historians such as John Sedgwick have developed statistical models to investigate interwar

---

[67] D. A. Ritchie, *Doing Oral History* (2nd edn, Oxford, 2003), p. 126.

[68] M. Jones, 'Memories of British cinema', in *The Routledge Companion to British Cinema History*, ed. I. Q. Hunter, L. Porter and J. Smith (Abingdon, 2017), pp. 397–405.

[69] Kuhn, *An Everyday Magic*.

cinema-going, and Sue Harper and Robert James have analysed film ledgers to demonstrate the tastes of specific social groups.[70] James, however, lamented that 'very few film ledgers remain extant, so it is extremely difficult to deploy this type of material to make definitive taste comparisons between the classes'.[71] Belfast and Sheffield, however, are relatively well served by records of cinema attendance. There are weekly summaries of Entertainments Duty for many Belfast cinemas, which provide the basis for a comparative assessment of the popularity of particular films.[72] For Sheffield, the records of the Rex, the Cartoon Cinema (later the Classic) and the Library Theatre provide an insight into various sites and forms of exhibition.[73]

The extensive scrutiny of local sources provides greater detail of regional developments, challenging the conclusions of historians who make broader generalizations about national trends in cinema-going. Newspapers reports in the *Belfast Telegraph* and the Sheffield *Star* show how changes in cinema-going were reported in regional contexts in relation to wider social and economic developments. In the period under review, the former had an estimated daily circulation of between 195,000 and 200,000 copies, and an adult readership of over 600,000.[74] Both papers were the most widely circulated in their respective cities and are those most commonly cited by cinema-goers in oral history interviews. It is likely that the journalistic processes of framing and selection adopted by these papers shaped the way that citizens understood the post-war decline in cinema attendance. The placement of articles within these newspapers also shows how cinema-going related to other aspects of daily life such as work, housing and alternative leisure activities. The use of council minutes reveals how Belfast Corporation and Sheffield City Council licenced and regulated cinemas. As Farmer stated, 'the power exercised by local laws and local licensing authorities and watch committees meant that cinema exhibition was shaped by the specificities of

[70] J. Sedgwick, *Popular Filmgoing in 1930s Britain: a Choice of Pleasures* (Exeter, 2000); S. Harper, 'A lower middle-class taste community in the 1930s: admissions figures at the Regent cinema, Portsmouth, UK', *Historical Journal of Film, Radio and Television*, xxiv (2004), 565–87; 'Fragmentation and crisis: 1940s admission figures at the Regent Cinema, Portsmouth, UK', *Historical Journal of Film, Radio and Television*, xxvi (2006), 361–94; R. James, 'Cinema-going in a port town, 1914–1951: film booking patterns at the Queens Cinema, Portsmouth', *Urban History*, xl (2013), 315–35.

[71] R. James, 'Popular film-going in Britain in the 1930s', *Journal of Contemporary History*, lxvii (2011), 271–87, at p. 274.

[72] PRONI, FIN/15/6/A-D, Ministry of Finance records of Entertainments Duty.

[73] Sheffield City Archives, MD7333, Rex Cinema (Sheffield) Limited.

[74] M. Brodie, *The Tele: a History of the Belfast Telegraph* (Belfast, 1995), p. 112; *Belfast Telegraph*, 1 March 1963.

place, evolving in response to local events, cultures, tastes and prejudices'.[75] These local sources are supplemented by reports in national weekly trade journal *Kine Weekly*, which although rarely read by cinema-goers, provides a rich source of information on exhibition, distribution and promotion. It often published columns dedicated to Belfast and Sheffield and included comprehensive reports on local branch meetings of the Cinematograph Exhibitors' Association (CEA). These sources are deployed to convey the diverse nature of the cinema industry and the importance of place as a determinant of cinema attendance. By assessing two local case studies alongside national developments, and by placing these findings in a broader social and cultural context, it is possible to provide the necessary detail for a more nuanced picture of post-war cinema-going across the UK.

The book is divided into five chapters that collectively show the extent to which residents of Belfast and Sheffield constituted distinct cinema communities. The first chapter investigates what the experience of cinema-going was like and how it corresponded to other aspects of daily life. Cinemas were social spaces and it examines audience behaviour and the social practices of cinema-going. It looks at the social and economic distinctions patrons made between cinemas, film reception and the relationship between cinema-going and the life cycle. Chapter 2 places these findings in the broader context of cinema's decline and assesses the extent to which television was responsible for the fall in cinema attendance. It then examines the impact of new forms of youth culture and the response of cinema exhibitors. Chapter 3 focuses on the relationship between cinema-going and the built environment and on the place of cinemas within the topography of Belfast and Sheffield. It explores the small number of cinemas that opened in this period, the greater number of cinemas that closed and the reasons the local press gave for these closures. It also looks at how perceptions of cinemas changed and how they were viewed within their respective cities. The final two chapters assess the operation of cinemas, the service they provided to customers and the ways that patrons consumed films. In these chapters, financial data is combined with programme listings to build a profile of film preferences and attendance patterns. Chapter 4 investigates the implementation of Entertainments Duty in Northern Ireland and uses quantitative records kept by the Northern Ireland Ministry of Finance to compare cinema programming and audience preferences in five Belfast cinemas from 1948 to 1961. The final chapter uses the records of three Sheffield venues to investigate film exhibition across the period. These records display the diversity of film exhibition in Sheffield and the relationship between programming, admissions and box-office revenue.

[75] Farmer, *Cinemas and Cinemagoing in Wartime Britain*, p. 12.

1. Cinema-going experiences

While all cinema experiences include the act of watching a projected film in a specially defined space, what it means to go the cinema has changed significantly since the first moving images were screened in the late nineteenth century. By the time cinema attendance peaked in 1946, cinema-going was a long-established social habit with its own rituals, customs and conventions. Despite the precipitous post-war decline in admissions and the changing nature of attendance, it remained a profoundly important cultural practice for millions of UK citizens. Scholars such as Sue Harper, Robert James and Mark Jancovich have investigated cinema-going habits in various regions, foregrounding age, class and gender as key determinants of attendance.[1] These studies consistently show that while similar mass cultural products were shown in venues across the UK, cinema-going habits were geographically diverse.

What follows is an investigation of cinema-going experiences told principally from the perspective of the cinema-goer. It draws from oral history testimony to examine four key aspects of post-war cinema attendance: the social and economic distinctions patrons made between cinemas, changes in cinema-going habits over the course of the life cycle, responses and reactions to films, and audience behaviour both in and outside the cinema auditorium. This analysis builds on the recent spatial turn in new cinema history, developing the interest in 'the relationship between memories of cinema-going, and geographical and topographical space'.[2] In adopting this approach, it looks beyond the physical venues of film exhibition to examine the relationship of cinema to everyday life and

---

[1] For instance, see S. Harper, 'A lower middle-class taste community in the 1930s: admissions figures at the Regent cinema, Portsmouth, UK', *Historical Journal of Film, Radio, and Television*, xxiv (2004), 563–88; R. James, '"A very profitable enterprise": South Wales miners' institute cinemas in the 1930s', *Historical Journal of Film, Radio and Television*, xxvii (2007), 27–61; R. James, 'Cinema-going in a port town, 1914–1951: film booking patterns at the Queens cinema, Portsmouth', *Urban History*, xl (2013), 315–35; H. Richards 'Memory reclamation of cinema going in Bridgend, South Wales, 1930–1960', *Historical Journal of Film, Radio and Television*, xxiii (2003), 341–55; M. Jancovich, L. Faire and S. Stubbings, *The Place of the Audience: Cultural Geographies of Film Consumption* (London: 2003).

[2] P. Ercole, D. Treveri Gennari and C. O'Rawe, 'Mapping cinema memories: emotional geographies of cinemagoing in Rome in the 1950s', *Memory Studies*, x (2017), 63–77, at p. 64.

rituals, assessing how it was structured by attachment to neighbourhoods, communities and cities. According to Kuhn et al., oral history research aims 'not to objectively reconstruct the past based on subjective memories of respondents, but to look at how memories of cinema-going are constructed and how they complement (or contradict) institutional, economic or text-based approaches to the historical study of film reception'.[3] By combining personal narratives with evidence from trade journals, local newspapers and sociological studies, it is possible to show how these experiences were shaped by wider external factors such as government legislation or the provision of cinemas in local neighbourhoods.

Social and economic distinctions

Within industrial cities such as Belfast and Sheffield patrons made clear distinctions between venues and frequented cinemas for various social and economic reasons. A comparison of two working-class communities – the Holyland in Belfast and Heeley in Sheffield – shows how the range of venues available in local neighbourhoods created distinctive cinema-going practices. The Holyland was a largely Protestant working-class community located about one mile south of Belfast city centre.[4] Though interviewees described the area as distinctly working-class, they also claimed it was 'respectable' and 'upwardly mobile'. Their nearest cinema, the Apollo, opened in October 1933 and was the first of two local cinema-going options available for Holyland residents. It was the first cinema constructed in Belfast since 1923 and, following the transition from silent cinema to 'talkies', advertised itself as the 'the first cinema in Belfast built for sound'.[5] The second option, the Curzon, opened three years after the Apollo. Its higher prices, larger seating capacity and grander décor marked it out as one of the more glamorous art deco suburban picture palaces built in 1930s Belfast.

While interviewees recollected attendance at both the Apollo and the Curzon, they emphasized the contrast between the two cinemas and highlighted the Apollo's convenience, cheaper ticket prices, favourable location and geographical accessibility. For Norman Campbell, the Apollo was a mid-market cinema: It 'wasn't quite a fleapit, but it wasn't just to the

---

[3] A. Kuhn, D. Biltereyst and P. Meers, 'Memories of cinema-going and film experience: an introduction', *Memory Studies*, x (2017), 3–16, at p. 10.

[4] For further details on the Holyland, see S. Manning, 'Post-war cinema-going and working-class communities: a case study of the Holyland, Belfast, 1945–1962', *Cultural and Social History*, xiii (2016), 539–55.

[5] *Belfast Telegraph*, 27 Oct. 1933.

same standard [as the Curzon]'.[6] Other participants were less complimentary, using adjectives such as 'grim' to describe its plain, unadorned interior. George Brown added that it 'was very downmarket. It was sort of a working-class cinema'.[7] Liz Smyth's comments highlight the perceived higher status of the Curzon: it 'was slightly more expensive and a wee bit more upmarket … the Apollo was a bit of a dump, but it was at the corner'.[8] Ann Gorman's remark that the Curzon was 'a little bit closer to bigger houses than what you would have had close to the Apollo' shows that it attracted patrons with greater amounts of disposable income and from a wider geographical area.[9] Both cinemas were recalled as mixed social spaces and participants highlighted socioeconomic rather than religious or national divisions. As Liz Smyth recalled, the Apollo 'was definitely a slightly rougher [cinema]. They were rougher boys who went of all religions'.[10]

A distinctive feature of the Holyland was its proximity to Queen's University and the Belfast Museum, which both offered alternatives to the mainstream commercial films shown in the local cinemas. Though membership of the Queen's University Film Society reached 858 during its first season in 1952 and rose to 1,200 in 1954, no participants recalled attendance at its screenings, held in the university's Whitla Hall.[11] Many Holyland residents, however, attended screenings at the museum. From November to March, free Saturday screenings in its lecture room provided an alternative cinema-going option and by 1949, 15,900 (11,950 'juveniles' and 3,910 adults) admissions were recorded.[12] It exhibited a range of educational films and emphasized the didactic nature of these screenings on subjects such as natural history, food supply and geography.[13] In 1954, the museum boasted that the screenings were 'well patronised by children and adult audiences and on a number of occasions we have had to turn

[6]   Interview with Norman Campbell, Belfast, 4 June 2014.
[7]   Interview with Anne Connolly, Belfast, 28 May 2015; interview with George Brown, Belfast, 26 Aug. 2014.
[8]   Interview with Ronnie and Elizabeth Smyth, Spa, County Down, 27 Aug. 2014.
[9]   Interview with Ann Gorman, Belfast, 23 Oct. 2014.
[10]   Interview with Ronnie and Elizabeth Smyth, Spa, County Down, 27 Aug. 2014.
[11]   *Belfast Telegraph*, 29 May 1952; *Irish News*, 14 June 1954.
[12]   City and County Borough of Belfast, *Report of the Committee of Belfast Museums and Art Gallery: for Year Ending 31ˢᵗ March, 1946* (Belfast, 1946), p. 3; City and County Borough of Belfast, *Report of the Committee of Belfast Museums and Art Gallery: for Year Ending 31ˢᵗ March, 1949* (Belfast, 1949), p. 3; City and County Borough of Belfast, *Report of the Committee of Belfast Museums and Art Gallery: for Year Ending 31ˢᵗ March 1952* (Belfast, 1952), pp. 4–5.
[13]   City and County Borough of Belfast, *Report of the Committee of Belfast Museums and Art Gallery: For Year Ending 31ˢᵗ March, 1949* (Belfast, 1949), p. 3.

members of the public away through lack of accommodation'.[14] Tickets for Saturday morning screenings were distributed to local primary schools and Ann Gorman recalled that 'we would have a mental arithmetic test at the end of class … the first ten hands in the air with the correct answers won the ten tickets'.[15]

Heeley is an inner-city area located one mile south of Sheffield city centre. Like the Holyland, it housed a largely working-class population and, in 1960, it was described as a 'thickly populated area of old houses on a steep hill not far from the city centre'.[16] There were three cinemas in the local area: the Heeley Coliseum, the Heeley Green Picture House and the Heeley Palace. In a similar fashion to residents of the Holyland, the Heeley interviewees made clear social and economic distinctions between these cinemas. Several participants recalled that the Heeley Palace was more expensive than the Heeley Coliseum, which was described as both a 'fleapit' and a 'working-class cinema'. The 1,450-seat Heeley Palace opened in 1911 and the 900-seat Heeley Coliseum opened in 1913.[17] The Coliseum was slightly more expensive than the Heeley Green Picture House and was described by David Ludlam as 'a bit of a bug hut'.[18] The proximity of the Coliseum and the Palace to the tram line on Chesterfield Road meant that they were likely to attract patrons from a wider geographical area.

Heeley residents recollected attendance at a range of cinemas in adjacent areas including the Abbeydale, the Woodseats and the Chantrey. The 1,512-seat Abbeydale cinema, located one mile west of Heeley, opened in 1920.[19] Interviewees described it as 'probably the best local cinema house' and as an upmarket alternative to the Heeley cinemas.[20] Many interviewees, however, favoured local cinemas for their convenience and geographical accessibility. While many participants frequented the Heeley cinemas in childhood, they were deemed as unsuitable for the teenage rituals of courtship. When Carol Palmer entered adolescence, she forgot 'about the Heeley Coliseum and poor Heeley Palace, they were childhood places'.[21] In a similar fashion

---

[14] Belfast Municipal Museum and Art Gallery, *The Museum in Pictures: Museum & Art Gallery, Stranmillis, Belfast, Souvenir (1929–1954): Illustrated Souvenir to Commemorate the Twenty-Fifth Anniversary of the Opening of the Museum and Art Gallery, Stranmillis, Belfast, in the Summer of 1929* (Belfast, 1954), p. 15.

[15] Interview with Ann Gorman, Belfast, 23 Oct. 2014.

[16] Yorkshire Regional Association of the National Association of Youth Service Officers, *Adventuring with Youth in Yorkshire, 1960* (1960), p. 22.

[17] Shaw, *Sheffield Cinemas*, p. 85.

[18] Interview with David Ludlam, Sheffield, 25 June 2014.

[19] *Kinematograph Year Book 1958* (London, 1958), pp. 336–8.

[20] Interview with David Ludlam, Sheffield, 25 June 2014.

[21] Interview with Andrew and Carol Palmer (pseudonyms), Sheffield, 7 Aug. 2015.

to Belfast's Curzon, the upmarket status of the Abbeydale meant that it attracted patrons from a wider geographical area. Several participants' memories connected their perceptions of the Abbeydale to its architecture and Bill Allerton described its décor as 'muted grandeur ... [it] was sort of this really nice halfway house where you felt you were having an experience something other than just going to watch something'.[22] David Ludlam's memories also emphasize its architectural features: 'it was magnificent, the décor was excellent. The standard of seating and so on was good ... certainly better than most other cinemas in the outlying districts'.[23]

In both cities, interviewees made clear distinctions between local neighbourhood cinemas and their often larger and grander city centre counterparts, which were noted for their different clientele, upmarket reputation and better facilities. Sheffield's Gaumont cinema was commonly described as 'posh' and its status was defined further by its large seating capacity (2,300) and high prices. Margaret Bruton grew up in the Parson Cross area of Sheffield and described her three local venues – the Forum, the Ritz and the Capitol – as 'working-class cinemas'. The Gaumont, meanwhile, 'was bigger and more classy ... It were in the centre of town and you would have got all middle-class people going into town'.[24] Helen Carroll added that 'the Gaumont was the one to go to ... but then there were some that were a bit grotty and you wouldn't go there unless you were desperate'.[25] Sheffield University newspaper *Darts* noted the lack of upmarket cinemas in Sheffield city centre, warning the new student whose 'first thought is the down-town cinemas' that he is 'bound to make pretty invidious comparisons with his home town'. It commented that there were only two modern downtown cinemas and that the other three were outdated theatres with aged décor and uncomfortable seating.[26] The arrival of a new ABC cinema in May 1961 changed perceptions of the cinema hierarchy in Sheffield. Robert Heathcote was born in 1950 and claimed that it was the most upmarket cinema in Sheffield city centre, with better seating than its 1930s counterparts and an undercover area for queuing.[27]

In Belfast, interviewees recalled the Ritz (renamed the ABC in 1963) as the most upmarket cinema and, like the Gaumont, its status was related to its large seating capacity, programming practices and suitability as a courtship venue. Noel Spence contrasted the Ritz to local neighbourhood cinemas,

[22] Interview with Bill Allerton, Sheffield, 27 July 2015.
[23] Interview with David Ludlam, Sheffield, 25 June 2014.
[24] Interview with Margaret Bruton (b. Sheffield), Belfast, 20 Oct. 2014.
[25] Interview with Helen Carroll, Sheffield, 23 July 2015.
[26] *Darts*, 5 March 1959.
[27] Interview with Robert Heathcote, Sheffield, 30 July 2015.

stating that its reputation was defined by its lighting, advertisements, restaurant and organ. Its well-attired manager, commissionaires and usherettes contrasted with smaller cinemas where 'the manager would arrive on a bike and he'd go inside and then the lights would flicker on and you'd go in and he'd sell you your ticket and then he'd come round the other side of the box and tear it in two and then he'd run down with a torch and show you to your seat if he could be bothered'.[28]

Patrons further defined cinemas by their programming practices. Some venues were simultaneously associated with high-brow foreign language films and low-brow 'continental' sex films. The fact that the Rank Organisation did not produce or exhibit 'X' certificated films meant that other producers had to rely on more specialized cinemas, with *The Economist* claiming that some venues 'will not accept films that they consider to be insufficiently pornographic'.[29] While *Darts* advised students that the Wicker cinema exhibited European films, interviewees emphasized its reputation for risqué 'X' certificated films. Comments such as 'the nude films were at the Wicker' and 'they used to do a lot of sex films' were common.[30] In 1958, the manager rejected the cinema's unsavoury reputation, claiming that it attracted a diverse range of respectable patrons: 'Doctors, dons, business men, working men and the usual teenage regulars make up the Wicker's patrons for the most part'.[31] In Belfast, the Mayfair cinema held a similar reputation and interviewees highlighted its reputation for subtitled films and salacious content. Meanwhile, student newspaper *The Gown* remarked that 'it is certainly a great joy to have the Mayfair, which is concerned almost entirely with Continental pictures'.[32] The 1959 conversion of the Mayfair into the News and Cartoon Cinema reflected the lack of popular appeal for foreign language films and the increased competition of television. *Kine Weekly* reported that this conversion meant 'that there is now no outlet in Belfast for Continental films. This seems a pity as there is a nucleus of film-goers in the city who want to see good Continental product'.[33] *Belfast Telegraph* reporter Martin Wallace added further that '[s]ub-titles have always been a problem but, if a foreign film was successful at the Mayfair, it had a chance of being shown in several towns in Ulster. Now the market has virtually

---

[28] Interview with Noel Spence, Comber, Co. Down, 26 March 2014.

[29] *The Economist*, 1 Jan. 1955.

[30] *Darts*, 10 Oct. 1957; interview with Mike Higginbottom, Sheffield, 20 Aug. 2015; interview with Ann and Bob Slater, Sheffield, 28 July 2015.

[31] *The Star*, 24 Jan. 1958.

[32] Interview with Noel Spence, Comber, Co. Down, 26 March 2014; *The Gown*, 12 May 1955.

[33] *Kinematograph Weekly*, 29 Jan. 1959.

closed'.[34] In 1962, it hosted the International Cinema Club and from 1964 to 1966, screened late night films for the Belfast Festival.[35] Journalist Barry White thought it was ironic that the films were being shown at the News and Cartoon Cinema, which, as the Mayfair, was the 'last home of the Continental cinema in Belfast before it succumbed'.[36]

Cinemas were multifunctional spaces that appealed to a variety of different audiences. A small number of cinemas screened foreign language films to cater for the increasing number of migrants making their homes in Britain's industrial cities. The 1961 census revealed that that 4 per cent of Sheffield residents were born outside of England, and its small but growing migrant population were catered for by special Sunday screenings.[37] From the mid 1950s, for example, the News Theatre screened a series of Indian films for members of the Sheffield Indo-Pakistan Society, the Wicker showed 'educational and cultural films' to members of the Pakistan International Friendship Society and the Star cinema hosted Polish film screenings for the Polska Young Men's Christian Association.[38] These screenings attracted migrant communities from a wide geographical area, with a 1961 report suggesting that Indian and Pakistani films were so popular at the Adelphi that up to 1,000 people regularly travelled from towns such as Barnsley, Chesterfield, Doncaster and Rotherham.[39] In contrast, by 1961, only 1 per cent of Belfast's population were born outside of the British Isles and the opportunities for migrant screenings were further limited by conservative attitudes towards Sunday screenings.[40] In 1963, the general secretary of the Belfast Pakistani Association stated that 'there are about one hundred Pakistanis living in Ulster and most of them in Belfast'. He requested permission for Sunday screenings of Indian and Pakistani films' in a similar fashion to other UK cities, 'to enable our folks to have some sort of contact with our domestic surroundings and environments'.[41] There is no evidence that these screenings came to

---

[34] *Belfast Telegraph*, 20 Dec. 1958.

[35] *Belfast Telegraph*, 25 May 1963; *Belfast Telegraph*, 7 Nov. 1964.

[36] *Belfast Telegraph*, 10 Nov. 1964.

[37] W. Hampton, *Democracy and Community in Sheffield* (London, 1970), p. 36.

[38] Sheffield Local Studies Library, minutes of Sheffield City Council Watch Committee, 21 Apr. 1955, p. 713; minutes of Sheffield City Council Watch Committee, 21 July 1955, p. 178; minutes of Sheffield City Council Watch Committee, 1956, p. 528; minutes of Sheffield City Council Watch Committee, 16 May 1957, p. 251.

[39] *The Star*, 17 Nov. 1961.

[40] Government of Northern Ireland General Register Office, *Census of Population 1961: Belfast County Borough* (Belfast, 1963), p. xxvii.

[41] PRONI, LA/7/3/E/9/24, Belfast Corporation General Purposes Committee, correspondence with the Belfast Pakistani Association, 1963.

fruition and there are no further press reports of screenings for migrant communities in the period under review.

Cinema-going and the life cycle

The oral history testimony shows a strong connection between time, place and memories of cinema attendance. The fact that all the interviewees were born between 1925 and 1950 provides the basis for an investigation of changes in cinema-going habits over the course of the life cycle, from childhood, to adolescence and into adulthood. Early experiences of cinema-going were linked to a small geographical area and children were confined often to the cheaper and more accessible venues available in their local neighbourhoods. These memories often display links to parental supervision and are associated with family and domestic life. For instance, Anne Gorman recalled that cinemas provided a convenient space for young mothers to take children and women often took babies in shawls.[42] The cinema was frequently used as a substitute for childcare and parents commonly provided money for cinema trips: 'my father would have given me the money … most of the kids I grew up with were the same. Everybody had the money to go'.[43] Children who were taken to the cinema by family members often had a different experience, and Mike Higginbottom's memories of Saturday night cinema trips with his parents highlight both the inter and intra-class distinctions of cinemas in Attercliffe, a working-class area in east Sheffield. He was only taken to the higher-priced balcony seats at the Adelphi and Pavilion cinemas. The Globe and the Regal, meanwhile, were considered unsuitable venues.[44] Childhood memories of cinema-going highlight the lack of mobility and movement from local neighbourhoods. Derek Yeardley, for instance, was born in 1949 and claimed that he 'never went into the town centre' until the early 1960s.[45] Margaret Mitchell added that travelling to Sheffield city centre was like 'going to other side of world'.[46] In working-class communities, such as the Holyland, cinemas like the Apollo 'tended to serve their districts, their communities … it was the people in the area who went to the local picture house'.[47] Norman Campbell added that the Apollo was a 'very local cinema. People wouldn't have travelled across town unless there was a particularly good film'.[48]

---

[42] Interview with Ann Gorman, Belfast, 23 Oct. 2014.
[43] Interview with George Brown, Belfast, 26 Aug. 2014.
[44] Interview with Mike Higginbottom, Sheffield, 20 Aug. 2015.
[45] Interview with Derek Yeardley, Sheffield, 25 June 2014.
[46] Interview with Margaret Mitchell, Sheffield, 27 June 2014.
[47] Interview with George Brown, Belfast, 26 Aug. 2014.
[48] Interview with Norman Campbell, Belfast, 4 June 2014.

Cinemas understood the need to cater for younger audiences and Saturday children's matinees were an important part of their programme. By 1953, 42 per cent of British cinemas ran these screenings, constituting 4 per cent of admissions.[49] For many interviewees, trips to children's matinees represented their first visits to the cinema away from parental supervision, providing an opportunity to socialize with other children and adopt new attitudes and behaviour. Many interviewees recalled the misbehaviour of children in inner-city cinemas, including firing spud guns, dripping ice from the balcony and letting in friends through the emergency exit. In 1957, the Belfast Gaumont manager claimed that while matinee screenings were noisy, there was no 'rowdyism': 'If a film does not raise some excitement in a bunch of kids, then it's not for them. We never have to check them for being too boisterous'.[50] In 1960, one Sheffield cinema manager ejected three hundred children following an egg-throwing incident, though he claimed that 'there has been no trouble at all in the past and I am sure there will be no further incidents at matinees'.[51] These findings correspond with Robert Shail's oral history study of Saturday morning cinema clubs, in which interviewees recalled memories of noisy audiences, misbehaviour, the role of usherettes, club songs, competitions, talent shows and birthday prizes. Shail observed that 'overshadowing the films themselves was the attraction of the clubs as a social event'.[52]

From 1953, the Belfast Curzon named its children's cinema club after Roy Rogers, the 'king of the cowboys', whose films appeared regularly at children's matinees. Manager 'Uncle' Sidney Spiers was recalled fondly, and participants highlighted the regular routines and social activities of the club. These recollections of innocent fun at children's matinees contrast with newspaper reports revealing them as sources of parental concern. One *Belfast Telegraph* reader commented that 'the attention of the public should be drawn to the practice in a Belfast cinema of admitting children to matinees on Saturday afternoons after all available seats are occupied'. A cinema manager replied that, while he believed that standing for long periods was not good for the children's health, 'it was easier to let them in than turn them away. Children surround the place on Saturdays, their only free afternoons and their only opportunity to see a show at a matinee price'.[53] The short multi-part serials shown at children's matinees routinely ended in cliff-hangers, ensuring that the audience returned the following week. They also had a clear influence on behaviour and dress. Derek Yeardley,

[49] *Kinematograph Year Book 1958* (London, 1958), pp. 509–10.
[50] *Belfast Telegraph*, 26 Jan. 1957.
[51] *The Star*, 21 Nov. 1960.
[52] R. Shail, *The Children's Film Foundation: History and Legacy* (London, 2016), p. 145.
[53] *Belfast Telegraph*, 24 Sept. 1952.

Figure 1.1. Children in Botanic Gardens, Belfast,
1950s (courtesy of Norman Campbell).

for instance, recalled imitating Zorro, the masked vigilante, stating that following screenings of these films, children with duffel coats used to 'fasten the collars up with a hood on, and go rushing out, flying through like they'd got a cape on'.[54] Similarly, David McConnell recalled that 'you could tell what kind of film it was by the way we came up Agincourt Avenue. Because if it was a western you shot your way up, if it was swashbuckler you buttoned your coat to make it a cape and fenced your way up'.[55] In the 1950s, greater affluence and amounts of disposable income meant that children were increasingly able to indulge these fantasies through the purchase of consumer goods, such as cowboy outfits (see Figure 1.1).[56] The influence of these western serials later waned and, in 1960, Heeley Coliseum manager Peggy Blaskey commented that '[s]pecial matinees put on for them do not appeal, they prefer a good "U" programme and do not like second feature

[54] Interview with Derek Yeardley, Sheffield, 25 June 2014.
[55] Interview with David McConnell, Belfast, 24 Sept. 2014.
[56] *The Star*, 22 Oct. 1954; *Belfast* Telegraph, 15 Nov. 1956.

Westerns – they see too many of them on television'.[57]

As children moved into adolescence, press reports linked the cinema to poor academic performance and school truancy. In March 1953, a 'worried mother' wrote to *The Star* to complain that her child was doing poorly at school and thought only of the cinema. 'Live letters' columnist Christine Veasey advised her not to ban her child from the cinema as 'this might lead to great temptation on her part'.[58] The fact that some adolescents were absconding from school was a source of concern for the Northern Ireland Child Welfare Council and its 1954 report on juvenile delinquency stated that '[t]he fact that cinemas may afford truant children sanctuary from school welfare officers creates a problem deserving consideration'.[59] George Brown recalled that, to avoid playing rugby at school, 'I used to sneak out on a Wednesday afternoon out of the game so I could go to the Apollo'.[60] Noel Spence recalled absconding from school to see *Psycho* (US, 1960): 'I was only about fifteen so I shouldn't have been allowed into it anyhow but it hadn't really taken the cinema-going public by storm at that stage … I went into the cinema in the afternoon for the one o'clock show and I was the only one in the whole cinema'.[61]

From 1959 to 1960, sociologist M. P. Carter interviewed 200 Sheffield secondary modern school leavers to investigate the transition from school to work. He found that cinema attendance increased and '[i]nstead of just meeting friends in the neighbourhood and around the streets and parks, children got into the habit of dressing up and "going out". Cinema-going and dancing increased considerably whilst attendance at youth clubs fell off: the former were adult activities, the latter childish'.[62] During adolescence, greater amounts of disposable income and access to public transport led to greater geographical mobility and attendance at the often larger, grander and more expensive city centre cinemas. Carter stated that young females especially preferred city centre cinemas as 'they had been given the taste by boyfriends who escorted them there, and it was in any case more of an occasion to dress up and parade in town instead of just slipping round the corner'.[63] He also revealed racial tensions in cinemas, interviewing one

[57] *The Star*, 5 Feb. 1960.

[58] *The Star*, 12 March 1953.

[59] Government of Northern Ireland, *Juvenile Delinquency, Interim Report of the Northern Ireland Child Welfare Council* (Belfast, 1954), p. 11.

[60] Interview with George Brown, Belfast, 26 Aug. 2014.

[61] Interview with Noel Spence, Comber, Co. Down, 26 March 2014.

[62] M. P. Carter, *Home, School and Work: a Study of the Education and Employment of Young People in Britain* (Oxford, 1962), p. 291.

[63] Carter, *Home, School and Work*, p. 297.

female who avoided a cinema 'because it is full of coloured people'.[64]

The comfortable, dark and warm space of the cinema auditorium had long made it a convenient venue for meeting members of the opposite sex. It was, as Claire Langhamer observed, the 'archetypal public space with a private dimension'.[65] Interviewees recalled sitting on back-row double seats and Malcolm Ayton's remark that 'the back row was predominantly the place to be' was typical of many male participants.[66] Carter observed that the cinema was a site for 'kissing and petting' and the foyer 'a meeting place for youths and girls who lounge about in groups, with some horseplay. The youths whistle at the girls, or jeer at their friend who is skulking shyly in a corner awaiting the arrival of his first date'.[67] As admissions fell in the 1950s, cinemas retained their status as sites for courtship. In 1958, Belfast journalist Gordon Duffield commented that adolescents would always favour the cinema as 'it provides an escape from parental authority and is a recognised phase in the conventional pattern of courtship'.[68] For Norman Campbell, 'courting was a big adventure that didn't start really until we were teenagers'. This also provided a means to impress the opposite sex and 'you tried to show off by taking the bus'. While the balcony at the Grand Opera House was popular with courting couples, a local neighbourhood cinema like the Apollo 'wasn't the sort of place that you would have taken your girlfriend, had you been trying to show off to her what sort of a good guy you were'.[69] In Sheffield, the local press reported that males often misbehaved to impress girls. One manager observed that they 'use the cinema as a giant picking-up ground … Of course the lads show off, trying to outdo each other. And the girls lap it up'.[70] Carter interviewed one female who stated that 'if there are boys sitting behind you, they torment you and ask if you have got any sweets. Then you get talking, and the boys ask if they can take you home'.[71] While children's matinees were easily affordable, using public transport such as buses or trams to travel to grander city centre cinemas required greater expenditure. Lack of money meant that many males attempted to evade payment for their partner's admission. Ann Slater stated that 'If you had a date with a lad, they used to say they'd meet you inside so they didn't

---

[64] Carter, *Home, School and Work*, p. 298.
[65] C. Langhamer, *The English in Love: the Intimate Story of an Emotional Revolution* (Oxford, 2013), p. 113.
[66] Interview with Malcolm Ayton, Sheffield, 24 July 2015.
[67] Carter, *Home, School and Work*, p. 298.
[68] *Belfast Telegraph*, 14 Feb. 1958.
[69] Interview with Norman Campbell, Belfast, 4 June 2014.
[70] *The Star*, 12 Sept. 1960.
[71] Carter, *Home, School and Work*, p. 299.

have to pay for you to go'.[72] Noel Spence linked this social practice to post-war austerity, claiming that 'we couldn't afford to be too romantic'.[73]

Courting couples generally frequented evening screenings and there were clear generational differences in the time and day of cinema attendance. In 1952, one cinema employee commented that 'there are fewer crowds in the afternoon than in the evening, but this is a favourite time for women of all ages – particularly if a domestic film, either comedy or drama is being shown. Children also enjoy the afternoon show, but their taste is for cartoons and westerns'.[74] Sylvia Fearn confirmed this, stating that, at the Crookes cinema, the first house was frequented by younger people and 'young mothers who wanted to get back to put the kids to bed'. In the second house, meanwhile, 'you could see that it was more older ones and courting couples'.[75] Friday and Saturday evenings were popular with adolescents and young adults. In their 1954 study of Sheffield's Wybourn estate, Mark Hodges and Cyril Smith noted that cinema-going 'on Friday evening is a regular routine for the young people. Most of them go once again during the week, and it is not infrequent to find adolescents who go as many as four times'.[76]

Entry into the workplace and greater amounts of disposable income affected cinema-going habits. Between the ages of thirteen to sixteen Bill Allerton frequented the Abbeydale twice a week: 'after that there was a huge gap in my cinema-going because I bought a motorbike when I was sixteen and a half. And I think that, unless you'd got a girl or a girlfriend to take, that was the end of my cinema-going for quite some time'.[77] For young female wage earners, cinema attendance depended on domestic responsibilities. During her training at Sheffield's Royal Infirmary Hospital, Helen Carroll stayed in Young Women's Christian Association accommodation: 'we could often finish work, quickly go and have our meal and then get out to the cinema. We had no washing up to do or anything like that'.[78] The cinema-going habits of young women were further determined by the working practices of male wage-earners, as Valerie Lowe recalled:

---

[72] Interview with Ann and Bob Slater, Sheffield, 24 July 2015.
[73] Interview with Noel Spence, Comber, Co. Down, 26 March 2014.
[74] *Belfast Telegraph*, 6 Dec. 1952.
[75] Interview with Sylvia Fearn, Sheffield, 1 July 2014.
[76] M. W. Hodges and C. S. Smith, 'The Sheffield estate', in *Neighbourhood and Community: an Enquiry into Social Relationships on Housing Estates in Liverpool and Sheffield*, ed. T. S. Simey (Liverpool, 1954), pp. 79–134, at p. 93.
[77] Interview with Bill Allerton, Sheffield, 27 July 2015.
[78] Interview with Helen Carroll, Sheffield, 23 July 2015.

I used to go the Abbeydale every Monday and Friday without fail, every Monday and Friday with my mother right from being a young teenager, perhaps ten or eleven. We used to go Monday and Friday because my father worked overtime on Tuesday, Wednesday, Thursday. So when he finished early on a Monday and Friday … he could stop at home and look after my little brother while me and my mother went to the pictures.[79]

In Sheffield, the leisure habits of young males were disrupted by the introduction of the 1948 National Service Act, which led two million men from England, Scotland and Wales to serve in the armed services between 1949 and 1963. Due to fears of civil unrest, men in Northern Ireland were excluded from this legislation. Adrian Horn's research shows how National Service created a period of limbo between school and work for young males and created a 'generational consciousness' among those who had shared similar experiences. His call for further research on the impact of National Service on youth culture, spending patterns and social activities is brought to bear by oral history testimony that highlights its impact on cinema-going habits.[80] Alan Lockwood was one of the 'hundreds of thousands [who] jumped before they were pushed and volunteered for regular service'.[81] While this disrupted his cinema attendance in Sheffield, he frequently attended the Astra Cinema, built to serve RAF servicemen working on the British nuclear test programme at Christmas Island.[82] The fact that a large number of young males left Sheffield to serve in the armed forces affected the social habits and courtship rituals of young females. In July 1956, as 'all lads my age were in the forces', sixteen-year-old Valerie went to the Abbeydale cinema with her future husband, twenty-four-year old Pete Lowe. He had failed his National Service medical and went 'to the pictures continuously' after his friends were conscripted.[83]

In 1960, the Screen Advertising Association claimed that from the age of twenty-five to thirty-four many 'young adults who have remained single so far get married. Families are started, homes established, and purchasing broadens to meet these challenging conditions. Even now, marriage does not break the cinema habit. Two-thirds of this group are cinema-goers and on average, they go to the cinema once a fortnight'.[84] It claimed that in the average audience 39 per cent were aged sixteen to twenty-four, 21 per

---

[79] Interview with Pete and Valerie Lowe, Sheffield, 28 July 2015.

[80] A. Horn, *Juke Box Britain: Americanisation and Youth Culture, 1945–60* (Manchester, 2010), p. 108.

[81] R. Vinen, *National Service: a Generation in Uniform 1945–1963* (London, 2014), p. xxvi.

[82] Interview with Alan Lockwood, Sheffield, 24 July 2015.

[83] Interview with Valerie and Pete Lowe, Sheffield, 28 July 2015.

[84] Screen Advertising Association, *Spotlight on the Cinema Audience* (London, 1962), p. 5.

cent were aged twenty-five to thirty-four, and 13 per cent were aged thirty-five to forty-four.[85] In 1957, one Sheffield cinema cashier commented that '[w]omen who have been in the house all day want a change of scene at night. They want to dress up and go out so I don't think television will have any great effect on cinema audiences'.[86] The interviews revealed, however, that the decline in adult cinema attendance of this generation was a result of increased television ownership, the poor service provided by cinemas and the onset of marriage and children. With the arrival of television, many adults no longer visited the cinema due to the increased comfort and ease of home-centred entertainment. Patrons increasingly criticized the service that cinemas provided. In 1957, one *Star* reader complained of cinema queues when seats were available, excessive advertising, poor second features and the sale of food and drink in an under-ventilated environment. He wanted proprietors to 'think of their customers as people and not as so many three-and-ninepences'.[87] The behaviour of fellow cinema-goers also deterred patrons and in 1960, one 'disgusted patron' complained that 'we paid 2s 6d each for balcony seats, but we were unable to enjoy the performance due to hooliganism in the stalls below … I for one will join the band of stay-away patrons until hooligans in the cinemas are controlled'.[88] In Belfast, W. Davidson complained of 'bad seating, too many intermissions, no assistance in trying to find a seat and no courtesy whatsoever'.[89]

Motherhood often meant that women were no longer able to attend the cinema. Childcare was a key issue for Belfast Ritz employee Stella Wilson: 'On her evenings off, and when a baby-sitter can be arranged for [her son] John, she and her husband may be found ice-skating, at the pictures, or as partners at an occasional dance. On her evenings at home, when the housework is done, Stella finds relaxation in a serious novel'.[90] The oral history testimony reveals the extent to which marriage and children disrupted cinema-going habits. Andrew Palmer commented that, after marriage, 'you had to start saving, so you couldn't really afford to go out … We used to stay in a lot and watch television then'.[91] Rosemary Topham was born in 1935. She married in 1959 and her eldest daughter was born in 1962. Before her wedding, she attended the Hippodrome with her future husband: 'after we got married we didn't go to the cinema at all because I

[85] Screen Advertising Association, *Spotlight on the Cinema Audience*, p. 7.
[86] *The Star*, 3 May 1957.
[87] *Belfast Telegraph*, 24 Oct.1957.
[88] *The Star*, 6 Jan. 1960.
[89] *Belfast Telegraph*, 15 Sept. 1962.
[90] *Belfast Telegraph*, 9 Dec. 1952.
[91] Interview with Andrew and Carol Palmer (pseudonyms), Sheffield, 7 Aug. 2015.

guess the children came along and that was it'.[92] The closure of many local neighbourhood cinemas limited the possibilities for parents' attendance. In his 1962 report on the decline of cinema-going, John Spraos commented that 'distance involves time and leisure time is a commodity in short supply and therefore valuable. In computing the true cost of travel to the cinema, the actual fare is a minor component; the value of the time spent in travelling is by far the greatest'.[93] Stuart Hanson later confirmed this finding, arguing that, as cinemas closed, the 'inconvenience of having to go out of one's area to visit the cinema may have deterred many people'. This, added to the deterioration in public transport services and the rise in car ownership, highlights that 'the location of the cinema in a neighbourhood was important in the formation and maintenance of the cinema-going habit'.[94] Sylvia Fearn was born in 1937 and married at the age of nineteen. While she previously attended the local Crookes cinema, it closed in 1960 and she rarely went to the cinema after the birth of her children:

> If I could get my mother, but she'd say 'only two hours' and by then the pictures were getting a lot longer so you'd either got to miss beginning or miss the end as well as get back to town and back. So it wasn't such a pleasure going, when you couldn't see the film out. Probably just used to pop down to the pub for an hour, just to get away from kids.[95]

In the 1950s, the sociologists who studied life on new housing estates observed the impact of marriage upon cinema-going habits. In Belfast, Dorita Field and Desmond Neill suggested that in 'the large poorer family, the higher rent and fares reduce the amount of money available for bought entertainment, and in all the families the larger house and garden make extra demands on the time and energies of the housewife'.[96] On Sheffield's Wybourn estate, Hodges and Smith observed that the cinema 'continues to be very popular with young housewives until they have small children to look after'.[97] They reported that one well-to-do single-child family kept their house to a standard 'which would more than meet the standards of a middle-class suburb'. Both parents spent their money on household goods such as their television and 'they never went to the pictures as they did not want to leave their son in anyone else's charge'.[98]

[92] Interview with Rosemary Topham, Sheffield, 17 Aug. 2015.
[93] J. Spraos, *The Decline of the Cinema: an Economist's Report* (London, 1962), p. 129.
[94] S. Hanson, *From Silent Screen to Multi-Screen: a History of Cinema Exhibition in Britain Since 1896* (Manchester, 2007), p. 101.
[95] Interview with Sylvia Fearn, Sheffield, 1 July 2014.
[96] D. Field and D. G. Neill, *A Survey of New Housing Estates in Belfast* (Belfast, 1957), pp. 60–3.
[97] Hodges and Smith, 'The Sheffield estate', p. 93.
[98] Hodges and Smith, 'The Sheffield estate', p. 88.

Film memories

Annette Kuhn has shown 'the extent to which interviewees' memories of cinema have revolved far more around the social act of cinema-going than around the films they saw. Memories of individual films have played only a small part in … recorded cinema memories'.[99] This observation applies equally to this oral history project where interviewees spoke at length about their cinema-going habits and behaviour. Given that attendance was often habitual and the films themselves were often seen only once, it is, Matthew Jones observed, 'perhaps understandable that the texts would fade away while the sociality of the activity remains prominent in memory'.[100] Participants were just as likely to recall the programming practices of cinemas as they were to remember particular films or film stars. These memories were often divorced from the content of films and focused on the regular routines of cinema attendance, such as the practice of continuous programming, whereby cinemas played their programme on a loop with patrons free to enter at any time. 'This is where we came in' was a commonly repeated phrase. Alongside the main and supporting features, programmes often contained adverts, cartoons, shorts and newsreels, though as the 1950s progressed the latter became a less valuable source of information. It is no surprise that after the BBC introduced regular news bulletins from 1955, Paramount News and Gaumont-British/Universal closed in 1957 and 1959 respectively.[101]

One of the difficulties of using oral history testimony to assess the popularity and impact of individual films is that there is often a contrast between those that were box-office successes and those that are subsequently remembered. Films that were reissued, later shown on television or released on other platforms are more likely to remain vivid in the public imagination. This, Jones claimed, means that that memories of individual films are better suited to telling us how films are now recalled than providing information on how they were understood at the time of their release.[102] In this project, memories of individual films were often connected to family life or important stages of the life cycle. For instance, Norman Campbell's first memory of cinema-going was seeing *The Desert Rats* (US, 1953) with

[99] A. Kuhn, 'What to do with cinema memory?', in *Explorations in New Cinema History: Approaches and Case Studies*, ed. R. Maltby, D. Biltereyst and P. Meers (Chichester, 2011), pp. 85–97, at p. 85.

[100] M. Jones, 'Memories of British cinema', in *The Routledge Companion to British Cinema History*, ed. I. Q. Hunter, L. Porter and J. Smith (Abingdon, 2017), pp. 397–405, at p. 400.

[101] T. Shaw, *British Cinema and the Cold War: the State, Propaganda and Consensus* (London, 2001), p. 32.

[102] M. Jones, 'Memories of British cinema', pp. 397–405.

his aunt, who took him because 'one of my relations had been involved in the attempt to kill Rommel'.[103] Memories of individual films were also linked to traumatic events and personal tragedy. Bill Allerton's father died of leukaemia at the age of forty-two. He recalled a hospital visit prior to his death:

> My dad took some money off the table at the side of his hospital bed and gave it me and said 'take your mum to the cinema, there's a picture she wants to see'. And it was *The Student Prince* with Edmund Purdom miming to Mario Lanza ... we sat there and watched this film and I kept looking at my mother and looking at the screen and I knew that neither of us were really watching the picture ... we sat there for a joyless two hours watching *The Student Prince*, neither of us wanted to be there but because my dad had asked me to take her and so she went. And it was a very moving experience, but not because of the cinema.[104]

Several films which received significant press coverage at the time of their release did not feature in the oral history testimony. In 1954, for instance, the upcoming release of *Martin Luther* (Germany/US, 1953) led the *Belfast Telegraph* to comment that:

> From the financial point of view, Northern Ireland is a place where religious films, of whatever shade of opinion can expect some success. In the past films like 'Song of Bernadette' and 'Boys' Town', sharing the Roman Catholic background which is the dominant one in the American cinema, were appreciated and enjoyed by Protestants no less than others. It is not unreasonable that the same measure of tolerance should be extended to 'Martin Luther'. We believe that it would be given by ordinary people, and that any suggestion of disturbances which might follow is less a prophecy than an incitement.[105]

One Roman Catholic reader responded that while Catholic-themed films such as *Going My Way* (US, 1944) 'did not falsify history or misrepresent the official teaching of any Protestant religious body. Catholics contend that the film *Martin Luther* is so inaccurate as to be anti-Catholic'.[106] Commercial cinemas did not screen the film, but it was shown at the centrally located Grosvenor Hall, a 2,000-seat Methodist hall which often held film screenings accompanied by 'illustrated hymns' and a 'silver service collection'. During its five weeks of exhibition in early 1955, 100,000 patrons saw *Martin Luther*. Exhibitor George Lodge claimed that this was twice as

---

[103] Interview with Norman Campbell, Belfast, 4 June 2014.
[104] Interview with Bill Allerton, Sheffield, 27 July 2015.
[105] *Belfast Telegraph*, 9 June 1954.
[106] *Belfast Telegraph*, 15 June 1954.

many patrons as he expected and attendance was especially high given the recent poor weather.[107]

Memories of films were often linked to the impact they had on behaviour and dress. Historians such as Mark Glancy and Adrian Horn qualify the impact that Hollywood films had on British audiences and demonstrate that the reception of American mass cultural products was mediated by local circumstances.[108] Leanne McCormick has also shown how women's impressions of the US troops who arrived in Northern Ireland in the Second World War 'were largely based upon national stereotypes, which in turn were derived mainly from Hollywood films'.[109] In the immediate post-war years, the absence of money limited the capacity of young people to impersonate their favourite film stars. David Ludlam, for instance, claimed that young people would 'affect an American drawl from time to time … not clothing so much, because that was always in short supply … But in gestures, in attitudes, the way you leaned against a pillar with your arm'.[110] In 1952, the *Belfast Telegraph* interviewed a female cinema employee who imitated ideas from the cinema screen: 'This, she recommends as an ideal way of keeping up to date. With one proviso – copy only the simpler styles and those worn by everyday characters like yourself'.[111] While the cinema provided a template for behaviour and dress, it was limited by parents' conservative attitudes towards gender, sexuality and respectability. Sylvia Fearn recalled that she permed her brother-in-law's hair 'because he wanted to look like Tony Curtis … His mother went crackers when he got home with all these massive curls'.[112] Adrian Horn noted that as 'home dressmaking was commonplace there were limitless individual adaptations of standard fashions … which were shown in the cinema'.[113] This was evident in the oral history testimony and several interviewees stated that austerity led them to make their own clothes. Jean McVeigh stated that seeing Doris Day on screen made her 'feel like going home and setting fire to my wardrobe

---

[107] *Belfast Telegraph*, 28 Feb. 1955.

[108] Horn, *Juke Box Britain*; M. Glancy, *Hollywood and the Americanization of Britain: from the 1920s to the Present* (London, 2014); J. Lacey, 'Seeing through happiness: Hollywood musicals and the construction of the American dream in Liverpool in the 1950s', *Journal of Popular British Cinema*, ii (1999), 54–66; P. Swann, *The Hollywood Feature Film in Postwar Britain* (London, 1987).

[109] L. McCormick, *Regulating Sexuality: Women in Twentieth-Century Northern Ireland* (Manchester, 2009), p. 152.

[110] Interview with David Ludlam, Sheffield, 25 June 2014.

[111] *Belfast Telegraph*, 6 Dec. 1952.

[112] Interview with Sylvia Fearn, Sheffield, 1 July 2014.

[113] Horn, *Juke Box Britain*, p. 158.

because it was just so beautiful'.[114] There was a stark contrast between the sartorial aspirations of young cinema-goers and the accessibility and affordability of clothing in their home cities. Malcom Ayton commented that while American film stars often had multiple suits, 'the average man at the time probably had one suit that wanted to be patched up for work'.[115]

The affluence and glamour presented in Hollywood films provided a fantasy space that contrasted with the austerity that residents of Belfast and Sheffield experienced on a day-to-day basis. American culture was particularly influential and Stuart Hanson argued that, for those in working-class neighbourhoods, 'identification with the pleasurable, seemingly classless and optimistic world of Hollywood films was easier than with that of a hidebound and rarefied British cinema'.[116] In her study of post-war female spectators, Jackie Stacey observed that interviewees often recalled the cinema 'as a physical space in which to escape the discomforts of their everyday lives'.[117] Anne Connolly recalled that she believed 'everything was wonderful in America … I was a child just after the war, I mean anything American, they just had everything. You know, the style and the beautiful houses and it just seemed to be everybody had it all in America'.[118] Ann Slater added that 'the musicals were the thing that we really liked as well. Anything that were a bit of a fantasy or just a dream. You had to pretend it were you it were happening to'.[119]

In contrast to Hollywood films, interviewees tended to connect their memories of British films to everyday life and personal experience. John Ramsden estimates that 100 British war films were produced between 1945 and 1960, far larger in number than Empire films or Ealing comedies.[120] These films were popular in Belfast and Sheffield: *The Cruel Sea* (UK, 1953), for instance, was the best attended film at the Sheffield Gaumont in 1953.[121] Malcolm Ayton served in the RAF and commented that 'the British films were pretty true, pretty accurate. Whereas the Americans glamorized them too much and they always seemed to add a love story to it'.[122] The reception of these films was often linked to class identity; Alan Lockwood also served in the RAF and claimed that British war films 'were a bit hoity-toity. They

[114] Interview with Jean and Terence McVeigh, 2 Apr. 2014.
[115] Interview with Malcolm Ayton, Sheffield, 24 July 2015.
[116] Hanson, *From Silent Screen to Multi-Screen*, p. 109.
[117] J. Stacey, *Star Gazing: Hollywood Cinema and Female Spectatorship* (London, 1994), p. 94.
[118] Interview with Anne Connolly, Belfast, 28 May 2015.
[119] Interview with Ann and Bob Slater, Sheffield, 28 July 2015.
[120] J. Ramsden, 'Refocusing "the people's war": British war films of the 1950s', *Journal of Contemporary History*, xxxiii (1998), 35–63, at p. 45.
[121] A. Eyles, *Gaumont British Cinemas* (London, 1996), p. 193.
[122] Interview with Malcolm Ayton, Sheffield, 24 July 2015.

don't talk like that in forces. They call you all things under the sun'.[123] Ann Gorman's testimony reveals generational differences in the reception of war films: 'I absolutely hated anything to do with the Royal Navy … I know it wasn't long after the war and there might have been older people who were interested but … that was not for us'.[124] The emphasis of these films on the winning of a just war and male bonding in dangerous situations meant that depictions of the Second World War were overwhelmingly masculine.[125] This accounts for Ann's comment that these films depicted 'too many men talking with pointers up at a board'. Participants, however, perceived tonal shifts in British films and she remarked that the 'kitchen sink' movies of the early 1960s 'were better because at least they spoke like normal people. I mean all the British movies, originally, everybody spoke like they were working for the BBC'.[126]

Audience behaviour

Participants frequently offered vivid descriptions of the communal experience of cinema attendance, recalling both the atmosphere of shows and the kinds of behaviour that occurred before screenings, within the auditorium and on the journey home. By assessing these recollections alongside further primary source material, it is possible to show how activities that were recalled as an innocent and everyday part of the cinema-going experience were often a source of great concern to exhibitors. For instance, several participants recalled the attempts by children to gain underage entry to the cinema. A common childhood experience was asking strangers to accompany children to gain entry to 'A' certificated films and several participants recalled getting into these films without an adult. Ann Slater was one of many interviewees who recalled the phrase 'will you take me in mister?'[127] Andrew Palmer added that 'if you went to see an 'A' film and you went without your mum and dad, and you didn't go with your parents, you had to wait in a queue obviously and you used to be asking people if they'd take you in because you weren't allowed to go in unless you'd got a parent with you or an adult'.[128] Local press reports reveal that this behaviour created a great deal of concern for exhibitors, who were often fined for allowing underage children into

[123] Interview with Alan Lockwood, Sheffield, 24 July 2015.

[124] Interview with Ann Gorman, Belfast, 23 Oct. 2014.

[125] P. Summerfield, 'Public memory or public amnesia? British women of the Second World War in popular films of the 1950s and 1960s', *Journal of British Studies*, xlviii (2009), 935–57.

[126] Interview with Ann Gorman, Belfast, 23 Oct. 2014.

[127] Interview with Ann and Bob Slater, Sheffield, 28 July 2015.

[128] Interview with Andrew and Carol Palmer (pseudonyms), Sheffield, 7 Aug. 2015.

their cinemas. For instance, in June 1950, Scala Cinemas were fined £20 for allowing eighty-three unaccompanied children to a screening of *Whispering Smith* (US, 1948) at the Woodhouse Picture Palace. Manager Harold Booth was fined a further £4 and claimed that although he had done everything possible to comply with regulations, he received no co-operation from the public and 'received insults and abuse from parents when he tried to keep children out'.[129] Sylvia Fearn recalled both gaining underage access to the cinema and paying for younger children to enter:

> as I got to about fourteen, I was quite tall and I looked old enough to get in for eighteen, so I used to put lippy on and go to one box to pay and get in. Probably take other children in because they used to say 'can you take one in, can you take two in, missus' and they used to do that. And when it was a U, I used to leave my lipstick off and pay half the price and get in as a child.[130]

Kine Weekly summed up the long and short of the matter when Sheffield CEA Chairman Frank S. Neale commented that 'some children turned up in long trousers for certain pictures and short ones for others'.[131]

As children reached adolescence, they often tried to gain entry to 'X' certificated films, a practice associated with smaller, local neighbourhood cinemas. Norman Campbell recalled that 'the standards were more lax in the Apollo than they would be in the Curzon, which was very correct. So certainly the first 'X' film that I ever saw was in the Apollo, and I was well under age. There's no way I could have passed for the age, but they were quite happy to take my money'.[132] In March 1962, *Star* reader Mrs D.B. complained that children who lied to gain access to 'X' certificated films were placing cinema operators in jeopardy. She suggested that the law regarding these films 'should be the same as the law regarding under-age drinking' and under-sixteens should be fined for purchasing tickets under false pretences. Columnist Richard Wilson replied that he believed 'the best solution to this problem lies with parents – not with a change in the law'.[133] In January 1961, Sheffield CEA discussed the penalties applied to cinemas for allowing entry to underage patrons. Peter Blake said that 'the ones to be charged should be those who got in under false pretences and lied about their ages'. Arnold Favell added 'It seems the law can prosecute those who let in, but not those who get in. It sounds silly to me'.[134]

[129] *Kinematograph Weekly*, 13 July 1950.
[130] Interview with Sylvia Fearn, Sheffield, 1 July 2014.
[131] *Kinematograph Weekly*, 1 June 1954.
[132] Interview with Norman Campbell, Belfast, 30 May 2014.
[133] *The Star*, 29 March 1962.
[134] *The Star*, 30 Jan. 1961.

Queuing was another everyday aspect of the cinema-going experience recalled by participants. John Mitchell remembered that 'It was part of the experience. You had to do it and it was just natural and you'd probably meet half a dozen friends and stand in this great big long queue for an hour, provided it wasn't raining'.[135] Margaret McDonaugh recalled that 'cinemas were always busy, you always had to queue. And no matter how many cinemas there were, you always seemed to have to queue outside and possibly wait in the rain'. Andrew Palmer's comments reveal that the length of queues was a key determinant of attendance: 'if there was a big queue and it was the best film, you used to wait a while. But if it was too big, then you used to go off somewhere else to another cinema and watch that one instead … you had to come early in the evening to try and miss the queue'.[136] His memories of queuing also show the popularity of particular screenings and he recalled that Sunday queues at the Gaumont were particularly large.[137]

Not all memories of queues were positive. Bill Gatt recalled that he nearly got crushed in the crowd: 'it was one of my experiences of queuing for the cinema that's lingered on in my mind for a long time because somebody saved me from being crushed. They actually rose me, they heard me screaming. I was going to be trampled'.[138] In Belfast, cinema queues were also sites of criminal activity. In 1948, cinema workers sought 'improvement in regulations concerning queues inside and outside Belfast cinemas'. Trade union representative W. H. McCullough stated that 'one or two serious incidents had occurred recently, when cinema attendants were mishandled while supervising queuing'.[139] In December 1951, the *Northern Whig* reported that a Woolworth's window was smashed 'when a crowd of people attempted to "crash" a queue which was filing into the Alhambra cinema … For a short space the crowd looked like getting out of control of the policeman on duty, and extra police had to be summoned before order could be restored'.[140]

Elements of audience behaviour, habits and dress were associated with certain days of the week. Despite opposition from the Belfast Corporation Watch Committee, the Army Act permitted cinemas to open on Sunday for uniformed members of the armed forces. In 1944, the Kelvin and the Imperial were the only cinemas to open on Sunday and 'the stern

[135] Interview with John Mitchell, Sheffield, 8 July 2014.
[136] Interview with Andrew and Carol Palmer (pseudonyms), Sheffield, 7 Aug. 2015.
[137] Interview with Andrew and Carol Palmer (pseudonyms), Sheffield, 7 Aug. 2015.
[138] Interview with Bill Gatt, Belfast, 18 March 2014.
[139] *Northern Whig*, 5 Nov. 1948.
[140] *Northern Whig*, 17 Dec. 1957.

Presbyterian grip on the Northern Ireland Sabbath' remained strong.[141] In 1947, soldiers were granted permission to attend the Imperial in plain clothes with their families 'with the proviso that their identities would be checked by the Royal Military Police'. Colonel E. V. Lang claimed that this prevented soldiers 'standing or strolling aimlessly about the streets of Belfast'.[142] In 1949, the Belfast Corporation Police Committee expressed concerns that people other than those in the armed forces were being admitted to Sunday screenings and voted in favour of changing the rules so that only uniformed members of the forces were allowed entry.[143] In 1952, the Deputy Town Solicitor told the Police Committee that Sunday opening for the forces was legislated for in the Army Act and 'the Corporation had no jurisdiction in the matter'. The Committee voted by four to two against the motion that 'representations be made to the Military Authorities to discontinue the use of the Imperial Cinemas on Sunday evenings'.[144] James Doherty recounts the testimony of a RAF radar technician, who in 1955 leant his pass to a young relative:

> One Sunday as he queued at the Cornmarket, an RAF military policeman arrived to do spot checks on the passholders. To his alarm and embarrassment my friend was hauled out of the queue, and taken away for interrogation, with the pass confiscated ... Two days later I was summoned before the camp Commanding Officer and dismissed in disgrace.[145]

In Sheffield, the first licence for Sunday cinema exhibition was granted in 1944. Despite opposition from the Sheffield Free Church Federal Council, the Sheffield Sunday School Union and the Lord's Day Observance Society, 27,199 voted in favour and 15,186 voted against retaining Sunday exhibition in a 1947 referendum. The number of Sheffield cinemas licenced for Sunday exhibition increased from nine in 1947 to twenty-seven in 1956.[146] Adolescent cinema-goers were frequently associated with rowdyism and misbehaviour, particularly in Sunday screenings. Children under school-leaving age were not permitted to enter cinemas on Sunday, though the oral history testimony suggests that many did enter these screenings.[147] One cinema

[141] *Kinematograph Weekly*, 13 Jan. 1944.

[142] McClay Library, minutes of Belfast Corporation Police Committee, 2 June 1949, p. 13.

[143] McClay Library, minutes of Belfast Corporation Police Committee, 16 June 1949, p. 13.

[144] McClay Library, minutes of the Belfast Corporation Police Committee, 21 Aug. 1952, p. 240.

[145] J. Doherty, *Standing Room Only: Memories of Belfast Cinemas* (Belfast, 1997), p. 85.

[146] Sheffield Local Studies Library, minutes of Sheffield City Council Watch Committee, 21 Nov. 1946, p. 30; 17 Nov. 1955, p. 432.

[147] In 1959, Sheffield City Council changed the regulations so that children under school-leaving age were allowed entry 'when accompanied by and in the charge of a parent or some

manager commented that 'Sunday night cinema-goers are by far the worst offenders' and he bemoaned that up to forty slashed cinema seats weekly led to a £500 annual repair bill.[148] Coliseum manager Harry Gent lamented the use of razor blades to slash seats and claimed that '[t]he law is far too lenient in matters of vandalism. It costs the small local cinemas packets to put the damage right. And it drives the respectable patrons away'.[149] Alan Lockwood recalled misbehaviour (though not criminal damage) at Sunday screenings, stating that teenagers 'used to take football rattles. They used to take whistles. They used to take anything that would make a noise. They used to go in and make as much noise, and some of my mates they used to take bags of rice. Take a bag of rice and spray the audience'.[150]Another cinema manager noted a direct correlation between disturbances and the film shown: 'Action and comedy films result in little misbehaviour in the cinema ... It is the film with a love theme that causes "restiveness" in this cinema where perhaps 70 per cent of the audience are "teen-agers"'.[151] Several Sheffield cinemas took measures to control this behaviour; the Plaza introduced 'a mad fifteen minutes to "clear the air"' and the Gaumont allowed teenagers to 'sing, dance, whistle or spread out and go to sleep' before Sunday screenings.[152] In Belfast, limited Sunday opening meant that Monday and Thursday were considered the worst nights for misbehaviour.[153]

From the mid 1950s, press reports of violent behaviour increased and this was often associated with the emergence of Teddy Boys. These reports should be treated with caution, for as Patrick Glen observed, the press created moral panic about young people who deviated from social mores and newspapers often 'represented discourses around teenagers rather than the voices of teenagers themselves'.[154] Despite the efforts of Sheffield cinema managers to control misbehaviour, a 1955 report highlighted that:

> Many of the smaller houses are long-suffering victims of exhibitionist hooligans who seem bent on destroying filmgoers' entertainments ... Most of these nuisances are 'Teddy Boy' types who find willing allies in their gum-chewing girlfriends ... Sunday evenings are the worst, says a film fan colleague ...

other person who appear to have attained the age of sixteen years' (Sheffield Local Studies Library, minutes of Sheffield City Council Watch Committee, 20 May. 1959, pp 49–50).

[148] *The Star*, 2 Jan. 1953.
[149] *The Star*, 9 July 1960.
[150] Interview with Alan Lockwood, Sheffield, 24 July 2015.
[151] *The Star*, 7 May 1954.
[152] *The Star*, 25 Apr. 1959; *The Star*, 11 Dec. 1959.
[153] *Belfast Telegraph*, 3 Sept. 1960.
[154] P. Glen, '"Exploiting the daydreams of teenagers": press reports and memories of cinema-going by young people in 1960s Britain', *Media History*, xxv (2019), 355–70.

Managers are fully alive to the problem, but it seems that as soon as offenders are 'banned' from the cinema, either temporarily or permanently, there are others to take their places.[155]

In September 1955, the severity of this behaviour led the Wicker and the News Theatre to refuse entry to Teddy Boys.[156] In November, the former claimed that '[t]he ban has had its desired effect and we are not now keeping out any youngsters who appear in Teddy Boy clothes … But we know of a crowd of about 50 trouble-makers who are now never allowed through the doors'.[157] Another manager believed that hooliganism had 'been on the up ever since the war. The trouble is now that organised gangs of toughs are coming out into the suburbs with the sole purpose of causing trouble'.[158] In July 1960, Sheffield City Council passed a by-law to counter rowdyism in cinemas and in the following year CEA secretary Arnold Favell claimed that it had led to improved behaviour.[159]

Memories of the rock 'n' roll films released from the mid 1950s offer an example of memories of (mis)behaviour that were directly linked to the images shown on screen. Alan Lockwood recalled watching *Blackboard Jungle* (US, 1955) at Sheffield's Phoenix cinema and claimed that 'people were up and dancing in aisles. In some cases they were ripping seats out. The manager used to come up on stage doing his nut'.[160] Ann Slater added that at one screening 'everybody were up dancing, they were doing rock 'n' roll in aisles'.[161] It is unsurprising that such conspicuous behaviour was widely reported in the press as it reflected contemporary concerns over youth culture and changing leisure habits. Several interviewees made a distinction between the behaviour of patrons in city centre cinemas and their local neighbourhood counterparts. John Mitchell recalled that, during screenings of *Blackboard Jungle* in city centre cinemas, Teddy Boys 'just went mad, they were ripping up seats and going crazy with all this rock and jive music'. When the film arrived at the local Crookes cinema 'there was a policeman stood outside and nothing happened. Everybody was getting ready for punch ups and things like this … there was just a policeman stood outside, looking left, looking right. What's it all about?'[162] In Belfast, John Campbell recalled seeing *Blackboard Jungle* at the Mayfair, where: 'when

---

[155] *The Star*, 14 March 1955.
[156] *The Star*, 9 Sept. 1955.
[157] *The Star*, 1 Nov. 1955.
[158] *The Star*, 12 Sept. 1960.
[159] *The Star*, 30 Jan. 1961.
[160] Interview with Alan Lockwood, Sheffield, 24 July 2015.
[161] Interview with Ann and Bob Slater, Sheffield, 28 July 2015.
[162] Interview with John Mitchell, Sheffield, 8 July 2014.

the boys heard the first blast of *Rock around the Clock*, a few of them threw their hats up in the air … the guy came down with a flash torch and threw the whole lot of us out, so we never seen the picture. They didn't stand for that sort of stuff up there.[163]

In his assessment of juvenile delinquency in Northern Ireland, David Fowler claimed that 'Teddy Boys were not prominent in Belfast in the late 1950s. In the local press they were treated as a novelty as late as April 1957 – four years after they had appeared in London'.[164] While concerns related to Teddy Boys reached Belfast later than many other parts of the United Kingdom (including Sheffield), by September 1956 *Kine Weekly* reported that though the 'Teddy Boy craze was slower in catching on in Belfast than in most cross-Channel cities … it has reached alarming proportions in some areas'.[165] Several members of the Northern Ireland CEA proposed to ban Teddy Boys from Belfast cinemas and the Forum's adverts stated that 'persons in Teddy boy dress or jeans' would be refused entry. A Rank official hoped that 'others will follow our lead and ban the lot'.[166] From 1957, local press reports suggest that there were increasing concerns about this youth subculture's behaviour. In 1958, Belfast Resident Magistrate R. M. Campbell went as far to describe 'Teddy-boyism' as a 'civic cancer' after twenty juveniles were either jailed, fined or sent to training school. These prosecutions related to several incidents of gang violence, including an altercation outside the downmarket Clonard Picture House.[167] In 1960, while *Kine Weekly* stated that hooliganism was 'not yet a major problem in Belfast', according to the *Belfast Telegraph* incidents 'involving gangs of young people are becoming commonplace in a number of city cinemas'.[168] It reported that disturbances were created by both sexes and confined largely to the front stalls. The newspaper claimed, however, that 'the blame cannot be laid entirely on rock 'n' roll and crime films. Trouble crops up no matter what is on the screen'.[169]

This conspicuous behaviour was a source of concern for the police, local authorities and cinema exhibitors, receiving considerable attention in the columns of newspapers and trade journals. Cinema-goers, however, were just as likely to recall everyday aspects of the cinema-going experience, such as smoking. In 1957, one Sheffield cinema manager estimated that 95 per

---

[163] Interview with John Campbell, Belfast, 30 May 2014.
[164] D. Fowler, *Youth Culture in Modern Britain, c.1920–c.1970* (Basingstoke, 2008), p. 109.
[165] *Kinematograph Weekly*, 27 Sept. 1956.
[166] *Kinematograph Weekly*, 27 Sept. 1956; *Irish Press*, 20 Sept. 1956.
[167] *Belfast Telegraph*, 28 Oct.1958.
[168] *Kinematograph Weekly*, 7 July 1960; *Belfast Telegraph*, 3 Sept. 1960.
[169] *Belfast Telegraph*, 3 Sept. 1960.

cent of his patrons were smokers.[170] A 1960 survey found that 72 per cent of male and 52 per cent of female adult cinem-agoers were smokers, and that this was significantly higher than the proportion of smokers in the general population.[171] For adolescent cinema-goers, the cinema provided a space to hide their smoking habits from parents. In 1959, one third of fifteen-year-old boys and 5 per cent of fifteen-year-old girls were regular smokers. Rates of smoking were higher in secondary modern than grammar schools.[172] David McConnell recalled that his pocket money of 2s 6d would 'get you in to the front stalls at the Curzon on a Friday night, and five cigarettes as well. And I just remember the smoke in the beam, and we must have stank when we came home. Which was good of course, because that way it was more difficult to be accused of having smoked yourself'.[173] While the smoke-filled environment of cinemas was often described as 'atmospheric', it was not always remembered fondly.[174] 'I never liked the smoke. So I tried not sit near anybody … that was smoking', recalled Sylvia Fearn.[175] 'With everybody smoking', added David Ludlam, 'sometimes it was difficult trying to see what was on the screen'.[176] In 1957, one *Belfast Telegraph* reader asked 'when do our cinema proprietors propose to do something for the convenience of non-smokers?' He claimed that, during a recent cinema he sat next to a woman, who 'smoked no fewer than seven cigarettes … my earnest wish was that she would burst into flames'. If cinemas were unable 'to set aside certain nights for non-smokers', he added, 'they should at least, issue goggles and antismog masks to alleviate our discomfort'.[177]

Following increasing concerns of the medical dangers of smoking and the launch of the first public health campaigns about this topic in the 1950s, the possibility of introducing a smoking ban was discussed in both Belfast and Sheffield. Cinema managers protested that any ban on smoking would inevitably lead to lower attendances. In 1957, one Sheffield cinema manager stated that a ban on smoking would be both impracticable and bad for business.[178] In 1962, Sheffield City Council discussed the possibility of a ban, though reports suggested that cinema-goers were generally against such legislation. 'No smoking, no cinema', asserted one accountancy student.

[170] *The Star*, 6 Sept. 1957.
[171] Screen Advertising Association, *Spotlight on the Cinema Audience*, p. 16.
[172] Study Group of the Public Health Department, 'Smoking habits of school children', *British Journal of Preventative & Social Medicine*, xiii (1959), 1–4.
[173] Interview with David McConnell, Belfast, 24 Sept. 2014.
[174] Interview with Malcolm Ayton, Sheffield, 24 July 2015.
[175] Interview with Sylvia Fearn, Sheffield, 1 July 2014.
[176] Interview with David Ludlam, Sheffield, 25 June 2014.
[177] *Belfast Telegraph*, 29 Nov. 1957.
[178] *The Star*, 6 Sept. 1957.

Steelworker Alec Ainsworth added that he could not 'enjoy a film if [he] couldn't smoke'. Newer Sheffield cinemas such as the ABC and the Odeon were against a ban on the grounds that their modern facilities prevented disturbance to other patrons: 'With the kind of air-conditioning you get in the best modern cinemas the only person who feels the effect of the cigarette is the smoker himself'.[179] In 1962, the Sheffield City Council Watch Committee decided not to ban smoking at local cinemas, except during performances wholly or mainly for children.[180] Alderman Harold Gent stated that no ban would be forced unless there was national legislation and commented that 'It would be impractical in the semi-darkness to find out who was smoking and the managements had no powers to enforce non-smoking'.[181] In 1964, a journalist claimed that eleven out of twelve patrons, nine of whom were smokers, felt that smoking should be banned in cinemas. John Wainwright stated that:

> I smoke between 25 and 35 cigarettes a day – and I'll be smoking in the cinema today. But I couldn't really argue against a ban on smoking in cinemas. It's only common sense really. If the cinema is full and every other person is smoking the atmosphere becomes unbearable. I think I could stand doing without if there was a film I really wanted to see.[182]

In 1957, Belfast Rural District Council discussed the possibility of introducing no-smoking nights. It wrote to the Alpha cinema, Rathcoole, and pointed out the link between smoking and lung cancer. A CEA spokesman responded that 'the branch was unanimous in the opinion that the recommendation was unrealistic because non-smoking nights would be bad for business'.[183] During the Stormont debate on the 1959 Cinematograph Bill, nationalist Cahir Healy again mooted the idea of non-smoking nights, claiming that smoke-filled auditoriums forced some people to leave the cinema.[184] Minister of Home Affairs W. W. B. Topping responded that it was an uneconomical policy restricting the rights of individuals.[185] Nationalist Harry Diamond added that the revenue generated from the sale of cigarettes aided cinemas at a time of declining attendances and increasing overheads. It would, he said, 'be unwise to interfere with the liberty of the

[179] *The Star*, 27 March 1962.
[180] *Kinematograph Weekly*, 3 May 1962; *The Star*, 1 Dec. 1962.
[181] *Kinematograph Weekly*, 6 Dec. 1962.
[182] *The Star*, 7 May 1964.
[183] *Kinematograph Weekly*, 26 Sept. 1957.
[184] Hansard (Northern Ireland), *Parliamentary Debates*, xlv (29 Oct. 1959), cols. 449–50.
[185] Hansard (NI), xlv (29 Oct. 1959), cols. 451–2.

majority'.[186] While the issue of smoking was discussed, no provisions for non-smoking nights were included in the final bill. The fact that tobacco company Gallahers were significant employers in Ballymena and Belfast may also have been a consideration.

At the end of the evening's performance, it was common for cinemas to play *God Save the Queen* (commonly referred as 'the Queen' by interviewees). While this was uncontroversial in a provincial English city such as Sheffield, it is understandable that cinemas in largely nationalist areas of Belfast refrained from this practice. It was a custom often associated with a rush to leave the cinema. In 1952, *Kine Weekly* reported that '[w]e all know there is a scramble to beat the playing of the National Anthem by many patrons, but in most cases … this is not due to disloyalty as much as the sheer necessity of catching the last bus home'.[187] In Belfast, many of those from a Protestant background shared similar sentiments and defiance of this practice was linked to youthful rebellion or a desire to return home, rather than disrespect for the monarchy or British institutions:

> My awareness coming from the Protestant side of the community was when the national anthem started … people left the cinema. Now, my understanding of it at the time, and it might well be naïve, was that these were the 'jack the lads', the people who were too cool to stay for that sort of thing. It didn't ever occur to me that this might be the Catholic population.[188]

Margaret McDonaugh stated that people:

> tried to leave because the cinema programme was over. It wasn't any political statement … I didn't like it when 'the Queen' came on because you wanted to get out, you wanted to get home, you wanted to do something else. But I was never aware amongst my friends that there was any problem with it.[189]

Other participants from a Protestant background recalled minor tensions: 'if there was a guy standing or sitting beside you, who didn't want to be there, and tried to get out, you stopped him. You just stood there'.[190] David McIlwaine grew up in a working-class area of west Belfast and recalled that in 'Catholic areas, only a quarter of them would have stood and the others would have very pointedly pushed past them to get out.[191] Participants often underplayed these tensions and Noel Spence recalled that at the Coliseum

---

[186] Hansard (NI), xlv (29 Oct. 1959), cols. 453.
[187] *Kinematograph Weekly*, 28 Feb. 1952.
[188] Interview with Norman Campbell, Belfast, 4 June 2014.
[189] Interview with Margaret McDonaugh, Belfast, 18 May 2015.
[190] Interview with John Campbell, Belfast, 30 May 2014.
[191] Interview with David McIlwaine, Cultra, Co. Down, 9 July 2015.

– located between Unionist and Nationalist communities – 'there was the potential for some sort of sectarian clashes but it never really came to anything'.[192] Peter Smyth claimed that the city centre Gaiety evolved a protocol whereby its patrons came from the largely nationalist Falls Road on three nights a week and the largely unionist Shankill Road on the other three, and this kind of behaviour perhaps prevented further trouble.[193]

Roman Catholic interviewees offered a greater sense of communal tension in their testimony and their memories display similar characteristics to the oral history testimony collected by Anna Bryson in mid Ulster. She investigated the ways that Protestants and Catholics presented their own past and observed 'two distinct communal narratives, each carefully reinforced with reference to both the recent and distant past'. While many Protestants depicted the post-war period as a 'golden age of community relations … many Catholics opened their recollections of the post-war period with references to both public and private discrimination against their community'.[194] This kind of 'golden age thinking' is not unique to Belfast and other oral history studies have shown how memories of the post-war years are filtered through subsequent events.[195]

One incident at the Strand cinema highlights the divisive nature of *God Save the Queen*. In 1954, the Belfast Education Committee arranged for 20,000 schoolchildren to view *The Conquest of Everest* (UK, 1953). One *Belfast Telegraph* reader complained that after a screening, a group of Roman Catholic children, under the instruction of two Christian Brothers, remained seated during the playing of *God Save the Queen*. They claimed that this action displayed disregard for the Crown and asserted that 'there is something here more deadly than the flying of a tricolour – an insidious canker that will take more than the shibboleth of the Border to cure when the children who successfully made their gesture yesterday have grown up'.[196] One Roman Catholic mother was 'disgusted and horrified by this behaviour … with threats of Communism and the atomic bomb hanging over us, I think our children should, at least, be taught tolerance and good manners'.[197] The incident was even debated by the parliament of Northern Ireland. Ulster Unionist Harry Midgley dismissed nationalist suggestions that Northern Irish cinemas should stop playing the national

---

[192] Interview with Noel Spence, Comber, Co. Down, 26 March 2014.

[193] P. Smyth, *Changing Times: Life in 1950s Northern Ireland* (Newtonwards, 2012), p. 73.

[194] A. Bryson '"Whatever you say, say nothing": researching memory and identity in mid-Ulster, 1945–1969', *Oral History*, xxxv (2007), 45–65, at p. 51.

[195] Jancovich, Faire and Stubbings, *The Place of the Audience*, p. 172.

[196] *Belfast Telegraph*, 26 Feb. 1954.

[197] *Belfast Telegraph*, 2 March 1954.

anthem when mixed audiences were present. He responded that, as local education authorities received grants, they should expect 'a greater measure of recognition for the patriotism and loyalty of this democratically-elected and administered part of the United Kingdom'.[198] While these debates were ostensibly concerned with the welfare of the children present, it is clear that they were used as a cipher to discuss Northern Ireland's position within the United Kingdom. In 1964, ABC introduced a ruling to play the national anthem at the start of performances, though it was not put into operation in Northern Ireland. ABC's Belfast manager Don Mackrell stated that '[w]hen I first came here I sensed a certain amount of sensitivity to the playing of the National Anthem. The people in Northern Ireland seem to respect it much more than they do in England and because of this I did not think a change was necessary'.[199]

In Sheffield, Mike Higginbottom's comments suggest generational divisions and he described the 'Gadarene rush to get to the top of the stairs before the music started … the rush was to get out before the music started because otherwise the old folk would glare at you'.[200] Ernest Walker recalled that, as a child, his aunt used to take him to the Unity cinema: 'they used to play the national anthem at the end of the showing. Most people couldn't be bothered and ran for the entrances. But Aunt Lisa was a patriot and we had to stand for "the Queen", much to our chagrin'.[201] In his letter to *The Star*, James Challis wrote that the behaviour of those who left during the anthem 'not only angers one, but embarrasses as well to think that a true Englishman could show such bad manners. This sort of behaviour will soon pull Sheffield down in the eyes of visitors'.[202] In the immediate aftermath of the Second World War, there was often tension between adolescent cinema-goers and those who had served in the armed forces. Bill Allerton stated that his girlfriend's father 'thought he was Nelson … he ended up falling out with someone in the cinema because he tried to get past him and he wouldn't let him pass. And people used to climb over the seats to get past people who were stood. It was a real division in local society at that time'.[203] Margaret Mitchell's father served in the navy, and she stated that during the anthem 'I laughed and so I got a swipe'.[204]

---

[198] Hansard (Northern Ireland), *Parliamentary Debates*, xxxviii (4 March 1954), cols. 1167–70.

[199] *Belfast Telegraph*, 16 May 1964.

[200] Interview with Mike Higginbottom, Sheffield, 20 Aug. 2015.

[201] Interview with Ernest Walker, Belfast, 26 Nov. 2014.

[202] *The Star*, 30 Apr. 1955.

[203] Interview with Bill Allerton, Sheffield, 27 July 2015.

[204] Interview with Margaret Mitchell, Sheffield, 27 June 2014.

Conclusion

The use of two local case studies offers fresh insights into the geographical diversity of cinema attendance during a period of declining audiences and instability in the film exhibition industry. Audience behaviour was rooted in place and there is a clear link between changing leisure habits, the evolving use of cinemas and the nature of post-war industrial cities. While social customs such as queuing or smoking were adopted by cinema-goers in both Belfast and Sheffield, these cities had distinctive local cinema cultures shaped by a range of wider social, economic and political factors. Disparities between these cities, such as responses to the national anthem or attitudes towards Teddy Boys, reveal the full extent of these factors on everyday leisure habits. Attitudes towards cinema-going practices also varied widely and were linked to local concerns about behaviour, morality and identity. This corroborates Richard Maltby's statement that 'close historical investigations of the everyday nature of local cinemagoing reveal how the resilient parochialism of individuals and communities incorporated and accommodated the passing content that occupied their screens to their local concerns and community experiences'.[205] More broadly, a comparison of Belfast and Sheffield challenges preconceptions of the former's post-war social history, affirming Marianne Elliott's observations that neighbourhood identity was often more important than sectarian divisions in Northern Ireland society.[206]

One of new cinema history's key characteristics is its 'acknowledgement of the diversity of the social experience of cinema and a concomitant resistance to compress that diversity into a single overarching account of the "cinema audience"'.[207] The use of local case studies further highlights the lack of a single, homogenous cinema-going experience – behaviour and social habits were diverse, shaped by the streets and neighbourhoods where people lived, the range of cinema-going options available to them and the films that were shown. A focus on space and place in oral history testimony confirms the findings of Pierluigi Ercole et al. that people 'persistently emphasize the spatial dimensions of those narratives, focusing on local topographies,

---

[205] R. Maltby, 'New cinema histories', in *Explorations in New Cinema History: Approaches and Case Studies*, ed. R. Maltby, D. Bilthereyst and P. Meers (Chichester, 2011), pp. 3–40, at p. 14.

[206] M. Elliott, *Hearthlands: a Memoir of the White City Housing Estate in Belfast* (Belfast, 2017), p. x.

[207] D. Bilthereyst, R. Maltby and P. Meers, 'Reflections and comments: introduction', in *The Routledge Companion to New Cinema History*, ed. D. Bilthereyst, R. Maltby and P. Meers (Abingdon, 2019), pp. 13–5, at p. 13.

travel to and from cinemas and the spaces of the remembered experience'.[208] Assessing these narratives alongside text-based archival sources such as newspaper reports or trade journals allows us to compare and contrast the views of cinema-goers to exhibitors, local authorities and other citizens. Only by doing this is it possible to provide a rounded picture of post-war cinema-going experiences across the United Kingdom.

---

[208] Ercole, Treveri Gennari and O'Rawe, 'Mapping cinema memories', p. 67.

2. The decline of cinema-going

UK cinema attendance fell from 1.6 billion in 1946 to 1.2 billion in 1955 and then to 327 million in 1965. The simultaneous expansion of television services brought moving images into millions of households and it is difficult to argue with Joe Moran's assertion that cinemas 'began seriously to decline in the late 1950s as their mainly working-class audiences acquired TVs on a large scale'.[1] Nevertheless, contemporary economists and subsequent social historians have debated the level of causation between the rise in television sales and the decline in cinema admissions. Population shifts, new forms of youth culture, increased affluence, the diversification of leisure activities and a shift towards home-oriented consumption are all cited as factors that fundamentally altered the way that people spent their time and money.[2] By considering the impact of these factors on cinema's decline, the following analysis answers Judith Thissen's call for proponents of new cinema history to engage with the arguments of social historians and adopt an outward-looking approach 'to better understand the place that cinema occupied in the lives of its audiences'.[3]

While the timing and nature of cinema's decline varied across the United Kingdom, post-war statisticians and government departments excluded Northern Ireland from their analysis, partly because records of cinema attendance were kept separately.[4] Though Barry Doyle placed 'the geography of the shrinking audience for film' at the heart of his research on the decline

---

[1] J. Moran, *Armchair Nation: an Intimate History of Britain in Front of the TV* (London, 2013), p. 115.

[2] J. Spraos, *The Decline of the Cinema: an Economist's Report* (London, 1962); D. Docherty, D. Morrison and M. Tracey, *The Last Picture Show? Britain's Changing Film Audiences* (London, 1987); S. Hanson, *From Silent Screen to Multi-Screen: a History of Cinema Exhibition in Britain since 1896* (Manchester, 2007).

[3] J. Thissen, 'Cinema history as social history: retrospect and prospect', in *The Routledge Companion to New Cinema History*, ed. D. Biltereyst, R. Maltby and P. Meers (Abingdon, 2019), pp. 124–33.

[4] H. E. Browning and A. A. Sorrell, 'Cinemas and cinema-going in Great Britain', *Journal of the Royal Statistical Society*, cxvii (1954), 133–70; Political and Economic Planning, *The British Film Industry* (London, 1952); Political and Economic Planning, *The British Film Industry 1958* (London, 1958), pp. 132–70; *Distribution and Exhibition of Cinematograph Films, Report of the Committee of Enquiry Appointed by the President of the Board of Trade* (Parl. Papers 1949 [C. 7837]).

of cinema-going in Great Britain, his findings again exclude Northern Ireland and lack the specificity provided by case studies and micro-historical research.[5] Here, the detailed local evidence shows that the displacement of television by cinema was more complex, and the coronation of Queen Elizabeth II less of a watershed, than historians usually suggest. It also shows distinct regional variations in the strategies adopted by cinema exhibitors to compete with rival attractions and combat declining admissions.

Television services in Belfast and Sheffield

The BBC television service opened in 1936 and started broadcasting to a limited audience in London and the Home Counties. The service was suspended in 1939, but, after it reopened in 1946, gradually spread throughout the UK regions (see Table 2.1). In August 1951, test transmissions from Yorkshire's Holme Moss transmitter led to increased demand for television sets in Sheffield and *The Star* predicted the sale of 15,000 television sets in Sheffield and Rotherham in the upcoming year. Broadcasts began in October 1951 and by December reports suggested that though the initial surge in television sales had passed, sales were increasing in the weeks before Christmas.[6] Belfast residents had to wait longer than their Sheffield counterparts and from May 1953, the temporary Glencairn transmitter relayed the BBC signal from Scotland's Kirk O'Shotts transmitter to Belfast and the surrounding area.[7] It was not until 1955 that the erection of the permanent Divis transmitter brought television signal to the majority of Northern Ireland.[8] While Northern Ireland was one of the last UK regions to receive television, an Irish service (RTÉ) did not begin until 1961.[9] In September 1955, commercial television arrived with the launch of ITV in London and the surrounding area. Granada television began in May 1956 and, in November 1956, the Emley Moor transmitter brought commercial

[5] B. Doyle, 'The geography of cinemagoing in Great Britain, 1934–1994: a comment', *Historical Journal of Film, Radio and Television*, xxiii (2003), 59–71, at p. 59.

[6] *The Star*, 3 Dec. 1951.

[7] Moran, *Armchair Nation*, pp. 74–5.

[8] For more on the introduction of television in Northern Ireland, see R. Cathcart, *The Most Contrary Region: the BBC in Northern Ireland* (Belfast, 1984); R. Savage, *A Loss of Innocence? Television and Irish Society 1960–72* (Manchester, 2010), pp. 318–82; S. Manning, 'Television and the decline of cinema-going in Northern Ireland, 1953–63', *Media History*, xxiv (2018), 408–25.

[9] Before the introduction of RTÉ, many Irish households received British television. Joe Moran claims that, following the introduction of UTV, there were 90,000 television sets in the Irish Republic and a 'feature of the skyline in Irish towns was the multitude of especially tall aerials erected to pick up the distant signals of British transmitters' (Moran, *Armchair Nation*, p. 129).

television to five million residents in the north of England, including those in Sheffield. Ulster Television (UTV), the ITV franchise in Northern Ireland, launched on 31 October 1959. Before its launch, a small minority of viewers received signal from Lancashire's Winter Hill transmitter, such as the residents of Belfast working-class Ardoyne district who attended a 'commercial TV party' in 1956.[10]

Table 2.1. Introduction of UK television services.

Region	BBC	ITV
Northern	1953	1959
Yorkshire East & West Riding	1951	1956
North Western	1949	1956
N. Midland	1949	1956
Midland	1949	1956
London & South East	1946	1955
South Western	1952	1961
Eastern	1955	1959
Southern	1954	1958
Scotland	1952	1957
Wales	1952	1958/62
Northern Ireland	1953	1959

Sources: B. Doyle, 'The geography of cinemagoing in Great Britain, 1934–1994: a comment', *Historical Journal of Film, Radio and Television*, xxiii (2003), 59–71, at p. 67. Figures for Northern Ireland added by author.

The *BBC Handbook* provides detailed figures of the number of UK television licences. It records the number of television licences in regions such as the north of England and Northern Ireland, and areas within those regions, such as Yorkshire and north Derbyshire, and Antrim and Down. While the handbook does not contain figures for individual cities, local newspapers featured several articles containing Post Office data on the number of television licences in Belfast and Sheffield. In November 1956, the *Belfast Telegraph* stated that 42,000 of Northern Ireland's 51,000 television licences were 'in the area of greater Belfast'.[11] These figures should be treated with caution as many television owners were either unable to purchase a television licence or felt that the authorities had little chance

[10] *Belfast Telegraph*, 4 June 1956; 11 June 1956.
[11] *Belfast Telegraph*, 3 Dec. 1956.

of catching them. In 1959, media research company Television Audience Measurement estimated that as many as 23,000 television sets in Northern Ireland remained unlicensed. A Post Office spokesman stated that the organization had sent 13,000 letters to Belfast householders suspected of having an unlicensed television and claimed that the problem was greater in Northern Ireland than in Great Britain.[12]

The coronation of Queen Elizabeth II

On 2 June 1953, over twenty million viewers watched the television broadcast of the coronation of Queen Elizabeth II. It is rightly cited as a catalyst for increased television ownership and the number of UK television licences increased by 52 per cent from 2.14 million in March 1953 to 3.25 million in March 1954. Close analysis of local evidence, however, offers a more nuanced picture of its impact than has been previously suggested, challenging David Kynaston's claim that 'there is little disputing the conventional wisdom that the Coronation "made" television in Britain'.[13] In Sheffield, the increase in television licence holders followed the national pattern and the number increased by 58 per cent from 31,469 in 1953 to 49,681 to 1954. In Northern Ireland, the number of television licences increased dramatically from an extremely low base of 558 in 1953 to 10,353 in 1954. Ninety-eight per cent of these licences were held in the most populous counties of Antrim and Down. Television sets were beyond the means of many working-class households and, in their 1954 survey of estates built by the Northern Ireland Housing Trust, Field and Neill found that only nine of 363 families had one in their own homes.[14] The relatively low levels of television ownership in Belfast and Sheffield meant that the coronation was experienced largely as a communal event and Joe Moran estimated that, excluding children, there was one set to an average of 7.5 people.[15] Approximately 20,000 Belfast residents watched television footage of the ceremony in a combination of private homes and public spaces.[16]

The use of oral history testimony builds on the work of Henrik Örnebring who used Mass-Observation material to assess the coronation's television audiences.[17] Memories of the coronation were linked to the absence of

---

[12] *Belfast Telegraph*, 17 Apr. 1959.
[13] D. Kynaston, *Family Britain: 1951–57* (London, 2009), p. 301.
[14] D. Field and D. G. Neill, *A Survey of New Housing Estates in Belfast* (Belfast, 1957), p. 43.
[15] Moran, *Armchair Nation*, p. 77.
[16] *Belfast News-Letter*, 3 June 1953.
[17] H. Örnebring, 'Writing the history of television audiences: the coronation in the Mass-Observation archive', in *Re-viewing Television History: Critical Issues in Television Historiography*, ed. H. Wheatley (London, 2007), pp. 170–83.

television in households and early experiences of television were often shared with friends and relatives. This reaffirms the findings of Jancovich et al. that early experiences of television were shared and communal rather than a retreat into privatized, domestic space.[18] As Sylvia Fearn stated, 'my auntie next door was the first one to get a tele and everybody went into their front room to look at it, the Queen's coronation'.[19] Jean McVeigh was raised in a Roman Catholic Belfast household and her house was so busy that she and her brothers were sent to the local cinema.[20]

For many people, however, the coronation was experienced both as televisual and then a cinematic event. David McIlwaine visited friends in the seaside resort of Bangor where he watched the ceremony. He recalled that 'it was really wonderful in 1953 to be able to see the coronation in black and white and on wee small screens. But, you could say, you could brag, I saw it on TV. And then you saw it in the cinema perhaps a week later'.[21] Mike Higginbottom recalled relatives obtaining a television in time for the coronation: 'everybody piled in to the front room. It was like a day out'. He was then taken to the cinema afterwards: 'I remember going to see the movie and my gran saying "you want to watch this because you might not see it again"'.[22]

Despite the communal nature of television broadcasts, low levels of television ownership meant that, alongside radio, press reports and local street parties, cinema screenings were central to coronation experiences. While cinema scholars such as Jeffrey Richards and James Chapman have discussed the way that coronation films portrayed and represented the monarchy, there has been little discussion of how these films were experienced and received by audiences.[23] Cinemas in both cities went to great lengths to obtain and promote newsreels and full-length feature films of the coronation and it is likely that this footage was viewed by more residents than the television coverage. In Belfast, on the evening of the coronation, the managers of the Crumlin and the Gaumont 'drove to Nutt's Corner [airfield] to pick up the shots of scenes along the Coronation

---

[18] M. Jancovich, L. Faire and S. Stubbings, *The Place of the Audience: Cultural Geographies of Film Consumption* (London, 2003), p. 161.

[19] Interview with Sylvia Fearn, Sheffield, 1 July 2014.

[20] Interview with Jean McVeigh, Belfast, 2 Apr. 2014.

[21] Interview with David McIlwaine, Cultra, Co. Down, 9 July 2015.

[22] Interview with Mike Higginbottom, Sheffield, 20 Aug. 2015.

[23] J. Richards, 'The coronation of Queen Elizabeth II in film', *The Court Historian*, ix (2004), 69–79; J. Chapman, 'Cinema, monarchy and the making of heritage: *A Queen is Crowned* (1953)', in *British Historical Cinema*, ed. C. Monk and A. Sergeant (London, 2002), pp. 82–91.

route for exhibition to their patrons at 10-30 o'clock the same night'.[24] The Crumlin offered free admission to its Gaumont-British Newsreel, going to great lengths to decorate its premises, celebrate the event and promote the film.[25] In Belfast, royalist decoration was a clear marker of identity and in the days preceding the coronation the *Manchester Guardian* reported that that what used to be the 'invisible dividing line' between nationalist and unionist districts 'is no longer invisible. It is strikingly clear where the flags, banners, and bunting end abruptly'.[26] On 3 June, further sequences were 'flown over by special plane' and were exhibited for the remainder of the week at both cinemas.[27] Anne Connolly's comments show that, even for those with access to television, the cinema held technological advantages: 'my mother took me to see it on the Pathé News because they were the only ones showing it in colour. We only had black and white television'.[28] The Belfast Corporation considered the event so important that they arranged for 25,000 schoolchildren to view the coronation footage.[29] Matinees were organized at several cinemas including the Gaumont, the Majestic, the Ritz and the Strand. On 4 June, one report suggested that the 2,000 children in attendance at the Royal Hippodrome 'cheered to the echo'.[30]

In 1953, the full-length Technicolor feature *A Queen is Crowned* (UK, 1953) was the highest grossing film at the British box-office and also performed well internationally.[31] The production of 309 copies, in comparison to around forty for a standard release, showed the faith of distributors in its popularity and ensured simultaneous distribution to almost all Odeon and Gaumont cinemas.[32] It broke the attendance record at Belfast's Imperial cinema when it was screened nine times daily for five weeks. The fact that the film was so popular in a centrally located cinema indicates that, despite its positive portrayal of monarchy and empire, it appealed to patrons from

[24] *Belfast Telegraph*, 29 May 1953.
[25] *Belfast Telegraph*, 1 June 1953.
[26] *Manchester Guardian*, 29 May 1953.
[27] *Belfast Telegraph*, 29 May 1953.
[28] Interview with Anne Connolly, Belfast, 28 May 2015.
[29] McClay Library, minutes of the General Purposes and Finance Committee, Belfast Corporation, 18 March 1953, p. 249.
[30] *Belfast Telegraph*, 4 June 1953; 5 June 1953.
[31] Chapman, 'Cinema, monarchy and the making of heritage', p. 82. At the Guild Theatre, New York, it did record business and to accommodate the crowds the cinema 'launched extra showings in the morning and evening, increasing the number of performances per day to 10' (*Motion Picture Daily*, 11 June 1953). It was the second best attended film at the Captiole, Ghent from 1953–71 (L. Van de Vijver, D. Biltereyst and K. Velders, 'Crisis at the Capitole: a cultural economics analysis of a major first-run cinema in Ghent, 1953–1971', *Historical Journal of Film, Radio and Television*, xxxv (2015), 75–124).
[32] A. Eyles, *Odeon Cinemas 2: from J. Arthur Rank to the Multiplex* (London: 2005), p. 57.

Figure 2.1. Ritz stage show, Belfast, June 1953 (*ABC News*, August 1953).

both sides of the community.[33] While the film clearly appealed to Unionist sentiment, the pageantry and spectacle of the occasion was also central to its attraction. As one *Belfast Telegraph* reviewer commented, 'Hollywood at its brightest and best has never produced anything as colossal'.[34] It was far more successful than ABC's rival film *Elizabeth is Queen* (UK, 1953) and shorter films such as Movietone's twenty-minute feature *Coronation Day* (UK, 1953). Despite this, the *Northern Whig* reported that patrons were 'in no mood to discriminate' between *A Queen is Crowned* and *Elizabeth is Queen*.[35] Screenings of these films were also combined with stage shows to enhance the spectacle of the event. ABC's in-house magazine reported that a stage show presented at the Ritz to accompany *Elizabeth is Queen* (see Figure 2.1) 'was the most successful they have ever run'.[36] Television brought the coronation into the domestic sphere, but it could not match the cinema for size, showmanship and spectacle.

Belfast cinemas also provided footage for those living outside the city. Following threats from Sinn Féin and the Irish Anti-Partition League, no Dublin cinemas exhibited footage of the coronation. The *Irish Examiner*

[33] *Belfast Telegraph*, 8 July 1959.
[34] *Belfast Telegraph*, 6 June 1953.
[35] *Northern Whig*, 9 June 1953.
[36] *ABC News*, Aug. 1953, p. 21.

stated that there was 'a genuine interest among thousands of ordinary people who profess no allegiance to the Crown'.[37] Many Dubliners took advantage of the Great Northern Railway's special fares and travelled from Dublin to Belfast to view coronation films. The Regent placed adverts in the Irish press, which emphasized that the cinema was only a five-minute bus ride from the Great Northern Railway station.[38] On 10 June, 400 passengers boarded the early train from Dublin to Belfast. So many people turned up at the train station, that an extra train left fifteen minutes later, carrying a further 500 passengers.[39] One Belfast cinema manager claimed that he had received 3,000 letters and anticipated that 30,000 of the 50,000 patrons who would see the film in its first week would travel from the Irish Republic. 'They are falling over themselves to come here', he claimed.[40] This figure was no doubt an exaggeration and the manager of a large Belfast cinema claimed that he received around 1,000 patrons from across the border. The manager of a smaller cinema stated that 'we probably had about 300 Southerners here during the week. We had expected a great many more'.[41]

In Sheffield, exhibitors also made great effort to promote and screen coronation films. Before the event, the Sheffield branch of the Cinematograph Exhibitors' Association decided that, to prevent patrons from 'bobbing up and down', the national anthem should be substituted for 'appropriate martial music' in coronation films and newsreels.[42] Some cinemas even relayed television footage of the coronation. The 540-seat Sheffield News Theatre charged patrons £1 5s for admissions to its six-foot by four feet 'large screen' transmission of the event, advertising that it included 'a packed lunch so that the audience will not miss any part of the programme'.[43] On 2 June, footage was flown to Doncaster, 'rushed from there by motor-cycle, and shown on the Sheffield screen little over an hour after it had been taken'.[44] The Gaumont's patrons sent a congratulatory telegram to the queen and Her Private Secretary's response asked manager Roy Raistrick to 'convey the Queen's sincere thanks to all those who joined with you in your kind and loyal message on the occasion of Her Majesty's Coronation'.[45] On 3 June, it screened a Gaumont-British newsreel of the

[37] *Irish Examiner*, 11 June 1953.
[38] *Irish Independent*, 3 June 1953.
[39] *Belfast Telegraph*, 10 June 1953.
[40] *Belfast Telegraph*, 3 June 1953; *Kinematograph Weekly*, 11 June 1953.
[41] *Sunday Independent*, 14 June 1953.
[42] *Kinematograph Weekly*, 5 Feb. 1951.
[43] *The Star*, 6 May 1953.
[44] *The Star*, 3 June 1953.
[45] *The Star*, 2 June 1953.

full procession and ceremony. While the nearby Cinema House closed both its cinema and café on coronation day, from 3 June it screened the Universal newsreel *The Coronation of Queen Elizabeth* three times daily.[46] On 6 June, *The Star* stated that the 'five cinemas in Sheffield's city centre will next week show colour films of the Coronation, and at four of them the films will be feature length'.[47] Both the Cinema House and the Gaumont screened *A Queen is Crowned*. On 13 June, the Lord Mayor and Lady Mayoress of Sheffield attended a special screening at the Gaumont where the Deputy Lord Mayor, the president of the Chamber of Commerce, the leader of the City Council and the editor of *The Star* were present.[48] The film was well attended at the Gaumont, where the manager commented that 'nothing but the highest praise has been showered on the production'. Patrons told him it was 'magnificent', 'truly a wonderful experience' and 'the finest film ever seen'.[49]

While the coronation led to increased sales of television sets, it did little to fundamentally alter patterns of cinema attendance in Belfast or Sheffield. Jancovich et al. noted that while television was shaped by its domestic setting, cinema-going represented freedom from the home and was closely associated with public space.[50] There were also clear generational differences and in October 1952 one local resident told the *Belfast Telegraph* that she wanted 'to meet someone who will let me "look-in" on Coronation Day. Eventually I hope my home will have T.V. but as a young person and a cinema fan I do not think it will keep people from the pictures. It will be very nice to see shows at home but getting out and meeting friends has more attractions'.[51] Table 2.2 shows that Belfast cinema attendance remained stable after the coronation and there were only minor fluctuations in the six month periods ending in March and September from 1952 to 1954. At Sheffield's Rex Cinema, gross box-office revenue remained almost static and the Gaumont's admissions increased slightly from 1952 to 1953, which may have been a result of the popularity of films such as *A Queen is Crowned*.

---

[46] *The Star*, 1 June 1953.

[47] *The Star*, 6 June 1953.

[48] *The Star*, 13 June 1953.

[49] Cinema Theatre Association Archive, Gaumont, Sheffield, weekly return forms, June 1953.

[50] Jancovich, Faire and Stubbings, *The Place of the Audience*, p. 177.

[51] *Belfast Telegraph*, 27 Oct. 1952.

Table 2.2. Belfast cinema admissions at six-monthly
intervals, March 1952–September 1954.

Six months ending	Admissions
March 1952	8,566,095
September 1952	8,023,412
March 1953	8,315,824
September 1953	7,950,164
March 1954	8,332,704
September 1954	8,083,061

Source: PRONI, FIN/15/6/A/10, Ministry of Finance, reduction in rates of Entertainments
Duty, 1954.

The impact of television on cinema attendance

In Belfast and Sheffield cinema attendance remained strong until the
late 1950s. As Table 2.3 shows, the 1951 introduction of BBC television
in Sheffield did little to alter the number of operating cinemas. Between
1945 and 1956 only one Sheffield cinema closed and this was due to the
expansion of Sheffield University, rather than the impact of television or
declining cinema attendances. Similarly, between 1945 and 1958 only a
single Belfast cinema closed. The number of Belfast cinemas even increased
in the mid 1950s, despite the introduction of BBC in 1953. There is a danger
in assuming that the content of television and cinema programmes were in
direct competition in the early to mid 1950s. As Sian Barber stated, rather
than being in competition with cinema, television 'was simply part of the
ongoing process of the domesticating of leisure and entertainment'.[52] In
both cities, the most precipitous declines in cinema attendance occurred
following the introduction of commercial television. In the United
Kingdom, ninety-one cinemas closed in 1955, 224 closed in 1956 and a
further 204 closed in 1957.[53] From 1957 to 1964 the number of Sheffield
cinemas drastically declined from fifty-one to twenty-three, and the number
of Belfast cinemas from forty-three to twenty-eight. In 1945, Sheffield had
twelve more cinemas than Belfast. By 1960 they had the same number,
though by 1964 Belfast had five more cinemas than Sheffield.

[52] S. Barber, 'Cinema and the age of television: 1950–70', in *The Routledge Companion
to British Cinema History*, ed. I. Q. Hunter, L. Porter and J. Smith (Abingdon, 2017), pp.
220–30, at p. 228.

[53] *Kinematograph Year Book 1958* (London, 1958), p. 509.

Table 2.3. Number of cinema licences granted in Belfast and Sheffield, 1945–64.

Year	Belfast	Sheffield
1945	41	53
1946	40	53
1947	42	53
1948	42	53
1949	42	53
1950	42	53
1951	42	54
1952	43	53
1953	43	53
1954	43	53
1955	43	52
1956	44	51
1957	43	51
1958	43	48
1959	41	45
1960	37	37
1961	34	33
1962	30	31
1963	28	26
1964	28	23

Sources: McClay Library, Belfast Corporation minutes, 1944–64; Sheffield Local Studies Library, Sheffield City Council minutes, 1945–64.

A simple count of cinema numbers, however, does not show the type and size of cinemas that closed or provide an indication of how overall attendances changed. Nor can it demonstrate the impact of television as these changes were related to a range of social economic factors such as population shifts and the pull of rival leisure activities. The records of the Rex show that its gross box-office revenue peaked in 1952, one year after the introduction of BBC television. From 1953 to 1957, box-office revenue remained stable. Following the introduction of ITV, however, it declined from £34,018 in 1956 to £23,870 in 1958.[54] This correlates to increased

[54] Sheffield City Archives, MD7333/5/1–2, Rex Cinema (Sheffield) Limited, Receipts Ledgers.

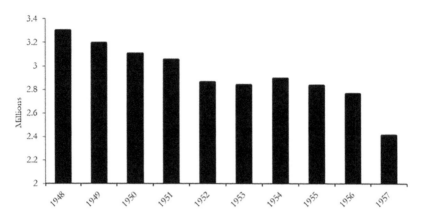

Figure 2.2. Recorded admissions in Northern Ireland cinemas, 1948–57 (PRONI, FIN/15/6/A/12, Reduction in rate of Entertainments Duty, 9 June 1958).

sales of television licences in Sheffield, which rose from 108,895 in 1956 to 146,963 in 1959. Figure 2.2 shows the decline in recorded admissions in Northern Ireland cinemas from 1948 to 1957. After the introduction of BBC television, admissions actually increased from 28.37 million in 1953 to 28.94 million in 1954. Belfast cinema admissions constituted the majority of Northern Ireland cinema admissions, which fell from 17.2 million in 1953 to 15.3 million in 1957. The number of recorded admissions only dropped significantly after 1957, though this has more to do with concessions for cheaper tickets in the rates of Entertainments Duty than actual declines in attendance.

In 1962, economist John Spraos questioned the isolated impact of the introduction of commercial television on cinema attendance and stated that 'there is a strong case against the hypothesis that the second programme has inflicted on the cinema damage additional to and distinct from that of a single programme'.[55] He identified three phases in television's impact on cinema admissions. In the first phase, during the early 1950s, the effect was small as a disproportionate number of televisions were purchased by those in high income groups who were least likely to be regular cinema-goers. In the second phase, from 1955, there was a dramatic increase in television ownership as sets became available to larger working-class families. From 1958, this gave way to a final phase when smaller families were increasingly represented in each year's new viewers, meaning that the loss of admissions measured against each new television declined.[56] The number of UK

[55] Spraos, *The Decline of the Cinema*, p. 28.
[56] Spraos, *The Decline of the Cinema*, p. 22.

television licences increased from 4.5 million in 1955 to 13.3 million in 1965. In Sheffield, the number of television licences increased from 108,895 in 1956 to 160,790 in 1960. In the same period, television licences in Antrim and Down increased more than fourfold from 23,535 in 1955 to 112,231 in 1960. While this marked a dramatic increase, table 2.4 shows that Northern Ireland had a much lower proportion of television licences than either the north of England or the United Kingdom as a whole. This may indicate both the lack of disposable income in Northern Ireland and the persistence of communal television viewing. Despite these low levels of television ownership, Northern Ireland cinema admissions still declined, though to a lesser extent than Sheffield and more cinemas remained open for longer periods of time.

Table 2.4. Percentage of families owning television licences, 1957–65.

Year	North of England	Northern Ireland	United Kingdom
1957	45.7	14.6	43.5
1958	53.2	19.6	50.3
1959	60.6	24.4	57.3
1960	67.6	32.6	64.5
1961	69.7	36.7	67.1
1962	72.6	40.1	70.5
1963	75.5	45.3	73.2
1964	77.4	47.9	75.3
1965	78.8	49.7	76.9

Sources: *BBC Handbook 1961* (London, 1961); *BBC Handbook 1966* (London, 1966).

Increased television ownership was crucial, for as one reporter suggested '[o]nce a set is bought or hired, the viewer likes to get value out of it – and probably has less to spend on other entertainments'.[57] While television sets were beyond the means of many working-class households, access to credit and rental agreements increased television ownership in Belfast and Sheffield. Joe Moran argued that the 'easing of restrictions on hire purchase in July 1954 was probably more important than the coronation in turning television into a mass medium'.[58] After the Westminster government lifted hire purchase restrictions, Belfast retailers expected a subsequent 'buying boom in television and radio sets, washing machines, refrigerators and

[57] *Belfast Telegraph*, 5 Oct. 1960.
[58] Moran, *Armchair Nation*, p. 81.

vacuum cleaners'. Some, however, were more cautious and one retailer stated that 'Northern Ireland people and the Scots are rather more cautious about involving themselves in lengthy hire purchases – much more so than the English'.[59] Field and Neill's survey found that while hire purchase was often used to 'to obtain furniture or household appliances … no case was encountered of payments on a television set'.[60] Here, television was not the only factor limiting cinema attendance and the extra expense of living on new estates, alongside the distance from amenities such as cinemas, libraries and sports facilities, also restricted available leisure time. The survey found that 40 per cent of 'housewives seldom or never went outside their homes, except on necessary errands or to visit friends or relations. For those housewives who did go out, cinema-going was by far the most important activity, and for more than half of them their sole activity'.[61] In 1954, Mark Abrams claimed that since the end of the Second World War the population had used its economic gains to improve domestic comfort through the purchase of home improvements and goods such as domestic appliances and television sets. He claimed that these advances had to be offset by declines elsewhere and 'the reductions have been made in expenditure on cinema admissions, clothing and footwear'.[62]

In September 1954, the *Belfast Telegraph* stated that the introduction of more attractive hire purchase terms, the announcement of a new licence detector van and an increased interest in BBC programming had led to a recent increase in television licence sales.[63] One Belfast confectionary wholesaler suggested an early shift towards home-centred consumption, stating that those who previously only purchased sweets at the cinema 'are now taking them home up to four or five times a week to share with their families around their sets in the evening'.[64] Spraos believed that the type of programme shown on television was not a key determinant of falling cinema attendance. Rather, it was the convenience of home entertainment, the diversion of household funds for rental and hire purchase payments and the fact that television had no repeat viewing costs. Television placed a high financial burden on working-class households and created restrictions on other expenditure.[65]

---

[59] *Belfast Telegraph*, 14 July 1954.
[60] Field and Neill, *A Survey of New Housing Estates in Belfast*, p. 43.
[61] Field and Neill, *A Survey of New Housing Estates in Belfast*, pp. 60–3.
[62] *Financial Times*, 8 June 1954.
[63] *Belfast Telegraph*, 27 Sept. 1954.
[64] *Belfast Telegraph*, 4 Oct. 1954.
[65] Spraos, *The Decline of the Cinema*.

The oral history testimony shows the reluctance of working-class households to engage in hire purchase agreements, revealing the extent some people went to purchase a television set outright. Televisions were expensive and in 1956, Belfast's Electrad store advertised a Philips seventeen-inch table television for seventy-six guineas (£79 16s).[66] David McConnell remembered that 'my dad had got a gold watch for twenty-five years in Gallaher's [tobacco factory]. And I remember being allowed to wear it once and I asked my brother years later what happened to it. And he said "did you not know, they sold it to get the television"'.[67] The introduction of commercial television in Great Britain had unintended benefits for Belfast consumers. In September 1955, one report suggested that '[t]elevision sets are being sold in Ulster for £10. In the past few days one Belfast dealer has disposed of more than 100. The sets were bought in bulk in London and shipped to Belfast in crates. They are obsolete there because – having only a single channel – they receive only B.B.C. programmes'.[68] David McIlwaine took advantage of a similar offer and recalled that, following his marriage in 1956, 'there was a firm in Bermondsey offering Bush television sets for £8. Send away, send your cheque or postal order and they would deliver. It was really for nothing. So we took the chance and I bought a postal order for £8'.[69]

Even by the end of the 1950s, many households preferred to rent their television than engage in hire purchase agreements. Hire purchase controls were lifted and reintroduced throughout the 1950s and deposits were out of reach for working-class households. In August 1959, the chairman of Ulster Telefusion stated that their seventeen-inch sets could be rented from 9s weekly and customers were offered free twenty-four-hour service. He claimed that 'most of our radios are bought for cash, or by hire purchase – but with television most customers prefer to rent'.[70] Customers preferred to rent more expensive items, such as televisions, as it removed the fear of them breaking down and placed the onus of repair on the rental company. Rental allowed Belfast residents to participate in the growing consumer society, and in 1960, UTV General Manager Brum Henderson told the Northern Ireland Radio Retailers' Association that 'Ulster is entering an age in which the average home will not be complete without a washing machine, refrigerator and television set'.[71]

---

[66] *Belfast Telegraph*, 9 Aug. 1956.
[67] Interview with David McConnell, Belfast, 24 Sept. 2014.
[68] *Belfast Telegraph*, 15 Sept. 1955.
[69] Interview with David McIlwaine, Cultra, Co. Down, 9 July 2015.
[70] *Belfast Telegraph*, 13 Aug. 1959.
[71] *Belfast Telegraph*, 25 March 1960.

Sheffield residents were better able to purchase televisions outright and displayed a greater willingness to engage in hire purchase agreements. In 1954, Malcolm Ayton used the money he saved in the armed forces to purchase his first television: 'A Bush twelve-inch, very expensive, I think I paid £80 … when the average working wage was about £8 10s'.[72] Helen Carroll worked as a nurse and recalled that 'I bought it on hire purchase because I couldn't afford to pay for it outright'.[73] There were, however, clear intra-city variations in rates of television ownership and this had a marked impact on cinema-going. In their 1954 study of community structure and neighbourhood on Sheffield's Wybourn estate, Hodges and Smith found that in 'relation to the number of dwellings, the estate appears to have only about half as many television licences as the rest of the city'.[74] The authors claimed that while there was some local interest in 'pig-keeping, gardening, angling and pigeon fancying', residents largely spent their leisure time 'at the cinema, the public house, and the "dogs"'.[75] In 1958, Ferdynand Zweig interviewed 161 English Steel employees at Sheffield's River Don Works and found that 62 per cent owned television sets. He claimed that the number was so low 'partly due to the lack of electricity in old-type houses'.[76]

By the end of the decade, more families were able to purchase televisions outright. In 1960, *The Star* commented on the ubiquity of television sets in households and one spokesman for a television sales firm commented that '[n]ewly-weds consider TV an essential and sometimes they have saved up to buy a set outright'. A spokesman for another firm stated that '[w]e are selling sets at the rate of 100 to 150 a week'.[77] Despite this, television rental was still common. Pete and Valerie Lowe married in 1961 and obtained their first television in 1962. Valerie stated that 'every March he got a bonus and you see you could rent your television, but you had to pay for the aerial. And we couldn't afford to pay for the aerial. So in March, every year, he used to get a bonus from work and that bonus paid for an aerial and somebody putting it up. Then we could rent the television'.[78] Bob Slater's comments show that homes with televisions were increasingly seen as sites of affluence: 'if you saw a big H aerial on the house, you'd think: "oh, they must have got

---

[72] Interview with Malcolm Ayton, Sheffield, 24 July 2015.
[73] Interview with Helen Carroll, Sheffield, 23 July 2015.
[74] M. W. Hodges and C. S. Smith, 'The Sheffield estate', in *Neighbourhood and Community: an Enquiry into Social Relationships on Housing Estates in Liverpool and Sheffield*, ed. T. S. Simey (Liverpool, 1954), pp. 79–134, at p. 87.
[75] Hodges and Smith, 'The Sheffield estate', pp. 92–3.
[76] Ferdynand Zweig, *The Worker in an Affluent Society* (London, 1961), p. 108.
[77] *The Star*, 9 Sept. 1960.
[78] Interview with Pete Lowe, Sheffield, 28 July 2015.

some money them"'.[79] Increased television ownership, smaller family sizes, an increase in space and better housing conditions all led to an increase in domestic leisure activities, and these changes affected a range of leisure activities other than cinema-going.[80] In 1959, for instance, the chairman of Sheffield's Owlerton greyhound stadium attributed declining attendances on the use of hire purchase to obtain television sets.[81]

Television ownership was one of many factors cited by local newspapers and trade journals as contributing to the decline of cinema attendance. Jancovich et al. found that, in Nottingham, cinema-owners also cited Entertainment Tax, the British Film Production Levy and the Sunday levy as key factors in cinema closures. It was only in the 1960s that television was seen as the central threat, due to the arrival of commercial television, the reduced price of television sets and the increasing number of films shown on television.[82] In Belfast, high rates of Entertainments Duty, rising overheads and alternative forms of leisure were all seen as key factors in the decline of cinema attendance; it was only towards the end of the 1950s that television was identified as the central threat. In 1956, *Kine Weekly* reported that the 'sales figure of TV sets in Belfast is nearly 40,000 – equivalent to the seating capacity of the city's cinemas'. Despite this, it added that the 'falling off in admissions is not yet so noticeable here as across the water, but Ulster has yet to receive commercial television'.[83] Alternative leisure activities and temporary attractions were viewed as a greater threat and it reported that the arrival of the Chipperfield Circus led to below average attendance: 'Belfast – where the total seating is 40,000 – is feeling the drain of the 8,000 to 10,000 people attracted by the circus daily'.[84] By 1958, the increasing competition of television, the continuation of Entertainment Tax and recent increases in valuation rates meant that Northern Ireland exhibitors were 'looking to the future with only cautious optimism'.[85] The *Belfast Telegraph* claimed that while the sense of occasion, technical advancement and the novelty of new films all drew patrons to the cinema, attendances were clearly in decline:

The great enemy is television. TV is the medium which has meant the beginning of the end for many a cinema. For as the TV aerials shoot up, so do the attendance figures shoot down. In Belfast the number of TV sets is roughly

---

[79] Interview with Bob Slater, Sheffield, 28 July 2015.
[80] Jancovich, Faire and Stubbings, *The Place of the Audience*, p. 150.
[81] *The Star*, 27 Aug. 1959.
[82] Jancovich, Faire and Stubbings, *The Place of the Audience*, p. 141.
[83] *Kinematograph Weekly*, 5 July 1956.
[84] *Belfast Telegraph*, 5 July 1956.
[85] *Kinematograph Weekly*, 2 Jan. 1958.

equivalent to the seating capacity of all the cinemas and I.T.V., which has been proved to have even greater drawing power than B.B.C., has yet to come.[86]

In the following month, it added that while cinema closures were inevitable, they 'can still hold a large place in the entertainment life of the community if the production side of the industry is able to maintain a flow of top quality films, and they are prepared to adopt the latest technical refinements'.[87] These reports suggest that it was only five years after the coronation that television ownership was perceived as the central threat to cinema attendance and, even then, cinemas believed they could stem the tide of people lured away by television.

The introduction of UTV was a key turning point in the decline of cinema-going in Belfast. The number of television licences in Antrim and Down increased from 86,094 in 1959 to 112,231 in 1960, the greatest year-on-year increase during the period under review.[88] Reports suggested that 'attendances dropped 20 per cent. in the first months of UTV' and from 1959 to 1960, Entertainments Duty payments from cinema tickets fell by 30 per cent.[89] UTV's focus on entertainment meant that it provided more direct competition than the BBC. Brum Henderson claimed that he wanted to provide television for the working-class Shankill and the Falls, rather than the more affluent Malone and Antrim roads.[90] In October 1960, *Belfast Telegraph* reporter Martin Wallace stated that Belfast's suburban exhibitors were pessimistic about the future as there were 'too many cinemas for the film-going population which remains – and too few films are being made to provide new "product"'.[91]

There were fewer reports on the decline of Sheffield cinema attendance in both *The Star* and *Kine Weekly*. The introduction of commercial television had a less immediate impact on television ownership in Sheffield and from 1956 to 1957, the number of television licences increased from 108,895 to 123,217. The impact was varied and city centre cinemas with larger seating capacities were better placed to cope with declines in cinema attendance. In 1958, the Rank Organisation appealed to Sheffield's local valuation court after an increase in the Odeon's rating value. City architect and surveyor W. R. Rothwell refuted the claim that commercial television would negatively

[86] *Belfast Telegraph*, 14 Feb. 1958.

[87] *Belfast Telegraph*, 28 March 1958.

[88] *BBC Handbook 1960* (London, 1960), p. 224; *BBC Handbook 1961* (London, 1961), p. 172.

[89] *Belfast Telegraph*, 5 Oct. 1960; *Digest of Statistics Northern Ireland 1961* (Belfast, 1961), p. 72.

[90] Moran, *Armchair Nation*, pp. 126–7.

[91] *Belfast Telegraph*, 5 Oct. 1960.

affect the cinema's revenue. He said that its impact was greatest on suburban cinemas and added that 'at the opening of the new cinema the managing director of the Rank Organisation said that the best way of meeting that competition was to build a cinema like that, at that point'. A. H. Bean, of Odeon cinemas, replied that '[c]ommercial television, coupled with easy purchase of cars and other things on hire purchase which had given people a higher standard of living had resulted in falling cinema attendances'.[92] However, the Gaumont's manager reports show that television also offered a boon to cinema attendance. He made several references to television advertising throughout 1956 and, for example, commented that *The Intimate Stranger* (UK, 1956) 'had a very good boost on T.V. and has reaped the reward in attracting patrons'.[93]

In 1962, *Sheffield Telegraph* journalist Anthony Tweedale reported on the state of the city's cinemas. While he assessed many factors, he claimed that television was cinema's 'arch menace … because of the simple alternative it had to offer to filmgoers … The public, fascinated by commercials, the mechanics of television and those interminable "personalities" thereon, hardly paid the cinema the same close, fond attention that they used to'. His comments suggest that television led cinema-goers to become more discerning in their film choices: 'Mass mentality seemed to change overnight, from a natural awe … to a vastly more detached – though not necessarily sophisticated – interest in the *occasional* things of the Cinema'.[94] These comments are reinforced by oral history testimony that demonstrates how perceptions of the cinema altered with the introduction of television. Bill Allerton's family obtained a television in the mid 1950s and he claimed that it 'changed the role of the picture house … Unless it was a really special film the only reason you were going was to see if there was any young ladies to pick up'.[95]

Affluence, leisure and youth culture

The reasons for the post-war decline in cinema admissions were far more wide-ranging and extensive than increases in television ownership and economic factors affecting the profitability of cinemas. Teenagers and young adults remained the cinema's core audience. However, greater amounts of disposable income and a more diverse range of leisure activities altered the ways that they spent their time and money. In the 1950s, the range

---

[92] *The Star*, 5 Nov. 1958.
[93] Cinema Theatre Association Archive, Gaumont, Sheffield, weekly return forms, 1956.
[94] *The Star*, 23 May 1962.
[95] Interview with Bill Allerton, Sheffield, 23 July 2015.

of commercial leisure options expanded and cinema-goers also spent their money in dance halls and cafés, and on consumer goods such as clothes and records. The use of two case studies to examine the impact of new forms of youth culture and entertainment expands on the work of Adrian Horn, who argued for the importance of local evidence above generalizations at a national level. He stated that an assessment of youth culture in Northern Ireland would be particularly fruitful, as it would present a non-English view.[96]

Cinema's decline was uneven and there were clear generational and geographical differences in the pace at which the cinema-going habit was lost. Following the Second World War, the young working-class were the most frequent cinema-goers. In the 1950s, the increased range of leisure opportunities available to this group meant that they stopped going to the cinema as regularly as they had done, although they remained proportionately significant within the total audience.[97] It was their parents' generation who were most likely to be drawn from cinemas to television sets. Children were also more likely to spend time at home rather than at the cinema. For instance, by December 1961, the headmaster of Belfast's Knockbreda Secondary Intermediate School found that six out of ten of his pupils now preferred television to cinema and there was a clear preference for UTV over BBC. Many children, he claimed 'seemed to be happy with the shock and crime programmes and the endless succession of Westerns'.[98] As audiences declined, and cinemas then closed down, cinema-going became a more expensive, youth-oriented leisure activity targeted at teenagers with greater amounts of disposable income. Attendance became less habitual and patrons were likely to attend on fewer occasions but travel further and spend more on individual cinema trips.

The oral history interviews revealed generational differences in the impact of television ownership. Norman Campbell stated that television ownership 'didn't affect my personal cinema attendance too much. But on reflection, I think it affected the cinema attendance for mothers and fathers, because it was now possible to sit in at night'.[99] Ann Gorman's family obtained their first television in 1958. She stated that this had a limited impact on her generation's cinema attendance as 'all we wanted to do was get out of

[96] A. Horn, *Juke Box Britain: Americanisation and Youth Culture, 1945–60* (Manchester, 2010), p. 193.

[97] S. Harper and V. Porter, 'Cinema audience tastes in 1950s Britain', *Journal of Popular British Cinema*, ii (1999), 66–82.

[98] *Belfast Telegraph*, 12 Dec. 1961.

[99] Interview with Norman Campbell, Belfast, 4 June 2014.

the house'.[100] As she moved into adolescence, her range of leisure activities expanded and Ann also frequented dance halls and a jazz club in Belfast city centre: 'You would have still gone out to the cinema … If a James Bond movie came along or something, you wouldn't have missed it. You have still made sure you went to the cinema to see it. There were still key movies you went to. But it wasn't your number one thing'.[101]

In her study of women's leisure in England, Claire Langhamer found that, despite the national decline in attendances, cinema remained a popular leisure pursuit for young girls in the 1950s. She noted a shift in adulthood from personal to family-oriented leisure, rooted in notions of duty and service to others. She stated that cinema trips often provided 'periods of momentary affluence' and 'allowed working-class girls access to a physical environment which differed markedly from their home experience'.[102] While television was watched in domestic settings, the cinema continued to provide a space for courtship and freedom from parental supervision. Norman Campbell recalled that, as cinema attendances declined, 'courting couples still went at night-times because you had to be quite far on in a friendship to be taking somebody home. But you could go to the cinema and be warm and dry'.[103] Margaret McDonaugh's testimony shows the contrast between experiences of television and cinema:

> you went to the cinema to get out and to be with friends or to be with a boyfriend or something. When television came, when we got television first of all it was just BBC. And then, then ITV came, but for a long time it was just two channels and if you'd been in with your parents, there's a lot of people, there might have been six of you in the room watching television.[104]

There were other places for teenagers to escape the household and, in the 1950s, an increasing range of commercial leisure activities competed with the cinema for their time and money. Docherty et al. believed that:

> the cinema audience was affected by a cultural revolution – the emergence of the teenager … Cinema could not withstand the onslaught of Rock and Roll, Trad Jazz, espresso (Bongo or otherwise), motorbikes, duffle coats and leather jackets, the Bomb, and the panoply of artefacts and opinions which made up youth culture from the mid-1950s.[105]

---

[100] Interview with Ann Gorman, Belfast, 23 Oct. 2014.
[101] Interview with Ann Gorman, Belfast, 23 Oct. 2014.
[102] C. Langhamer, *Women's Leisure in England* (Manchester, 2000), p. 61.
[103] Interview with Norman Campbell, Belfast, 4 June 2014.
[104] Interview with Margaret McDonaugh, Belfast, 18 May 2015.
[105] Docherty, Morrison and Tracey, *The Last Picture Show?*, pp. 26–7.

This statement, however, places too much emphasis on the teenager as a post-war phenomenon. As Adrian Horn suggested, while post-war youth were not the first generation of teenagers, increased media attention, greater amounts of disposable income and improved education meant they were more distinctive than earlier counterparts.[106] Many interviewees connected their experiences of cinema-going to their broader leisure lives. As Jack Riley stated 'you might go to pub one night and picture palace next night. You might even go twice a week, and you might go dancing. You varied, my activities and my pleasures really. It weren't as though I were just hooked on films'.[107]

In the immediate post-war period, the popularity of cinema-going was inflated due to the limited range of commercial leisure options available. James Nott argued that post-war economic and social circumstances favoured existing commercial leisure activities, as there were few consumer goods to spend money on and building restrictions limited the ability of leisure providers to construct new facilities. Money poured into existing leisure activities such as cinema, dancing and spectator sports.[108] Andrew Palmer's recollections show how post-war austerity led to more frequent cinema trips:

> The '47 winter was terrible, it were really bad. And rationing … [was] worse after the war than it were during the war. And the only pleasure you got were going to the cinema. And we used to love going to the cinema … at least four times a week. Sometimes five and six if you'd got money.[109]

The failure of companies to invest in new leisure facilities and infrastructure boosted cinema attendance. In 1954, the *Belfast Telegraph* stated that '[i]ce skating had attained a big following when the only rink in the city at King's Hall, Balmoral, was closed early last year'.[110] Despite plans to open a new rink, in 1956 it reported that for '5,000 of Belfast's 65,000 teenagers, this winter will again be dull and uninteresting. After two years' fighting – with much talk but no action – ice-skating fans are still without a rink'. It added that 'one only has to think of the numbers who spend their holidays in cross-Channel towns simply because of the ice-rinks there. But it looks as if it's back to pictures and dancing for ice-skaters here'.[111] When an ice rink

---

[106] Horn, *Juke Box Britain*, p. 109.
[107] Interview with Jack Riley, Sheffield, 26 June 2014.
[108] J. Nott, *Going to the Palais: a Social and Cultural History of Dancing and Dance Halls in Britain, 1918–1960* (Oxford, 2015), p. 84.
[109] Interview with Andrew and Carol Palmer (pseudonyms), Sheffield, 7 Aug. 2015.
[110] *Belfast Telegraph*, 17 Feb. 1954.
[111] *Belfast Telegraph*, 8 Sept. 1956.

opened at the King's Hall in 1964, its promoters suggested that television had played a key role in popularizing this activity.[112]

Despite this failure to invest in new facilities, local newspaper articles reveal the range of everyday leisure habits of both sexes. The use of these sources is particularly important because, as Adrian Horn suggested, the study of leisure habits often favours conspicuous and threatening male behaviour, at the expense of the everyday habits of their more discreet female counterparts.[113] From 1952 to 1953, the *Belfast Telegraph* interviewed a range of women in different professions for its 'Ulster types' column. It reported that the social life of five shop girls aged between seventeen and twenty-two 'has one thing in common – they all like dancing. Their other interests include collecting "boogie" records … filmgoing and swimming'.[114] For eighteen-year-old trainee nurse Jean Cobain, 'when text books are closed country walks, reading, the cinema and the radio – in that order – claim her time. She has little interest in games or in dancing, and always wanted to be a nurse'.[115] Twenty-year-old Pat Smith worked as a telephonist at the Ulster Weaving Company. She enjoyed 'dancing, and when she has a few hours to spare in the evening is usually found at the Orpheus'. It added that she enjoyed radio and cinema, was 'keen on housework, follows the fortunes of Crusaders Football Club and plays the piano'.[116] Work and domestic duties, however, often impeded leisure activities: 'Not the cinema or the dance hall for dark-haired Miss Ruby Halfpenny when the last customer is served. Ruby, who works in the Midland Hotel, hurries home to attend to her invalid mother'.[117]

By the beginning of the 1960s, many teenagers had more disposable income and there was a greater range of goods and services to spend their money on. When asked what people of her age did in the evening, eighteen-year-old Pauline McCourt responded that '[t]elevision's only for young children and old people. Jiving's the thing – that's what most of us do around this part of Belfast at night'.[118] Nineteen-year-old Irene Murland worked as a florist and spent £1 10s 'weekly on herself – one dance, once to the cinema and a little for a continental holiday every two years'. This level of consumer spending and an aspiration to spend a holiday abroad would have been unimaginable in the austerity of the immediate post-war years.

---

[112] *Belfast Telegraph*, 28 Dec. 1964.
[113] Horn, *Juke Box Britain*, p. 148.
[114] *Belfast Telegraph*, 25 Nov. 1952.
[115] *Belfast Telegraph*, 2 Dec. 1952.
[116] *Belfast Telegraph*, 5 Dec. 1952.
[117] *Belfast Telegraph*, 9 Dec. 1952.
[118] *Belfast Telegraph*, 14 Sept. 1960.

Nineteen-year-old Thomas Hewitt earned £5 17s a week and claimed 'I buy a lot of clothes, smoke 15–20 cigarettes a day and have a 5s flutter every Saturday on the pools. Two dances and one night a week at the pictures – that's not too much entertainment'.[119] In 1963, Ian Cromb opened a roller-skating rink in Belfast, claiming that 'there is a need for other forms of teenage entertainment in Belfast beside dancing and the pictures. I think that the cinema is now dead and that the dances are too common place. Roller skating is now something new'.[120]

In 1947, there were an estimated three million weekly admissions to 450 UK venues used exclusively for ballroom dancing. Rowntree and Lavers estimated that 'there were at least 2,000 halls in England and Wales, in addition to the palais-de-danse, where dancing takes place regularly'. They observed that the large majority of dancers were working- or lower-middle class aged between sixteen and twenty-four.[121] The reasons for the rise and fall of cinema and dancing activities broadly correlate and James Nott has observed that after the Second World War:

> the popularity of social dancing in Britain soared to new heights, before rapidly declining. The golden age of the dance hall was the 1950s. Buoyed up by an era of full employment and rising prosperity, dancing became Britain's pre-eminent leisure activity ... But the prosperity that created the boom was also responsible for the bust. Despite appearing entrenched in Britain's social and cultural life, the dance hall disappeared with surprising speed. By the end of the 1960s, superseded by nightclubs, and later discos, the palais was no more.[122]

In 1955, the *Belfast Telegraph* estimated that '30,000 people attend dances each week in Belfast during the winter months'.[123] These figures, however, were still far lower than cinema attendance and, in the year ending March 1957, there were 293,530 weekly recorded admissions to Belfast cinemas.[124] The figures for Sheffield are less precise, but there are several reports that indicate the popularity of dancing. In 1955, large crowds were such a problem that Sheffield licencing magistrates introduced attendance limits at eighteen city dance halls.[125] While cinema admissions were far higher than those for dance halls, admissions to dance halls were concentrated in

[119] *Belfast Telegraph*, 27 Sept. 1960.
[120] *Belfast Telegraph*, 4 Dec. 1963.
[121] S. Rowntree and G. R. Lavers, *English Life and Leisure: a Social Study* (London, 1951), pp. 279–85.
[122] Nott, *Going to the Palais*, p. 72.
[123] *Belfast Telegraph*, 16 Oct. 1956.
[124] PRONI, FIN/15/6/C/1/75–100, Entertainments Duty weekly returns, 1956–7.
[125] *The Star*, 6 Sept. 1955.

a narrower age range and may have been just as popular for teenagers and young adults as the cinema.

Dancing had a strong connection to certain days of the week. One Sheffield City Hall official offered two reasons for the popularity of Friday night dancing: 'it is pay night, and late night dancers can now lie-in on Saturday, since the introduction of the five-day week'.[126] Carol Palmer confirmed this when she stated that the City Hall 'was the place to go. You didn't go to the cinema at the weekend, you went to the dancing and that was the City Hall'.[127] David Ludlam stated that he never went to the cinema 'on a Saturday night, because that was the dance hall. That was in town. The City Hall or Cutler's Hall, and out of town the Abbeydale had a good dance there, but there tended to be a rougher crowd went there. And there was usually some sort of scrapping went on outside'.[128] This social distinction between dance halls was also made in Belfast and this appears to have been a greater determinant of attendance than religion. In their 1962 study of *The Northern Ireland Problem*, Denis Barritt and Charles Carter observed that '[t]he informal activities of youth in the commercial dance-halls are of course free from any distinctions on grounds of religion, but we have not been able to assess which community uses these dance-halls most'.[129]

Cinemas and dance halls were both important public sites for courtship and many interviewees commented on their interconnected nature. Brian Hanna stated that 'there was lots of ballrooms all round Belfast … and of course the fact that young men want to meet young girls, that was the opportunity to do it. And if you were going with somebody, you would go to the cinema as well. So these kind of things connected together'.[130] In 1957, *The Star* emphasized the role of dance halls in courtship and commented that '[m]any meet here, later marry. Dancing is the world's greatest matrimonial agency. With more and more youngsters under 21 marrying than ever before, many come expressly looking for a wife. The proprietors don't mind. It's healthy, and it's good for business'.[131] One key difference, however, was that while both were sites for courtship, you were more likely to meet a partner at a dance hall than you were at the cinema. As Rosemary Topham stated, dance halls were 'where you got to know the lads that you went to the cinema with later on'.[132]

[126] *The Star*, 22 June 1953.
[127] Interview with Andrew and Carol Palmer (pseudonyms), Sheffield, 7 Aug. 2015.
[128] Interview with David Ludlam, Sheffield, 25 June 2014.
[129] D. P. Barritt and C. F. Carter, *The Northern Ireland Problem* (London, 1962), p. 146.
[130] Interview with Brian Hanna, Belfast, 5 May 2015.
[131] *The Star*, 12 Aug. 1957.
[132] Interview with Rosemary Topham, Sheffield, 17 Aug. 2015.

In the 1950s, the range of social spaces available to young people expanded and cafés and coffee bars provided alternative social spaces to the cinema. Ann Slater recalled that 'the only other thing before coffee bars started was going to the pictures. There weren't really a lot else and then when coffee bars come in then that become very popular'.[133] Ann Gorman recalled attendance at the Kingsmoor Café and her comments highlight that it was often a cheaper alternative to the cinema: 'we'd see if we had enough money to get in and get a coke and stay inside. And then when the woman, who was quite strict, she'd say "if you're going to sit over that all night, get out"'.[134] They were also spaces free from parental influence and supervision. One female patron of Sheffield's El Mambo coffee bar commented that young people went to 'enjoy ourselves, listen to the kind of music we like, and meet boys – exactly what people go to dances for. Would people rather we went into pubs to hear juke boxes? Or hang around street corners'.[135] Cafés often housed juke boxes, which as Horn has shown, disseminated American music and allowed audiences to bypass the limited range of music played on BBC radio.[136] *The Star* stated that cafés would be:

> out of business if they tried to attract teen-age custom without a juke-box. A cup of coffee costs nine pence. The entertainment goes on all night, as teen-agers queue with their shillings at the glass and chrome machine which makes loud music as efficiently as it makes big money. The customers like what they know. The same number may be played a dozen times an evening.[137]

Horn adds that '[y]oung people wanted their own space and used youth-cafes as alternatives to the unwelcoming, older-generation-dominated public houses'.[138] This generation gap, however, has perhaps been overstated and in 1960, *The Star* claimed that 'teenage drinkers don't seem to "dig" all that youth club stuff'. Eighteen-year-old Trevor admitted to underage drinking and claimed that there was 'nothing else to do … I was fed up with pictures and too young to go steady with anyone'.[139]

Teenagers had greater disposable income but spent their money on an increasing range of consumer goods, including recorded music. The value of the British record industry rose from £6 million 1953 to £27 million in

[133] Interview with Ann Slater, Sheffield, 28 July 2015.
[134] Interview with Ann Gorman, Belfast, 23 Oct. 2014.
[135] *The Star*, 6 March 1959.
[136] Horn, *Juke Box Britain*, p. 85.
[137] *The Star*, 12 Aug. 1957.
[138] Horn, *Juke Box Britain*, p. 180.
[139] *The Star*, 12 Feb. 1960.

1958. In the latter year, sales of singles peaked at 64.6 million.[140] In 1956, the *Belfast Telegraph* reported that record sales in Northern Ireland had tripled since the war.[141] Two years later, the paper visited the record department of a Belfast radio and television shop and found that 'for every adult there were eight under 21-year-olds' amongst the customers'.[142] Norman Campbell recalled that:

> we were the first family in the Holyland, I think, to have a record player that you didn't wind up ... It was a Dansette, it was a good quality one, and we were starting to buy and hire LPs, you could hire LPs from Dougie Knight's shop on Botanic Avenue. You'd have them for a week and take them back again, and I think that cost about a shilling.[143]

There was also a social element to record collecting and another report suggested that teenagers formed groups to purchase and swap 45 rpm records.[144] The owners of Belfast's Golden Disc record shop instructed the architect to make it a 'young shop'; it advertised a 'stereophonic listening booth' and claimed it was the first Belfast record shop to run on 'self-service' lines.[145]

In 1957, *The Star* suggested that teenagers spent up to 15s on records weekly and that 'teenage tempo is bringing prosperity to the record shops, where youngsters are counted as the backbone of the business. Donegan and Presley, the loudest of them all, are Sheffield's reigning kings'. One record shop manager stated that teenagers 'come in crowds every lunchtime ... And as often as not they'll each go out with the same record'.[146] In 1958, one reported that '[n]o sooner has that honey-toned bell announced the end of afternoon school than they are swooping down on the city's record shops before their money burns holes in their gymslips or trousers'. The shop's owner suggested that their spending habits depended on their family's affluence and that for 'most of them the record race begins when Father buys them that long awaited record player'.[147] In 1959, Sheffield record shop owners estimated that teenagers constituted 60–75 per cent of their trade and *The Star* claimed that 'the majority of Sheffield teenagers spend more money on records than on any other single thing'. Eighteen-year-old shop assistant Anita Kenney estimated

---

[140] Nott, *Going to the Palais*, p. 97.
[141] *Belfast Telegraph*, 27 Dec. 1956.
[142] *Belfast Telegraph*, 3 Feb. 1958.
[143] Interview with Norman Campbell, Belfast, 4 June 2014.
[144] *Belfast Telegraph*, 3 Feb. 1958.
[145] *Belfast Telegraph*, 2 Sept. 1958.
[146] *The Star*, 12 Aug. 1957.
[147] *The Star*, 29 March 1958.

that some teenagers spent £3 a week on records, and that the average teenager bought at least one 6s record a week.[148]

While the money spent on recorded music meant that it was a rival to cinema attendance, they often had an interconnected relationship with one reinforcing the appeal of the other. Sue Harper and Vincent Porter argued that, as cinema attendance declined, the cinema industry was forced to acknowledge the greater range of leisure activities enjoyed by young consumers.[149] The fifteen to twenty-four age group had increasing amounts of money to spend on themselves and they accounted for a large proportion of the cinema audience. Both music and films were central to the way teenagers received popular culture. Andrew Caine argued that the 'preference for American consumer products existed not only through new types of consumer goods, typified by jeans, but also through the musical and cinematic artefacts offered to young people. The key catalyst for this process centred around the emergence of rock 'n' roll'.[150] From the mid 1950s, film companies started to produce films directed specifically at a youthful audience. The emphasis of 1950s and 1960s rock movies 'lay on the spectacle of performance offered by ... new recording acts ... that directly appealed to teenagers'.[151] Cinemas took advantage of rock 'n' roll's popularity and, for instance, Tommy Steele performed at the Ritz in October 1958. Mike Higginbottom's comments highlight the interrelated nature of music and cinema: 'I can remember going on my own to see Cliff Richard's *The Young Ones* because I'd got the record and we'd got a record player and I was buying singles'.[152] Such films were increasingly popular and in March 1962, *The Young Ones* (UK, 1961) set a new box-office record on the Saturday of its first week at the Belfast Ritz.[153] In 1963, Sheffield ABC manager I. J. Drummond reported 'four glorious weeks' exhibiting *Summer Holiday* (UK, 1963) as 80,000 patrons passed through its doors.[154]

As the 1950s progressed, both sexes had more disposable income and spent more on fashion. In 1956, *The Star*'s 'It's a Man's World' column reported that the key customers for Sheffield's tailors are 'not the higher wage-earning adults – with – responsibilities, but the rock-and-rolling teenagers'.[155] These

[148] *The Star*, 29 Aug. 1959.

[149] S. Harper and V. Porter, *British Cinema of the 1950s: the Decline of Deference* (Oxford, 2003), pp. 246–7.

[150] A. Caine, *Interpreting Rock Movies: the Pop Film and its Critics in Britain* (Manchester, 2004), p. 41.

[151] Caine, *Interpreting Rock Movies*, p. 89.

[152] Interview with Mike Higginbottom, Sheffield, 20 Aug. 2015.

[153] *Kinematograph Weekly*, 1 March 1962.

[154] *Kinematograph Weekly*, 4 Apr. 1963.

[155] *The Star*, 26 Oct. 1956.

fashions were partly influenced by rock 'n' roll films. In 1960, *The Star* claimed that the young working class were the greatest spenders on fashion and stated that the 'rest of their money goes on cigarettes, dances and the cinema'.[156] Lynda Walker started work in 1960 and earned £3 10s a week. She recalled putting a deposit on a £17 three-quarter astrakhan coat and then paying in instalments.[157] *The Star* was critical of such developments and placed the blame for this frivolous spending on parents whose 'lives are geared to the relentless cogs of the never-never land of H. P. tick, overspending and keeping up with the Joneses'.[158] This increased consumer spending by young adults may have reduced their ability to frequent the cinema as they prioritized consumer goods. In 1962, Belfast department stores stated that they were increasingly reliant on teenagers as they have 'more freedom, more money and more security than the youth of a generation ago'. A spokesman for the Belfast Co-Operative Society stated that '[f]ashion makes first claim on the spending money of our teenage customers … Running a very close second are cosmetics, hair sprays, shampoos, lipsticks – anything that's new and a "gimmick" will attract the teenager'.[159]

While teenagers were increasingly spending their money on alternative leisure activities, they were simultaneously spending their leisure time farther from home. Caproni's dance hall was located in the seaside resort of Bangor and was a popular destination for Belfast dancers. In 1955, it advertised a combined travel and dance ticket for 5s 6d, with a bus leaving Belfast City Hall at 7.45pm on Saturday evening.[160] By 1961, these teenagers were less reliant on public transport and the *Belfast Telegraph* claimed that groups of dancers who used to frequent Belfast dance halls were now visiting a variety of destinations: 'Almost any Friday or Saturday night you can see them motoring out of town in cars hired or for which the petrol has been paid for out of a joint fund'.[161] This fits with the assertion of Jancovich et al. that while television kept people at home, cars and holidays also took them further afield: 'Rather than a retreat into privacy, this period saw a major transformation of many people's experience of space, which profoundly affected the experiences and meaning of locality'.[162] Ferdynand Zweig observed that car ownership allowed Sheffield residents to spend their leisure time further afield: 'Those who have a car move out of the reach of the

---

156 *The Star*, 6 Dec. 1960.
157 Interview with Lynda Walker (b. Sheffield), Belfast, 26 Nov. 2014.
158 *The Star*, 6 Dec. 1960.
159 *Belfast Telegraph*, 8 Jan. 1962.
160 *Northern Whig*, 15 Sept. 1955.
161 *Belfast Telegraph*, 28 Oct. 1961.
162 Jancovich, Faire and Stubbings, *The Place of the Audience*, p. 145.

"local". Previously they visited their own public house or club or other local centre of amusement where they could see their friends and neighbours. With a car they can visit more distance places of entertainment'.[163] As the number of cars increased, the importance of public transport and its use for cinema-going declined. In October 1956, the Belfast Corporation stated that they planned to reduce the frequency of services on several routes. The Belfast Corporation Transport Department blamed the decline in numbers using the service on increased motor vehicles, new housing estates and increased television ownership.[164] Similar developments occurred in Sheffield and the number of passengers carried by trams and buses fell from 260 million in 1958 to 254 million in 1959. Sidney Dyson, chairman of the Sheffield Transport Committee offered three reasons for this decline: the increased use of private transport, the increase in television ownership and resistance to increased costs of travel.[165]

The response of cinema exhibitors

How did cinema perceive the threat of television and what strategies did they adopt to combat declining attendances? The first response of many was to assert the technical superiority of cinema over television and to introduce new technologies such as 3D, CinemaScope, Todd-AO and VistaVision. Stuart Hanson states that the 'underlying idea in the application of these new forms of technology was that audiences had to be reminded that the projected, photographic image was superior to that of the broadcast television image'.[166] Docherty et al. added that the 'film industry believed that its fight was with a new alternative technology for delivering moving pictures. Instead of re-siting the cinemas and following the audience to the new housing estates, the film industry struck back at the technological level'.[167] American cinema audiences declined earlier than in Britain and when Hollywood production companies introduced new technologies, such as 3D, UK cinema audiences were still strong. In April 1953, the Belfast Royal Hippodrome screened the short *A Day in the Country* (US, 1953), and from July, the Ritz screened the full-length feature *House of Wax* (US, 1953).[168] 3D exhibition was expensive as it required special glasses, the use of two projectors, a new screen, polarizing filters and required extra

[163] Zweig, *The Worker in an Affluent Society*, p. 107.
[164] *Belfast Telegraph*, 20 Oct. 1956.
[165] *The Star*, 17 June 1959.
[166] Hanson, *From Silent Screen to Multi-Screen*, p. 119.
[167] Docherty, Morrison and Tracey, *The Last Picture Show?*, p. 28.
[168] *Belfast Telegraph*, 4 Apr. 1953; 10 July 1953.

power and lighting.[169] The Ritz acquired 6,000 pairs of 3D spectacles for the screenings, which were hired to patrons for 6d each. The *Northern Whig* reported that 'if any of them are not returned to the lending company, the cinema management are obliged to cover their value'.[170]

From 4 May 1953, the Sheffield News Theatre screened short 3D films, alongside its normal programme, and on 7 July it advertised its 'Sensational New Screen Entertainment: Stereo Technique Type 3-Dimensional Films'.[171] Several interviewees recalled the poor quality of 3D technology and the problems associated with the accompanying glasses. Noel Spence stated that it 'didn't work. I mean after five minutes the picture was blurry and you got, a sort of a sore head and you wanted to take the things off. They were very, very poor. It was a gimmick really to try to combat the rise of TV'.[172] Contemporary reports used similar language and *The Economist* described 3D as 'a showman's "gimmick" that Hollywood has exalted into a talisman'.[173] Local exhibitors were sceptical of 3D technology and voiced caution in installing expensive new projection equipment. In March 1953, Sheffield CEA member Harold Brocklesby believed that the introduction of 3D films was 'a rather feverish effort to divert attention from TV, and if they would only stand out until they had lost a bit of money, as in the early days of the talkies, they would do better than follow a stampede which some people seemed determined to set up'.[174] In June, the Sheffield CEA recommended that exhibitors should not install equipment until standardization was assured and asked members 'to exercise great caution in entering into any commitments with any particular type of 3-D installation'.[175]

The introduction of widescreen formats, such as CinemaScope, which increased the size and spectacle of cinema, was far more successful. A 1958 Political and Economic Planning report suggested that, by 1954 'it was clear that 3-D stereoscopy had lost the battle to the "wide screens", no doubt because audiences found tedious the necessity of wearing polaroid glasses'.[176] In Sheffield, the Cinema House and the Roscoe both installed new large curved screens in July 1953.[177] In September 1953, the Belfast Ritz installed a new thirty-seven-foot-wide screen, which it claimed was the first

---

[169] *The Economist*, 4 July 1953.
[170] *Northern Whig*, 6 July 1953.
[171] *The Star*, 12 March 1953; 7 July 1953.
[172] Interview with Noel Spence, Comber, County Down, 26 March 2014.
[173] *The Economist*, 27 June 1953.
[174] *Kinematograph Weekly*, 5 March 1953.
[175] *Kinematograph Weekly*, 4 June 1953.
[176] Political and Economic Planning, *The British Film Industry 1958* (London, 1958), p. 140.
[177] *The Star*, 11 July 1953; 17 July 1953.

of its kind in Ireland. It stated that '[p]ictures appear deeper and there is, of course, a far greater impression of width. The screen is particularly suitable for outdoor shots and when the film is in colour the enjoyment is greater'.[178] The public viewed the screen for the first time at a Midnight Matinee featuring the Northern Ireland premiere of *The Master of Ballantrae* (UK, 1953) and a personal appearance of film star Yvonne Furneaux. The *ABC News* claimed that 'the film was well received, and gathered more press space, adding to the large amount of editorial and photographs published in all the Belfast newspapers'.[179] In 1954, the arrival of CinemaScope at Belfast's Royal Hippodrome led the *Belfast Telegraph* to comment that 'cinema managements will rush to secure this new genie with the same haste as when pictures first started to talk'.[180] The Royal Hippodrome also screened films in Paramount's VistaVision, which was first used in November 1954 at a trade screening of *White Christmas* (US, 1954).[181]

Despite the expensive changes required for conversion to CinemaScope and other similar formats, over half of Britain's cinemas were equipped to project widescreen films by the end of 1955.[182] In June 1953, Sheffield exhibitors voiced concerns at the cost of structural alterations to accommodate new widescreen formats. Herbert Oliver stated that he 'could visualise a difficult future for exhibitors' as this outlay was added to increased heat and lighting costs, rates and assessments.[183] These changes were of particular concern to small cinema owners and, in 1955, the National Association of Theatrical and Kine Employees (NATKE)'s NI regional manager stated that because 'of the development of CinemaScope, fewer films suitable for old-type screens are being made, and the owners of small kinemas are faced with the prospect of installing costly equipment or closing down'.[184] Memories of CinemaScope foreground the extra spectacle that these films provided, though it is difficult to determine if they actively drew people away from television. Ted Bagshaw's comments show that, while he enjoyed CinemaScope films, the fact that his cinema attendance was habitual meant that he often only realized a film was a different format after he arrived at the cinema:

> When CinemaScope came, the curtains opened a little bit further, the screen opened a little bit wider and then the CinemaScope film come on obviously.

[178] *Belfast Telegraph*, 30 Sept. 1953.
[179] *ABC News*, Nov. 1953, pp. 16–7.
[180] *Belfast Telegraph*, 8 Jan. 1954.
[181] *Belfast Telegraph*, 2 Nov. 1954.
[182] *The Economist*, 4 July 1953; S. Holmes, *British TV & Film Culture in the 1950s: Coming to a Screen Near You* (Bristol, 2005), p. 223.
[183] *Kinematograph Weekly*, 4 June 1953.
[184] *Kinematograph Weekly*, 17 March 1955.

And it were a different tune on 20th Century Fox for a CinemaScope film. There were an extra bit of music on the opening title so we always knew when it was going to be a CinemaScope film, this extra bit of music come in.[185]

In the late 1950s, the production of large blockbuster films stimulated interest in new cinema technologies. In 1958 Todd-AO, a 70mm widescreen film format, was introduced for screenings of *South Pacific* (US, 1958) in large first-run cinemas in cities such as London, Manchester and Brighton. When the Royal Hippodrome was then surveyed for the installation of Todd-AO, *Kine Weekly* reported that 'Belfast trade has always shown itself quick to capitalise on new techniques which might draw in more crowds … If the system is installed Belfast will be the first centre in Ireland to have taken advantage of the new advance in screen presentation'.[186] The Ritz, however, was the first Belfast cinema to install the technology at a cost of £25,000 and *South Pacific* was screened from Christmas Day 1958. One report stated that the film had 'got off to a flying start … and a run of at least two months is expected'.[187] Similarly, in November 1958, the Odeon was the first cinema in South Yorkshire to install Todd-AO equipment and *South Pacific* was then screened from Boxing Day.[188] During its twenty-one-week run at the Sheffield Odeon, *South Pacific* attracted 300,000 patrons.[189] Historians have questioned the extent to which these new widescreen formats drew patrons away from their televisions sets. Steve Chibnall claimed that the acceleration in the decline of cinemas attendances in 1958 was 'indicative, perhaps not only of the rise in television licences and the regional spread of ITV, but also the way in which new exhibition formats such as CinemaScope and VistaVision were losing their novelty value and could no longer arrest the loss of the cinema-going habit'.[190]

Exhibitors also attempted to fight the decline in admissions by improving cinema décor. Following Rank's expansion into Northern Ireland, Odeon (NI) managing director R. V. C. Eveleigh stated that he was 'determined to fight television locally' and, with the competition of ITV looming, he was 'engaged in a programme of reconstruction in several of its buildings to attract patrons back to the cinema'.[191] In July 1956, the Belfast Gaumont

[185] Interview with Ted Bagshaw, Sheffield, 16 July 2015.
[186] *Kinematograph Weekly*, 14 Aug. 1958.
[187] *Kinematograph Weekly*, 8 Jan. 1959.
[188] *The Star*, 5 Nov. 1958.
[189] *Kinematograph Weekly*, 24 Sept. 1959.
[190] S. Chibnall, 'Banging the gong: the promotional strategies of Britain's J. Arthur Rank Organisation in the 1950s', *Historical Journal of Film, Radio and Television*, xxxvii (2017), 242–71.
[191] *Belfast Telegraph*, 12 Apr. 1958.

'completed a big renovation programme which included the installation of an ante-proscenium screen giving a 39-ft. picture with Cinema-Scope and stereophonic sound ... an enlarged sales kiosk in the foyer and a reconstructed canopy'.[192] In 1960, Rank sold the Gaumont and modernized its most important sites. Two years later, *Ideal Kinema* reported that Rank had 'brought a "new look" to cinemas in competitive, but forward-looking times'.[193] In November 1959, the Sheffield Gaumont closed for two weeks for improvements, including a new moveable screen, a new orchestral pit, new carpets and female toilets.[194] In 1962, the *Sheffield Telegraph* commented that there was now less of an emphasis on the films themselves and more on the cinema buildings. It claimed that 'it is the cinemas – the splendid buildings, the lively managements – that are providing the big distraction from the fireside'. Rather than being white elephants, new cinemas such as the Odeon and the ABC showed that 'the only way to influence families and couples to pay five shillings to see a film is to offer them luxury'.[195]

Stuart Hanson argued that US exhibitors were more responsive than their British counterparts and developed drive-in cinemas in response to increased car ownership, population growth in the suburbs and high construction costs.[196] In 1957, there were 4,500 drive-in cinemas in the United States alongside its 13,700 standard cinemas.[197] One exhibitor was undeterred by Belfast's unpredictable climate and low levels of car ownership. In 1959, student newspaper *The Gown* reported that Ulster's first drive-in cinema on Hazelwood Plateau had received great attention. A screening of musical *Walking My Baby Back Home* (US, 1953) attracted over a hundred cars and their occupants 'for some, as yet unexplained, reason made full use of the advertisers' announcement that cars could be parked from 11.15'.[198] The implication here is that a key attraction of drive-in cinemas is that provided young people the freedom from parental supervision to engage in sexual activity. Drive-in cinemas were clearly far more suited to the teenagers of Berkeley than Belfast and there was no further mention of these screenings.

Sheffield exhibitors combatted the decline of adult audiences by making greater efforts to attract family audiences to the cinema. The Heeley Palace encouraged patrons to follow the example of Mohammed and Doreen Ali, who regularly attended the cinema with at least ten of their seventeen

---

[192] *Kinematograph Weekly*, 26 July 1956.
[193] *Ideal Kinema*, 8 Feb. 1962.
[194] Cinema Theatre Association Archive, Clifford Shaw, The Regent, Barker's Pool.
[195] *Sheffield Telegraph*, 23 May 1962.
[196] Hanson, *From Silent Screen to Multi-Screen*, p. 97.
[197] *Kinematograph Year Book 1958* (London, 1958), p. 510.
[198] *The Gown*, 1 May 1959.

children.[199] In October 1958, the family were awarded a £5 cheque and a month's free admission to the cinema for winning a competition to find the country's largest cinema-going family.[200] In 1958, Star Cinemas encouraged Friday evening family attendance to help 'break the monotony of television'. Woodseats Picture Palace manager Winifred Crookes stated that 'Friday night was always the family's night out at the cinema. The custom has died out and we are trying to revive it'.[201] The Hamilton family claimed that they had not spent an evening away from their television since 1952 and, in 1960, Gaumont manager Harry Murray intended to show them 'what cinema-going is really like' by taking them to the cinema by limousine, placing them in the most expensive seats and providing them with a special tea afterwards.[202] Exhibitors also offered discounted admission to children. In November 1958, Murray introduced half price child's admissions, except for Saturday. He estimated that while there were 41,000 eight- to fourteen-year-olds in Sheffield, an average of only four children visited his cinema on week days. This he believed, was the result of high ticket prices and the fact that many cinemas only offered discounted rates to children before 4pm.[203]

In Belfast, exhibitors were more likely to diversify their programme to attract more patrons. In September 1958, *Kine Weekly* reported that '[c]ine-variety is catching on in Belfast' and renter Syd Durbridge had attracted patrons back to suburban cinemas by introducing a twenty- to twenty-five-minute variety interlude between films. His decision was surely influenced by the tax concession received by cinemas that devoted 25 per cent of a show to live performances.[204] In the early 1960s, some suburban cinemas such as the Troxy and the Lido staged performances, such as pantomimes. The Lido's manager claimed that if the show was a success he would consider replacing Tuesday's cinema programmes with live variety theatre.[205] Large city centre cinemas increasingly adopted similar practices. In 1962, the Ritz abandoned its normal programme for a performance by Helen Shapiro and Eden Kane. One report suggested that 'most of the seats have been

[199] *The Star*, 12 Sept. 1958.

[200] *The Star*, 10 Oct.1958.

[201] *The Star*, 21 Aug. 1958. Prior to the Second World War Harry Murray had previously served as general manager of the Royal Hippodrome, Belfast. After managing two cinemas in Holywood, he returned to the Royal Hippodrome 'in May 1942 as adviser for stage shows, booking films and arranging troop shows'. He also worked in the American Red Cross in Armagh and with the Gibraltarians in Saintfield, before returning to Yorkshire in 1944 (*Motion Picture Herald*, 1 Dec. 1945).

[202] *The Star*, 24 Apr. 1960.

[203] *The Star*, 7 Nov. 1958.

[204] *Kinematograph Weekly*, 11 Sept. 1958.

[205] *Belfast Telegraph*, 27 Dec. 1961; 6 Jan. 1962.

booked, so its success may point the way to more live variety on cinema stages. Certainly the idea has proved popular in many of the A.B.C. houses across the water'.[206] The Belfast ABC then hosted a range of performers in the 1960s, including the Beatles, Tom Jones, Roy Orbison and the Rolling Stones.

Despite the elaborate promotional campaigns of some Belfast exhibitors, in 1960, *Kine Weekly* argued that the promotional efforts of Belfast's cinemas lagged behind their counterparts in other parts of the United Kingdom: 'critical observers are asking why there is not a greater sense of showmanship in the promoting of films. It is only occasionally, for example, that one sees a Belfast cinema boost its product in anything but the conventional way. Exhibitors seem still to be hesitant to "go out and get" their patrons'.[207] While the introduction of UTV damaged cinema attendance, it also provided new opportunities for promotion. Su Holmes has argued that though television has consistently been viewed as cinema's biggest rival, it simultaneously played a key role in promoting it through television programmes such as *Picture Parade* and *Film Fanfare*.[208] *Preview,* UTV's entertainment magazine programme, featured clips of newly released films and was one of the most watched programme in Northern Ireland in 1962.[209] Nevertheless, *Kine Weekly* believed that, with the exception of *Hercules Unchained* (Italy, 1958), Northern Ireland exhibitors had not made the most of television promotion. It stated that as 60 per cent of the UTV audience was within Belfast 'a campaign mounted even by a cinema itself could be directly beneficial'.[210] In 1963, *Kine Weekly* claimed that a 'vitality has come into press coverage of the film industry in Northern Ireland ... Certainly the cinema trade cannot complain that it is not being taken notice of'.[211] The following year it reported on the growth in showmanship in Northern Ireland and the ABC's trainee manager stated that the lack of campaigns submitted to the journal 'must give managers from other parts of Great Britain the idea that we lag behind in showmanship'.[212]

Across the United Kingdom, the cinema industry displayed particular anxiety at the increasing number of films shown on television. In 1958, prompted by ABC Television's purchase of twenty-five Korda films and the BBC's acquisition of over 100 RKO films, five trade associations formed

[206] *Belfast Telegraph*, 3 Nov. 1962.
[207] *Kinematograph Weekly*, 20 Oct. 1960.
[208] Holmes, *British TV & Film Culture in the 1950s*, pp. 113–48.
[209] *Kinematograph Weekly*, 11 Oct. 1962; 13 Dec. 1962.
[210] *Kinematograph Weekly*, 15 June 1961.
[211] *Kine Weekly*, 14 Feb 1963.
[212] *Kine Weekly*, 17 Sept. 1964.

the Film Industry Defence Organisation (FIDO), which used a farthing levy from the sale of cinema tickets to purchase film rights and prevent television screenings.[213] Though 925 films were removed from the market by 1964, Edward Buscombe claimed the scheme 'was doomed from the start. It took funds from a constantly declining revenue base, the cinema box-office, and used them to compete in the market with a rival whose economic strength was increasing with every year that went by'.[214] John D. Ayres discussed 'the manner by which film adjusted and responded to the emergence of television as a domestically based rival to its supremacy in the British public's affections', including an assessment of FIDO.[215] However, by looking at evidence from local CEA branches it is possible to show regional variations in support for the scheme. In October 1958, the Northern Ireland CEA refused to join the scheme as it believed that:

> FIDO's aims are 'negative' and insufficient to meet the problems raised by the competition of television. It takes the stand that keeping old films away from TV screens is possibly only making room for better material. It also thinks that FIDO's policy is ineffective when it is considered that the major film studios are now turning out new material for television.[216]

In December, FIDO asked Northern Ireland CEA members to reconsider their verdict and two months later, national CEA president Teddy Hinge and secretary Ellis Pinkney visited George Lodge.[217] Despite the visit, the Northern Ireland CEA confirmed their decision not to join FIDO and members maintained that it was not 'equipped to achieve the purpose for which it was designed'.[218] CEA headquarters expressed 'considerable disappointment' at this decision and still hoped to persuade Northern Ireland exhibitors to join the organisation'.[219] This refusal to join may have been due partly to the fact that television had not affected their cinemas to the same extent as other UK regions.

While Sheffield exhibitors participated in the scheme, their support was far from unanimous. In March 1958, Harold Gent outlined FIDO to branch members. He recommended supporting the plan, as 'while it meant

[213] D. Hill, 'Defence through FIDO', *Sight & Sound*, xxviii (1959), 183–4.
[214] E. Buscombe, 'All bark and no bite: the film industry's response to television', in *Popular Television in Britain: Studies in Cultural History*, ed. J. Corner (London, 1991), pp. 197–208, at pp. 205–6.
[215] J. D. Ayres, 'The two screens: FIDO, RFDA and film vs. television in post-Second World War Britain', *Journal of British Cinema and Television*, xiv (2017), 504–21, at p. 505.
[216] *Kinematograph Weekly*, 2 Oct. 1958.
[217] *Kinematograph Weekly*, 26 Feb. 1959.
[218] *Kinematograph Weekly*, 23 Apr. 1959.
[219] *Kinematograph Weekly*, 30 Apr. 1959.

the exhibitor once more dipping his hand into his pocket he should look upon it as an insurance policy towards stamping out a very big competitor, and one which, in the course of years might be the means of putting a lot of exhibitors out of business'. Jack Reiss was less enthusiastic and believed that FIDO 'had no arrangements as to how much they would pay for the films. He added that the scheme was fatuous and the 'whole thing was riddled with improbabilities ... The answer was that old films should be junked'. Sidney Kirkham added that the 'farthing levy would immediately increase the value of the product they were buying, and eventually they may have to pay a half-penny levy or even more'.[220] In August 1958, Gent reaffirmed that while 'he did not want to part with any more money, he could see that it was the only possible way to keep from TV a large percentage of films which had been brought into the country'.[221] There is no doubt that the organization placed a greater burden on exhibitors already struggling with increased operating costs. The Rex started payments to FIDO in September 1958, and in the year ending July 1959, contributed £192. Its contribution declined to £69 in 1962 and payments ceased in November 1964.[222] The organization disbanded in December 1964 and the rights were offered back to the distributors who sold them to FIDO.[223]

Conclusion

In 1945, few leisure activities were able to compete with cinema-going, which dominated citizen's leisure lives. During the 1950s, attendances declined dramatically and cinema-going became a more youth-oriented activity. John Spraos observed that, by the end of 1960, the cinema remained a 'social and cultural force', adding that for 'the young it is still the principal form of entertainment'.[224] A 1960 survey by the Screen Advertising Association found that 67 per cent of the average audience were young adults aged between sixteen and thirty-four. This age group, however, were increasingly drawn to a wider range of leisure activities and consumer goods. It had a higher proportion of petrol buyers, record player owners, record buyers and holiday makers. It was more 'clothes conscious' and the use of cosmetics was substantially above average.[225] By 1965, the cinema was still popular, but increases in television ownership and the rise of youth culture meant that it

---

[220] *Kinematograph Weekly*, 6 March 1958.
[221] *Kinematograph Weekly*, 7 Aug. 1958.
[222] Sheffield City Archives, MD7333/4/1–2, Rex Cinema (Sheffield) Limited, payments ledgers.
[223] *The Economist*, 12 Dec. 1964.
[224] Spraos, *The Decline of the Cinema*, pp. 165–6.
[225] Screen Advertising Association, *Spotlight on the Cinema Audience*, p. 24.

was no longer *the* ubiquitous leisure activity in the United Kingdom.

The history of cinema's post-war decline can only be understood fully by placing the everyday experiences of cinema-goers in the context of broader social change and economic developments. By engaging with recent debates in cultural and social history, this chapter answers Judith Thissen's call for new cinema historians to 'grapple with broad themes even when they investigate film culture through the prism of a of a distinctive local community'.[226] In cities such as Belfast and Sheffield, television did not simply replace cinema. Cinema screenings were central to experiences of the coronation and though it was an important televisual event, its impact on cinema attendance has often been overstated. Micro-historical research shows that local newspapers and trade journals placed the blame for cinema's decline on a broad range of factors that were geographically diverse. These sources reveal the 1950s as a dynamic decade when attitudes to leisure were fundamentally altered by increased affluence, new forms of entertainment and the development of youth culture. These changes, however, were geographically uneven. One key difference between Belfast and Sheffield was timing and Belfast residents often had to wait longer to feel the effects of social and economic change, and to enter into new forms of consumption. These findings also need to be understood in relation to broader international trends. Though cinema attendance peaked earlier than in many European countries, the earlier decline in the USA had an impact on the supply of Hollywood films and the response of exhibitors within the United Kingdom. An outward-looking assessment of changing leisure habits in Belfast and Sheffield reveals the confluence of local, national and international factors that led to cinema's decline.

---

[226] J. Thissen, 'Cinema history as social history', pp. 124–33.

3. Cinema-going and the built environment

The recent spatial turn in new cinema history has led to an increased interest in the relationship between sites of film exhibition and the built environment.[1] The outbreak of war brought the 1930s cinema building boom to an abrupt end as building restrictions prevented the construction of new premises. Many cinemas suffered physical damage and others went into disrepair as money and resources were diverted into the war effort. By 1946 there were 4,709 cinemas operating in Great Britain and a further 107 in Northern Ireland.[2] The number of cinemas declined dramatically in the period under review and by 1963, these figures were 2,181 and 107 respectively.[3] While six new cinemas opened in suburban areas of Belfast or adjacent towns, eighteen Belfast cinemas closed between 1955 and 1962. In Sheffield, though two new city centre cinemas were constructed, the number of licensed cinemas fell from fifty-two in 1955 to twenty-three in 1964. Social experiences of cinema-going and the decline of cinema need to be understood in the wider context of post-war recovery and the urban development of industrial cities. A comparative assessment of the opening and closure of cinemas in Belfast and Sheffield leads us to question the impact of urban planning policies, population shifts and the development of leisure infrastructure on cinema exhibition and attendance. The case studies presented here complement the work of scholars who have turned their attention to the geography of this decline and the impact of cinema closures across the UK.[4] This assessment also builds on several recent studies

[1] J. Klenotic, 'Putting cinema history on the map: using GIS to explore the spatiality in cinema', in *Explorations in New Cinema History: Approaches and Case Studies*, ed. R. Maltby, D. Biltereyst and P. Meers (Chichester, 2011), pp. 58–84; D. Biltereyst, R. Maltby and P. Meers, 'Exhibition, space and place: introduction', in *The Routledge Companion to New Cinema History*, ed. D. Biltereyst, R. Maltby and P. Meers (Abingdon, 2019), pp. 199–201.

[2] Central Statistical Office, *Annual Abstract of Statistics 1949*, no. 86 (London, 1949), p. 75; *Kinematograph Year Book 1946* (London, 1946), pp. 594–8.

[3] Central Statistical Office, *Annual Abstract of Statistics 1964*, no. 101 (London, 1964), p. 86; *Kinematograph and Television Year Book* (London, 1963), pp. 353–6.

[4] For instance, see B. Doyle, 'The geography of cinemagoing in Great Britain, 1934–1994: a comment', *Historical Journal of Film, Radio and Television*, xxiii (2003), 59–71; M. Jancovich, L. Faire and S. Stubbings, *The Place of the Audience: Cultural Geographies of Film Consumption* (London, 2003).

'Cinema-going and the built environment', in S. Manning, *Cinemas and Cinema-Going in the United Kingdom: Decades of Decline, 1945–65* (London, 2020), pp. 91–127. License: CC-BY-NC-ND 4.0.

that 'share an interest in how local microhistories of individual cinemas or companies connect with larger histories of cinema circuits, systems of exhibition, and regional or national commercial practices'.[5]

New Belfast cinemas

In the 1930s, Belfast witnessed a cinema building boom. Seventeen new cinemas were constructed and the majority of these were located in inner-city and suburban areas on the main arterial roads leading away from the city centre. The Forum, Crumlin Road, opened on 20 November 1937, was the last new cinema in Belfast before the outbreak of the Second World War. The 2,200-seat Ritz was the largest Belfast cinema and was the only one of these 1930s cinemas located in the city centre. It was part of a cluster of cinemas around Great Victoria Street, including the Royal Hippodrome and the Mayfair. Another group of city centre cinemas centred on Cornmarket and included the Classic, the Imperial and the Royal. Before the construction of the Ritz, the Classic, which opened in 1923, was the newest cinema in Belfast city centre. There were four further city centre cinemas: the Alhambra and the Gaiety on North Street, the Picture House on Royal Avenue and the Central Picture Theatre on Smithfield. The Alhambra, the Royal Hippodrome and the Gaiety were all opened originally as theatres and then converted into use as cinemas. Of the cinemas that remained in the centre at the end of the Second World War, seven were built between 1910 and 1916. In the immediate aftermath of the war, many Belfast cinemas were operated by small circuits or independent exhibitors.[6] In 1947, the two largest chains operating in Northern Ireland were local companies, Curran Theatres and Irish Theatres, which operated six and four Belfast cinemas respectively.[7] Meanwhile, large British exhibitors held a small but significant presence in Northern Ireland. Gaumont operated a single city-centre cinema, the Classic, and the Union circuit (owned by ABC) operated three cinemas: the Majestic, the Ritz and the Strand.

Belfast suffered serious physical damage during the 1941 Blitz, including the destruction of four cinemas: the Lyric, the Midland, the Popular and the Queen's. In the aftermath of the Second World War, the Belfast Corporation understandably prioritized the reconstruction of housing and factories above places of entertainment and did not issue building licences for new

---

[5]   Biltereyst, Maltby and Meers, 'Exhibition, space and place', pp. 199–201.
[6]   K. Rockett with E. Rockett, *Film Exhibition and Distribution in Ireland, 1909–2010* (Dublin, 2011), pp. 80–4.
[7]   *Kinematograph Year Book 1947* (London, 1947), pp. 431–3.

cinemas.[8] While the Corporation, citizens and the press acknowledged that there was a demand for greater leisure facilities, no new Belfast cinemas were constructed until 1954. In June 1945, the Northern Ireland CEA presented a report to the Ministry of Commerce on the construction of cinemas in Northern Ireland. They believed that first priority licences should be granted to the owners of the four cinemas damaged in the war.[9] Only the Popular, 'which was badly damaged in the blitz', upgraded its auditorium and reopened in November 1946.[10] Some existing cinemas were permitted to upgrade their premises and the Kelvin reopened as the Mayfair.[11] Building restrictions, however, were tight and architect R. Sharpe Hill received a £100 fine for exceeding a £3,000 Ministry of Finance building licence.[12] This fine led CEA members to complain 'that they were not getting "fair treatment" in the matter of building licences or licences for the repair and reconstruction of their premises'.[13] In May 1946, the Ministry of Finance told exhibitors that '[l]icences for building kinemas in Northern Ireland will not be granted for a considerable time to come'.[14]

Independent exhibitors expressed concern that by permitting building licences, the Ministry of Finance would allow large British exhibitors to expand into Northern Ireland at their expense. In February 1946, *Kine Weekly* reported that exhibitors in Northern Ireland 'are preparing a secret plan of campaign to combat possible infiltration tactics by cross-channel invaders'.[15] In August, it suggested that Odeon had moved into the Northern Ireland market and purchased the Picture House from the Barrow Trust. It claimed that Rank planned to demolish the building and construct a 3,000 seat cinema.[16] This deal was never completed and local chain Curran Theatres purchased the Picture House in March 1947. *Kine Weekly* reported that 'when permits are available for building, the Picture House will be pulled down to make way for a new kinema'.[17] The *Belfast Telegraph*, however, reported that 'it is the intention of Curran Theatres to

---

[8] P. Larmour, 'Bricks, stone, concrete and steel: the built fabric of twentieth-century Belfast', in *Enduring City: Belfast in the Twentieth Century*, ed. F. W. Boal and S. A. Royle (Belfast, 2006), pp. 30–55, at p. 42.

[9] *Kinematograph Weekly*, 21 June 1945.

[10] *Kinematograph Weekly*, 21 Nov. 1946.

[11] *Kinematograph Weekly*, 7 Nov. 1946.

[12] *Kinematograph Weekly*, 26 June 1947; *Belfast Telegraph*, 23 May 1947; *Belfast Telegraph*, 13 June 1947.

[13] *Kinematograph Weekly*, 3 Jan. 1946.

[14] *Kinematograph Weekly*, 30 May 1946.

[15] *Kinematograph Weekly*, 28 Feb. 1946.

[16] *Kinematograph Weekly*, 1 Aug. 1946.

[17] *Kinematograph Weekly*, 6 March 1947.

close the newly-purchased cinema and restaurant in August for complete renovation and refurbishing, and it is probable that the cinema will be re-opened, on completely up-to-date lines, within two months from the date of closing'.[18] The Picture House was renovated and reopened as the Regent in September 1947. Undeterred from their failure to purchase the Picture House, Rank assessed other Belfast sites. In January 1947, *Kine Weekly* reported that Gaumont were 'planning widespread developments to materialise as soon as building restrictions are lifted' and that 'negotiations are in progress for the acquisition of a number of sites. The first of these – to be acquired from the Belfast Corporation – will probably be on the Antrim Road'.[19] While Estates Committee chairman W. J. Gillespie agreed to the construction of a cinema on the site of the Dromart supermarket, protestors argued that the site would be better used for housing and this cinema was never constructed.[20]

In 1948, the Belfast Corporation granted Odeon permission to construct a 3,000-seat city centre cinema, alongside offices and shops, on a bomb-damaged city centre site.[21] Major British circuits were keen to expand into Northern Ireland and *Kine Weekly* believed that 'owing to the near-critical unemployment position in Northern Ireland … the Government is likely to be more liberal in the issue of permits'.[22] These reports were unfounded and, in July 1948, the Stormont senate made it clear that Rank had not been granted permission and reaffirmed that its present policy was not 'to approve the issue of a building licence for the erection of any cinema in Northern Ireland'.[23] In May 1954, the *Belfast Telegraph* reported that the Rank Organisation planned to start construction in Autumn and had 'served notices to quit on tenants in a block in Fountain Mews'. They understood, however, 'that negotiations are not yet completed between the organisation and all tenants on the site'.[24] In October, it reported that the site was being cleared and building work was due to start imminently. The 1,750-seat cinema was to 'become the Northern Ireland "shop window" of the Odeon group' and the plans included provision for shops and office accommodation.[25] In March 1955, J. Arthur Rank told the *Belfast Telegraph* that he hoped to return to Belfast for the opening of this new £200,000

[18] *Belfast Telegraph*, 27 Feb. 1947.
[19] *Kinematograph Weekly*, 9 Jan. 1947.
[20] *Belfast Telegraph*, 1 Jan. 1947.
[21] *Belfast Telegraph*, 2 Feb. 1948.
[22] *Kinematograph Weekly*, 19 Feb. 1948.
[23] *Belfast Telegraph*, 8 July 1948.
[24] *Belfast Telegraph*, 11 May 1954.
[25] *Belfast Telegraph*, 14 Oct. 1954.

cinema.[26] However, this building was never developed and, in January 1958, *Kine Weekly* reported that the site 'may now be used for a 20-storey office block instead … Rank plans for the building of a super cinema in the city centre have been in the air for a number of years. The alternative to a new building is the reconstruction of the Regent which is the only first-run hall owned by Odeon (N.I.) Ltd.'.[27]

A key characteristic of Northern Ireland's post-war cinema exhibition industry was the Rank Organisation's late arrival in the province. At the end of the Second World War, the company controlled one Belfast cinema, the Classic, which was renamed the Gaumont in 1950. By 1962, Odeon (NI) Ltd. operated eleven Belfast cinemas and the 1,250-seat Tivoli in the Finaghy suburb.[28] Except from the Tivoli, which was purchased from Irish Theatres during its construction, Rank was unable to build any new Belfast cinemas and expanded by purchasing cinemas from local chains.[29] This provided a more cost-effective means of expansion, as the cost of Rank's proposed Fountain Street cinema was 'estimated at £100 a seat compared with £40 a seat before the war'.[30] In February 1955, Rank subsidiary company Odeon (NI) Ltd. completed the £500,000 purchase of eleven cinemas from Irish Theatres. George Lodge, a director of Irish Theatres, was appointed as managing director of the new company and claimed that his task was to 'bring the theatres up to the standards of Odeon theatres across the water'.[31] ABC also expressed an interest in expanding its Northern Ireland operations and, in November 1948, inspected a site on Crumlin Road for the construction of a new cinema.[32] In November, reports suggested that both ABC and Rank were interested in purchasing the twelve cinemas owned by Curran Theatres in a deal that could rise to more than £500,000. In January 1956, Curran Theatres accepted a £660,000 offer from the Rank Organisation.[33] The deal was completed in December 1956 to hand over eleven cinemas, including the Apollo, Astoria, Broadway, Capitol, Lyceum, Regal and Regent.[34]

The relaxation of building restrictions in the 1950s offered independent exhibitors the opportunity to construct suburban cinemas to serve new

---

[26] *Kinematograph Weekly*, 7 Apr. 1955.
[27] *Kinematograph Weekly*, 9 Jan. 1958.
[28] *Kinematograph Year Book* (London, 1963), p. 231.
[29] *Belfast Telegraph*, 17 June 1955.
[30] *Belfast Telegraph*, 11 May 1954.
[31] *Belfast Telegraph*, 7–8 Feb. 1955.
[32] *Belfast Telegraph*, 13 Nov. 1948.
[33] *Belfast Telegraph*, 14 Jan. 1956.
[34] *Kinematograph Weekly*, 4 Oct. 1956; 13 Dec. 1956.

housing developments. The location of these cinemas reflects post-war population shifts and the delayed impact of television in the areas where they opened. The 1,050-seat Lido was the first cinema constructed in post-war Belfast. At its official opening on 26 March 1955, former Lord Mayor Sir James Norritt stated that it 'filled a long felt want in that growing district of the city'.[35] Reports of the cinema's opening emphasized its comfort and technological advances. *Kine Weekly* believed that the absence of a balcony led to a greater focus on seating accommodation and observed that 'special emphasis has been laid on the distribution of sound'.[36] The *Belfast News-Letter* commented that architect John McBride Neill had retained 'maximum comfort for patrons and at the same time [kept] construction costs within manageable bounds'. The fact that the cinema was designed to accommodate widescreen presentation meant that 'the first impression one receives on entering the auditorium is the great width of the proscenium'. It remarked that the Lido and its café-shop 'has given this rather drab stretch of road an almost Continental aspect' (see Figure 3.1).[37] The cinema was popular among local residents and, in 1956–7 it recorded 354,857 admissions, a figure comparable to many other inner-city cinemas.[38] The Tivoli opened in June 1955 and reports again emphasized the cinema's technological capabilities: 'extraordinary care has been taken to make the auditorium as acoustically perfect as the latest knowledge of this subject will allow'.[39] The *Irish Builder and Engineer* noted that its ventilation system and high fidelity sound reproduction 'embodies important modifications of some features of auditorium design that were commonplace in cinema before the war'. The 'contemporary' interior was noted for its plain textured surfaces, use of pale pastel shades and green moquette seating.[40]

In September 1956, the Belfast-based Supreme Group opened two new cinemas in Northern Ireland: The Reo in Ballyclare and the 1,000-seat Metro in Dundonald, located just outside the Belfast city boundary.[41] The latter cost £50,000 and was the first post-war cinema in Northern Ireland with a balcony.[42] Press reports continued to emphasize the cinema's technological aspects in an attempt to persuade audiences of the benefits of cinema over television. *Kine Weekly* praised the Metro's 'anamorphic

---

[35] *Belfast News-Letter*, 28 March 1955.
[36] *Kinematograph Weekly*, 7 Apr. 1955.
[37] *Belfast News-Letter*, 28 March 1955.
[38] PRONI, FIN/15/6/C/1/91, Entertainments Duty weekly returns, Lido, 1956–7.
[39] *Belfast Telegraph*, 17 June 1955.
[40] *Irish Builder and Engineer*, 2 July 1955.
[41] *Kinematograph Weekly*, 27 Sept. 1956.
[42] *Irish Builder and Engineer*, 22 Sept. 1956.

Figure 3.1. Lido, Shore Road, Belfast, 1955 (*Irish
Builder and Engineer*, 10 September 1955).

projection' and the *Belfast Telegraph* stated that its forty-foot CinemaScope
screen compared favourably with the large city centre cinemas.[43] Owner
T. J. Furey claimed that while the competition of television and high levels
of Entertainments Duty made the Metro a 'calculated risk', it 'had long
been needed at Dundonald'.[44] On 1 September, Secretary to the Northern
Ireland cabinet Sir Robert Grandsen performed the opening ceremony and
congratulated the owner on a 'magnificent new cinema'. He hoped that
the people of Dundonald, 'a rapidly growing district, would appreciate
what efforts were being made to bring the best in cinema entertainment
their way'.[45] Oral history interviewees recalled the unusual decision to open
the Metro and Noel Spence stated that he considered it 'strange to open
a brand new custom-built cinema in 1957 when the danger signs were on
the horizon'.[46] It lasted only until March 1961, when the *Belfast Telegraph*
reported that the building was available to let. It claimed that '[f]or two
years after its opening the Metro attracted large crowds. But in 1958, when
the general fall-off in picture-going began, it also felt the effect'.[47]

[43] *Kinematograph Weekly*, 30 Aug. 1956; *Belfast Telegraph*, 31 Aug. 1956.
[44] *Belfast Telegraph*, 31 Aug. 1956.
[45] *Kinematograph Weekly*, 6 Sept. 1956.
[46] Interview with Noel Spence, Comber, Co. Down, 26 March 2014.
[47] *Belfast Telegraph*, 21 Apr. 1961.

From 1953–4, Dorita Field and Desmond Neill surveyed housewives on new housing estates built by the Northern Ireland Housing Trust, commenting that the distance from amenities was a factor that reduced or prevented cinema attendance. Their survey suggested that 'for housewives who did go out, cinema-going was by far the most important activity, and for more than half of them their sole activity ... Of those who did go to the cinema, about 60% went at least once a week, and about 30% once a month'.[48] Rathcoole was one of the post-war housing estates constructed by the Northern Ireland Housing Trust and Figure 3.2 shows the areas transition from rural farmland in 1936 to a suburban housing estate in 1961. In December 1955, reporter Eric Waugh claimed that the most common complaints among residents were the frequency of public transport and access to amenities in Belfast city centre. He added that 'the impression is unavoidable that already the city's jobs, its shops, its cinemas and ballrooms are influencing Rathcoole so much as to set it in the standard mould of a new Belfast suburb'. One resident lamented that 'the estate empties at nine o'clock on Saturday morning and it's that way till late at night – all the entertainment's in Belfast'.[49]

Cinema exhibitors were responsive to the local demand for leisure facilities on the new estates. In July 1956, *Kine Weekly* reported that Curran Theatres were awaiting completion of the Alpha in Rathcoole: 'This is the first of three which should be built in the next two years. The others are a 1,600-seater at Andersontown and a 1,300-seater at Cregagh, Belfast'.[50] While the latter were never constructed, the 918-seat Alpha opened in April 1957 under the ownership of a newly registered company, Rathcoole (Entertainments) Ltd. Its opening night featured a screening of *The Caine Mutiny* (US, 1954) and a personal appearance of celebrity pin-up and actress Sabrina.[51] *Kine Weekly* reported that the Alpha 'is in the middle of a new housing estate with a present population of about 6,000. The area has a potential population of 10,000 to 12,000'.[52] The cinema's opening night programme acknowledged the distance from Belfast city centre stating that a 'shopping centre has already been established, excellent churches have been provided, and now comes the opening of this beautiful cinema'.[53] Reports

---

[48]   D. Field and D. G. Neill, *A Survey of New Housing Estates in Belfast* (Belfast, 1957), pp. 60–3.

[49]   *Belfast Telegraph*, 5 Dec. 1955.

[50]   *Kinematograph Weekly*, 12 July 1956.

[51]   Interview with John T. Davis, Holywood, Co. Down, 8 Apr. 2014.

[52]   *Kinematograph Weekly*, 4 Apr. 1957.

[53]   Gala opening, Alpha Cinema, Rathccole, souvenir programme. Courtesy of Film Hub NI.

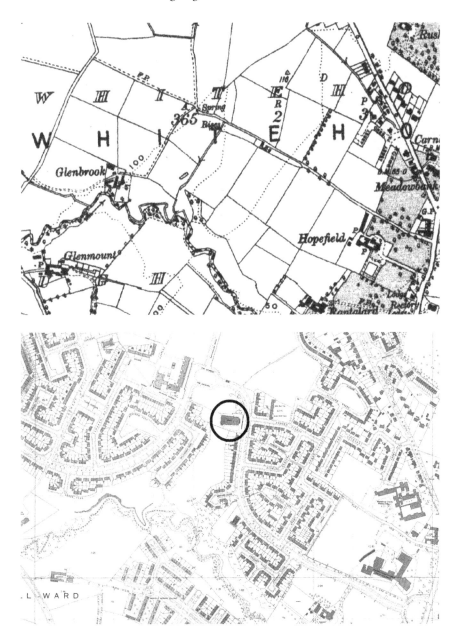

Figure 3.2. Rathcoole, 1936 and 1960–1 (Alpha circled) (Ordnance
Survey, National Grid 1:2500. © Crown Copyright and Landmark
Information Group Limited 2016. All rights reserved. 1936–61).

focused on McBride Neill's functional design and *Ideal Kinema* stated that 'one sees an extremely straightforward solution to many problems which have worried exhibitors for years and, indeed, the very simplicity of the planning, décor and furnishings is the outstanding feature of the building'. It also commented on the technological benefits over other cinemas and stated that the 'architect has given considerable thought to the acoustic treatment of the auditorium'.[54] The addition of a ground floor café and milk bar in 1959, the first in a Northern Ireland cinema, shows the exhibitors desire to attract young audiences by offering a range of social spaces.[55]

In December 1957, the new Comber cinema hoped to draw patrons from the new estates in south-east Belfast, four miles away. Noel Spence grew up in Comber and commented that while 'the new cinema was very classy', the decision 'to build a new cinema in fifty-seven was kind of an act of faith with TV becoming a real menace – but they did it anyhow and for many years Comber cinema was very successful and very popular locally'.[56] *Kine Weekly* commented that the construction of new cinemas provided '[e]vidence of the faith of independent exhibitors in the prosperity of the industry in Northern Ireland' and suggested that either small circuits had confidence in the future of the local cinema industry, or large British circuits did not build new cinemas as they considered the health of the industry in the United Kingdom as a whole.[57]

Several Belfast cinemas responded to changing audience preferences by renovating their premises and reopening under different names. In July 1958 Capital and Provincial News Theatres director, Eric Rhodes, visited Belfast to negotiate a deal to convert the Mayfair into Ireland's first news theatre. The *Belfast Telegraph* informed its readers that the programme lasted just over an hour and that news theatres were 'designed particularly for the city shopper and the person who has not enough time for longer programmes'.[58] Rhodes stated that 'I am sure a news theatre would do well in Belfast – it is most unusual for a city of this size not to have one'.[59] *Kine Weekly* informed its readers that it if the company 'does acquire a cinema in Belfast its programme will be mainly composed of cartoons with possibly one newsreel'.[60] In October, Capital and Provincial News Theatres purchased

---

54   *Ideal Kinema*, 13 June 1957.
55   *Belfast Telegraph*, 2 Oct. 1959.
56   Interview with Noel Spence, Comber, Co. Down, 26 March 2014.
57   *Kinematograph Weekly*, 26 Dec. 1957.
58   *Belfast Telegraph*, 2 July 1958.
59   *Kinematograph Weekly*, 10 July 1958.
60   *Kinematograph Weekly*, 10 July 1958.

the Mayfair and revealed a five-week conversion plan.[61] It stated that the conversion was designed to help the cinema compete with new media forms: '[it] is one type of cinema which to-day is successfully competing against television. It offers something which can't be got on TV – coloured cartoon and coloured travelogues. The latter are becoming very popular'. The cinema's central location was key to its appeal. Its marketing campaigns targeted travellers and mothers with domestic duties, claiming it is 'handy for the railway and bus stations' and 'handy to leave the children whilst mother does her shopping'.[62] In 1965, manager Sally Feenan claimed that many parents left children at the cinema during shopping trips: 'We keep them all in the back rows, where the usherettes can keep an eye on them'.[63]

From 1960 to 1962, Odeon (NI) completed a programme of 'modernisation, renovation and reorganisation' in its most important cinemas.[64] In November 1960, it purchased the Grand Opera House and the Royal Hippodrome and confirmed that it had 'no plans or intentions to convert either ... to a bowling alley or to use either for purposes other than entertainment'.[65] In April 1961, Eveleigh announced that the Royal Hippodrome was to receive 'extensive renovations and improvements' and that 'alterations in equipment and seating' were to take place in the Grand Opera House.[66] Eveleigh stated that these renovations were a temporary measure and 'in no way a forerunner of any change in the basic policy of either house'.[67] Odeon was anxious to preserve the Grand Opera House's character while modernizing it to 'present-day standards'. Its balcony's seating capacity was reduced to give 'maximum comfort' and licensed bars with a 'trim sophisticated look' were opened.[68] After these renovations, Norman Campbell claimed that the steeply tiered balcony was especially popular with courting couples: 'I have this image of the Grand Opera House filled from the top downwards, and at a particular time in the evening, it would have been top heavy, because nearly everybody there was in the balcony ... [it] would have been covered with couples who were all courting'.[69] From 26 June, the Royal Hippodrome underwent renovations and its seating

[61] *Kinematograph Weekly*, 23 Oct. 1958.

[62] *Belfast Telegraph*, 17 Dec. 1958; Belfast Central Library Cinema Collection, promotional leaflet for Belfast News and Cartoon Cinema, Dec 1958.

[63] *Belfast Telegraph*, 7 Apr. 1965.

[64] *Ideal Kinema*, 8 Feb. 1962.

[65] *Belfast Telegraph*, 18 Nov. 1960.

[66] *Kinematograph Weekly*, 27 Apr. 1961.

[67] *Belfast Telegraph*, 20 Apr. 1961.

[68] *Ideal Kinema*, 8 Feb. 1962.

[69] Interview with Norman Campbell, Belfast, 4 June 2014.

capacity was reduced.[70] In October 1961, it reopened as the Odeon and the *Belfast Telegraph* commented that the exterior had received a 'thorough facelift' and '[g]enerous leg-room between rows and swivelling seats, which make "popping up and down" unnecessary, and a lowered ceiling – achieved by eliminating the gallery – will be among the improvements'.[71] In 1965, buoyed by the success of previous renovations, Odeon (NI) spent £100,000 modernizing the Regent. In June, it reopened as the Avenue with its seating capacity increased from 675 to 800.[72]

Cinema closures in Belfast

In Belfast, the later arrival of television and lower levels of affluence meant that cinema closures occurred later than in many other parts of the United Kingdom. The most intense period of cinema closures occurred from 1958 to 1962, and seventeen cinemas closed their doors. The majority of these were older buildings and the Apollo was the only 1930s cinema to close in the period under review. Following the demise of the Apollo in December 1962, no Belfast cinemas closed until 1966. The first Belfast cinemas to go were generally smaller, older and independent cinemas. John Campbell was born in 1936 and lived in the York Street area of North Belfast. While he mainly frequented his local cinemas such as the Duncairn and the Lyceum, he also travelled to the city centre: 'When I was young, I would have went to the cheaper cinemas in the town centre. An old music hall called the Gaiety. Or the Gay-ity, as we called it. And there was another one in the centre of town called the Central, and it really was the pits'.[73] When the Gaiety ceased business in 1956, the *Irish Independent* claimed that it was 'the North's first casualty in the cinema versus television war'.[74] The Central, meanwhile, closed in 1958.[75] The 500-seat Shankill Picturedrome opened in 1910 and closed in 1958. It was one of the cheapest cinemas in Belfast and prices ranged from 3*d* to 6*d*. The building's conversion to a Spar Foodliner store in 1962 represents changing habits and the use of space within inner-city residential areas.[76]

---

[70] *Belfast Telegraph*, 16 June 1961; *Ideal Kinema*, 8 Feb. 1962.
[71] *Belfast Telegraph*, 28 Sept. 1961.
[72] *Belfast Telegraph*, 29 May 1965.
[73] Interview with John Campbell, Belfast, 30 May 2014.
[74] *Irish Independent*, 1 June 1957; *Kinematograph Weekly*, 23 Apr. 1959.
[75] *Kinematograph Weekly*, 6 March 1958.
[76] *Belfast Telegraph*, 27 Nov. 1962.

In 1958, Northern Ireland CEA chairman George Lodge stated that unless Entertainments Duty was abolished, 'a number of cinemas in the Province are bound to close'.[77] *Belfast Telegraph* reporter Gordon Duffield claimed that the Belfast cinema industry was 'fighting for its life'. While he highlighted television as cinema's 'great enemy', he agreed that Entertainments Duty placed an unfair burden on cinema exhibitors.[78] To survive, cinemas required a regular supply of quality films and to invest in their premises: 'it takes courage to invest money in cinema renovation and reconstruction. Running costs and overheads have increased from anything from 200 to 400 per cent. since the war – yet cinema prices have gone up only a fraction of that figure'. One method of increasing revenue, he suggested, was to open cinemas on Sunday: 'films are being shown in the majority of homes – through TV – on Sunday night. Should the cinema owner who wants to show his films on Sunday night be discriminated against?'[79] Sabbatarian interests and fears of a 'continental Sunday' meant that no Belfast cinemas opened on Sunday during the period under review, except for members of the armed forces. In October, Lodge told the *Belfast Telegraph* that '[p]eople will not go to the cinema to see an "ordinary" film. The good ones are still pulling in the crowds as they did before – but the public will not put up with mediocrity'. He claimed that there 'are many cinema-owners in Belfast who, if they could use their cinemas for some more remunerative purpose than films would seize the opportunity with both hands'.[80]

In 1959, four cinemas closed down: the Alhambra, the Coliseum, the Diamond and the Imperial. In July, the latter was sold for £110,000 and, following its final performance on 28 November, was converted into a branch of Sterling's fashion store. This change reflected increased affluence and the fact that young people were spending more of their disposable income on consumer goods, such as clothes. The *Belfast Telegraph* reported that 'while the Imperial was not losing money the general recession in the cinema trade and high overhead expenses had led to the decision to put it on the market'. The cinema's managing director added that the 'tremendous increase in rates a few years ago really tipped our heels'.[81] While the Alhambra and the Coliseum both closed in 1959, Odeon (NI) had attempted to offload these cinemas after purchasing them from Irish Theatres in March 1955. In March 1956, the Lyric Light Opera Company wrote to the Rank Organisation and

---

[77] *Kinematograph Weekly*, 6 March 1958.
[78] *Belfast Telegraph*, 14 Feb. 1958.
[79] *Belfast Telegraph*, 14 Feb. 1958.
[80] *Belfast Telegraph*, 3 Oct. 1958.
[81] *Belfast Telegraph*, 8 July 1959.

requested that they sell either the Coliseum or the Alhambra for use as a national theatre in Northern Ireland.[82] In September, *Kine Weekly* reported that 'negotiations are under way for the sale of the Belfast Coliseum – a 600-seater and one of the oldest theatres in the city – to the Northern Ireland Council for the Encouragement of the Music and the Arts' (CEMA).[83] While the Northern Ireland Government considered providing a £50,000 grant to CEMA to purchase the Coliseum, it eventually rejected the plan 'on grounds of general financial policy'.[84] Odeon (NI) managing director Victor Powell stated that the cinema was still on the market for use as a theatre or 'for other purposes'.[85] In April 1958, *Kine Weekly* reported that even if the Northern Ireland Government reduced the Entertainment Tax to similar levels as in Great Britain, 'it is unlikely to mean a reprieve for the Alhambra and Coliseum in Belfast. These two cinemas – formerly variety theatres – belong to Odeon (N.I.) Ltd., and have been on the market for some time'.[86] In October 1958, the Rank Organisation announced a national rationalization policy and intended to close 110 of its 494 cinemas, to merge the Odeon and Gaumont circuits and to convert some cinemas into dance halls.[87] Despite rumours of closures, Eveleigh stated that Odeon (NI) was registered as a separate company within the Rank Organisation and 'that the circuit did not envisage the closing of any other cinemas in Northern Ireland'.[88]

In May 1959, the Coliseum was sold to Silver Cabs Limited, who planned to convert the building 'to provide additional accommodation for their fleet of 200 cars'.[89] The company's director stated that it would be impossible to use the building for entertainment purposes as there was 'a covenant in the deeds prohibiting it'.[90] On 10 September 1959, a suspect fire partially destroyed the interior of the Alhambra. A spokesman for the Rank Organisation stated that '[i]t is no secret that the Alhambra has been up for sale for some time now. At this stage I cannot comment on its future – whether it will be sold as it now stands or whether it will re-open again as a picture house'.[91] It never reopened and by 1966 was reconstructed as a supermarket.[92]

[82] *Belfast Telegraph*, 20 March 1956.
[83] *Kinematograph Weekly*, 27 Sept. 1956.
[84] *Belfast Telegraph*, 18 Sept. 1956.
[85] *Belfast Telegraph*, 18 Sept. 1956; *Kinematograph Weekly*, 26 Dec. 1957.
[86] *Kinematograph Weekly*, 24 Apr. 1958.
[87] *The Economist*, 11 Oct. 1958.
[88] *Belfast Telegraph*, 3 Oct. 1958.
[89] *Belfast Telegraph*, 22 May 1959.
[90] *Belfast Telegraph*, 22 May 1959.
[91] *Belfast Telegraph*, 11 Sept. 1959.
[92] M. Patton, *Central Belfast: a Historical Gazetteer* (Belfast, 1993), p. 247.

From the introduction of UTV in October 1959 to the end of 1962, twelve Belfast cinemas went out of business. The majority of these were inner-city and suburban cinemas and, following the introduction of commercial television in Northern Ireland, reports of cinema closures tended to place greater emphasis on the impact of television. They also underlined potential future uses of these buildings, showing how their perceptions of the city were changing.

In May 1960, the *Belfast Telegraph* reported that an undisclosed cinema was for sale that was 'ideally suited for conversion into a supermarket or arcade'. The reporter claimed further that 'two more cinemas – described as suitable for motor works, shops or dance halls – in the same area are to be offered for sale soon'.[93] In December 1960, reports suggested that the Royal was to close in the following year and be replaced with an office block. Reporter Gordon Duffield believed that its proposed redevelopment, alongside Rank's recent acquisition of the Grand Opera House and the Royal Hippodrome, showed that 'major changes are pending in the city's cinema trade. It is rumoured that the Opera House and Royal Hippodrome will be pulled down to make room for a new super cinema and that the Gaumont and the Regent will be sold for their site values'.[94] In September 1961, the *Belfast Telegraph* included a picture of the partially demolished Royal cinema and highlighted that the cinema was 'fast disappearing to give place to a block of shops and offices … A part of the city's history is vanishing'.[95] When John Tyler and Sons' shoe shop opened on its former site, it stated that it 'is one of the block of modern buildings that have risen on the site of the old Royal Cinema, which dominated one side of Arthur Square for about 45 years'.[96]

In 1960, Martin Wallace reported on the recent spate of cinema closures in the *Belfast Telegraph*. Following the downturn of cinema-going in Great Britain, he claimed that 'Ulster cinemas, too, are feeling the cold wind of change. Close to a dozen have closed in recent years, and others will follow'. Belfast's suburban cinemas were hardest hit as 'most districts now have too many cinemas for the film-going population which remains – and too few films are made to provide new "product"'. The concurrent decline of cinema attendance in the US led Hollywood producers to make fewer films, with Harper and Porter observing that the 'choice of films available to cinema managers became even more restricted from 1954 onwards, when

---

[93] *Belfast Telegraph*, 26 May 1960.
[94] *Kinematograph Weekly*, 29 Dec. 1960.
[95] *Belfast Telegraph*, 14 Sept. 1961.
[96] *Belfast Telegraph*, 2 Aug. 1962.

the number of new American films fell sharply'.[97] Wallace believed that many suburban cinemas were competing for the same cinema-goers and there was simply not enough new material to keep viewers interested. In contrast, 'city centre cinemas are doing fairly well, although the queues of earlier years have largely vanished'. He stated that while 'a visit to the city centre is still a "night out" – a visit to the local cinema is not. It is the old, uncomfortable, cheaper cinemas which have mostly closed'. Wallace noted the interest of property speculators in city centre sites that might be put to a more profitable use. While many suburban owners wished to sell, their sites offered less potential than their city centre counterparts. Despite the impact of television and Entertainments Duty, Wallace believed that cinemas could do more to attract customers with greater showmanship, more variety in programming, greater comfort and improved advertising. Overall, he argued 'cinemas can still count on a young audience, particularly as teenagers have more money in their pockets. But this is not the basis of a large and profitable industry'.[98]

At the end of the Second World War, there were three cinemas on the Shankill Road: the Shankill Picturedrome, the Stadium and the West End Picture House. The latter closed in 1960 and a representative stated that it could not 'compete any more with television and the growth of motoring and outside sport ... People's habits are changing, and a night out at the cinema doesn't mean the same as it did. Independent owners haven't a chance today'.[99] The Stadium was one of the larger inner-city cinemas opened in the 1930s and was purchased by Odeon (NI) from Irish Theatres. In April 1958, the Rank Organisation claimed that it was 'determined to fight television locally' and was reconstructing many of its Northern Ireland cinemas to attract larger audiences.[100] It renovated its more profitable suburban cinemas, such as the Regal, the Stadium and the Astoria and there was greater standardization in their décor and fittings. An advert in November 1961 announced that the Stadium was reopening after 'complete modernisation'. It claimed that the cinema 'has been brought up to London West End standards for the comfort, pleasure and entertainment of the cinema-going public of Belfast'. It reopened with a screening of *The Guns of Navarone* (US/UK, 1961), which was shown concurrently with the first-run Odeon.[101] This policy of screening first-run films in suburban cinemas

---

[97] S. Harper and V. Porter, *British Cinema of the 1950s: the Decline of Deference* (Oxford, 2003), p. 245.

[98] *Belfast Telegraph*, 5 Oct. 1960.

[99] *Belfast Telegraph*, 16 May 1960.

[100] *Belfast Telegraph*, 12 Apr. 1958.

[101] *Belfast Telegraph*, 25 Nov. 1961.

'quickly caught the imagination of a public which was used to "going down town" for its films'.[102] By October 1961, *Kine Weekly* claimed that while a number of cinemas hade closed, '[t]here are strong signs of the virility of the industry ... In Belfast major conversions are taking place and even the smaller circuits have shown themselves willing to pour money into better accommodation and good publicity'.[103]

When the Metro closed in March 1961, the *Belfast Telegraph* reported that while it was 'one of the finest suburban cinemas to be equipped for Cinema-Scope', the owners 'have decided to let the 1,000-seater picture-house possibly as a supermarket, warehouse, small factory or garage'.[104] The fact that it had opened in 1956 made its closure especially surprising and the other post-war cinemas remained open much longer. The Alpha, Lido and Tivoli remained in operation until 1973, 1970 and 1975 respectively. The Capitol and the Lyceum were both located on Antrim Road and were both part of the Odeon (NI) circuit. On 17 April 1961, the *Belfast Telegraph* reported that the Lyceum, which was built in 1916, was 'available for sale'.[105] The cinema closed on 29 April and manager Kevin McConnell stated that '[w]e are having our normal three Saturday shows and after the final curtain falls we will lock up as usual and go home ... Anyone who is here to-night will be here simply because they decided to go to the pictures, not because the Lyceum is closing'.[106] The Gaumont cinema ceased business on 30 September 1961 and the staff were relocated to the newly renovated Royal Hippodrome. In April, Eveleigh denied that it had been sold to House of Fraser in a £350,000 deal, yet it was reported 'that a number of cross-channel organisations are showing interest in the cinema and representatives have inspected the building'.[107] In August 1961, the *Belfast Telegraph*'s property correspondent claimed to have been told 'that £325,000 has been paid by British Home Stores for the Gaumont Cinema'.[108] Construction of the new store began in July 1964 and the new BHS opened in December 1965.[109]

The closure and conversion of cinemas into shops and offices altered people's use of the city centre and changed the social life of Belfast. In November 1961, the *Belfast Telegraph* claimed that Belfast at night was a dying city: 'The pavements are silent. The hum of life is almost gone

---

[102] *Ideal Kinema*, 8 Feb. 1962.
[103] *Kinematograph Weekly*, 12 Oct. 1961.
[104] *Belfast Telegraph*, 21 Apr. 1961.
[105] *Belfast Telegraph*, 17 Apr. 1961.
[106] *Belfast Telegraph*, 29 Apr. 1961.
[107] *Belfast Telegraph*, 17 Apr. 1961.
[108] *Belfast Telegraph*, 3 Aug. 1961.
[109] *Belfast Telegraph*, 21 July 1964; 5 Nov. 1965.

and overhead arc lights throw unbroken shadows on the deserted streets'. After the three Cornmarket cinemas closed down, 'the public started to abandon the district after 6-30'. Consequently, surrounding shops were closing earlier, pubs were losing trade and the British Legion car park had lost business. A spokesman for Gardiners, a tobacconist with premises in Arthur Square, stated that the 'disappearance of the cinemas has certainly affected us. The area is still a good place to have a business during the day, but after six o'clock the place is deserted'. A. W. Allen, secretary of the British Legion car attendants, stated that now they were operating at a loss in the Cornmarket area: 'Although business has increased for us around the Ritz and Odeon, this has not made up for the collapse of Cornmarket'.[110] In 1963, the *Irish Independent* reported on changes in Belfast over the past decade. It claimed that television, 'with its stay-at-home audiences', had altered the social life of the city: 'London property men have virtually torn the heart out of Belfast's cinema and theatre-land and left behind a great emptiness, especially at night, a wilderness of shop fronts, office blocks, banks and insurance offices ... A city cannot lose its places of entertainment without losing its character as well'.[111] In Northern Ireland, licensing laws for bingo were stricter than in the rest of the United Kingdom and public games of bingo were permitted only on a club basis. In 1963, four men were convicted of running illegal bingo games in the former Sandro cinema.[112] Two months later, the Royal Ulster Constabulary warned that most bingo sessions in Northern Ireland were operating illegally. One report suggested that the Northern Ireland CEA had been keeping in close touch with the situation as 'the likely future of bingo is of some considerable concern to cinema proprietors'.[113]

Three more cinemas closed in 1962: the Popular, the Crumlin Picture House and the Apollo. The latter was one of the cinemas purchased by Rank from Curran Theatres in 1956. Eveleigh stated that '[t]he Apollo is a family theatre, but, as it stands at the moment, I do not consider it satisfactory for public use. The amenities in it are bad and, unfortunately, it is too small to lend itself to improvement'.[114] The *Belfast Telegraph* reported that 'the site was so confined that it would have required complete rebuilding to make it into the type of cinema Odeon operates'.[115] In many districts, there were too many cinemas to serve the population and large exhibitors were unwilling to

---

[110] *Belfast Telegraph*, 10 Nov. 1961.
[111] *Irish Independent*, 5 Aug. 1963.
[112] *Belfast Telegraph*, 11 March 1963.
[113] *Belfast Telegraph*, 23 May 1963.
[114] *Northern Whig*, 29 Nov. 1962.
[115] *Belfast Telegraph*, 29 Nov. 1962.

invest in smaller and less profitable cinemas. Writing in the *Belfast Telegraph*, Martin Wallace foresaw the closure of suburban cinemas and observed that '[m]ost districts now have too many cinemas for the film-going population which remains'. He claimed that, as cinema attendances decline further, 'it is quite possible that, in each district only the best cinema will survive – the one that is most comfortable, the one that has traditionally offered the best programmes'.[116] In the early 1960s, Belfast residents attended the cinema less frequently than they had done in the previous decade. There is evidence, however, that increasing wages and greater amounts of disposable income meant that they were prepared to spend more on individual cinema trips and preferred to visit more upmarket venues. The oral history testimony suggests that adolescents became more discerning in their film choices and as one cinema-owner commented to the local press: 'people don't go to the pictures anymore … they go to see a particular film. The bread-and-butter programme doesn't bring them in any more'.[117]

Suburban cinema exhibition in Sheffield

In 1945, there were only four first-run cinemas in Sheffield and large British exhibitors held a relatively small presence. ABC operated the Hippodrome and Rank operated the Regent. The latter opened in 1927 and was the last cinema built in Sheffield city centre before the war. In the 1930s, Rank attempted to increase its presence in Sheffield and though construction of the Sheffield Odeon began in 1939, the outbreak of war interrupted its progress. The majority of Sheffield's cinemas were either owned independently or under the control of local chains. In 1947, for instance, Sheffield and District Cinematograph Theatres owned the Carlton, the Cinema House and the Globe.[118] In 1959, this chain was purchased by Mappin and Webb Ltd., a London and Sheffield silversmiths.[119] By 1965, Sheffield had only twenty licenced cinemas. ABC relinquished the Hippodrome in 1948 and opened a new cinema in 1961, and Rank had increased its presence to two cinemas with the completion of the Odeon in 1956. Many small chains and independently-owned cinemas had closed down and the largest circuit was Star Cinemas, which operated the Abbeydale, the Heeley Palace, the Lyric, the Oxford, the Pavilion, the Star and the Wicker.[120]

---

[116] *Belfast Telegraph*, 5 Oct. 1960.

[117] *Belfast Telegraph*, 5 Oct. 1960.

[118] *Kinematograph Year Book 1947* (London, 1947), p. 505.

[119] *The Star*, 7 March 1959; *The Star*, 9 March 1959; *Kinematograph Weekly*, 2 Apr. 1959; *The Star*, 7 Apr. 1959.

[120] *Kinematograph and Television Year Book 1963* (London, 1963), pp. 306–7.

After the Second World War, no new cinemas were constructed to serve Sheffield's suburban housing developments. In March 1950, the Sheffield City Council Estates Committee allocated eight sites on housing estates for cinema construction: Stradbroke, Manor Park, Nab Lane, Greenhill, Broadway, Norton and two in Parson Cross.[121] The Sheffield CEA then appointed a sub-committee 'to go into the allocation of sites for new cinemas in the city suburbs'.[122] Secretary Arnold Favell requested that applicants state if they had at any point owned cinemas in slum clearance areas and the committee would then allocate the available sites in terms of priority.[123] No suitable exhibitors came forward and, in 1955, Sheffield CEA arranged a meeting for 'members interested in being allocated kinema sites on the new housing estates'. The number of sites available was reduced to four: 'Hackenthorpe, Greenhill, Manor Park and Gleadless Valley, with the first three ready for immediate development'. Favell claimed that since 1950 'there had been many changes. Some of the original sites had been abandoned and others added, and some of the companies allocated sites may not wish to go on with them'. Sheffield City Council, furthermore, 'were anxious to lease the sites expeditiously'.[124] Exhibitors were unwilling to invest in new cinemas as audiences were already declining and suburban cinemas were faring worse than their city centre counterparts. At the 1956 Sheffield CEA's annual meeting, Favell stated that although 'several kinema sites had become available on corporation housing estates CEA members had made little response'.[125]

Many interwar housing developments were served by cinemas in neighbouring districts. From 1951 to 1952, sociologists Mark Hodges and Cyril Smith investigated social relationships on the Wybourn Estate, built to provide housing for families relocated as part of an interwar slum clearance scheme.[126] They observed that it was well served by amenities and commented that the foot of the estate 'runs into a working class shopping centre with a cinema'.[127] One mother believed that 'without the cheap cinema nearby there would be nothing for the children to do'.[128] Many residents also used public transport to access city centre cinemas: 'in the

---

[121] *The Star*, 7 March 1950.
[122] *The Star*, 25 March 1960.
[123] *Kinematograph Weekly*, 30 March 1950.
[124] *Kinematograph Weekly*, 19 May 1955.
[125] *Kinematograph Weekly*, 9 Feb. 1956.
[126] M. W. Hodges and C. S. Smith, 'The Sheffield estate', in *Neighbourhood and Community: an Enquiry into Social Relationships on Housing Estates in Liverpool and Sheffield*, ed. T. S. Simey (Liverpool, 1954), pp. 79–134, p. 8.
[127] Hodges and Smith., 'The Sheffield estate', p. 80.
[128] Hodges and Smith, 'The Sheffield estate', p. 93.

evenings there is an outward movement to the cinema (as one person remarked, "You'll never find anybody in after seven on the estate. They're all at the pictures")'.[129]

Although exhibitors were unwilling to invest in new sites, press reports reveal the demand for cinemas on new housing developments. In 1958, residents of High Green, a village on the northern outskirts of Sheffield, lamented the lack of amenities and believed that more was needed to cater for bored youth. 'There are no pictures and no-where to go', pleaded one seventeen-year-old male accused of joyriding in court. *The Star* reported on 'the sad paradox of the large "For Sale" notice outside the village's only cinema – its doors closed for the last time through lack of audiences. "Paradox" because almost everyone we interviewed cited the lack of a cinema as one of the village's main deficiencies'.[130] Cinemas were not the only amenity absent from these areas. *The Star* later named seven-year-old Manor Park as Sheffield's 'forgotten estate', as its 5,000 residents lacked a post office, a chemist, a haberdasher, a cinema and a public hall or community centre.[131] Hackenthorpe resident Arthur Stocks told the paper that '[t]here's no cinema, no proper community centre and no playground for the kids ... They're building some shops now, but it's taken them a year and this estate is six years old. It makes anyone feel they're forgotten'.[132] In 1961, Anthony Tweedale, writing in *The Star*, cited population shifts as a significant factor in cinema closures:

> the people are being snatched away from the cinemas by re-development. Their homes are transplanted to foreign parts, leaving the local picture houses looking strangely imperishable but very naked – often still showing films – surrounded by unoccupied shells of houses ... Several magnificent housing estates have appeared since the war, and none of them has a cinema, though a site in each case has been provided for one.[133]

His comments suggest that the problem for independent exhibitors was not only that they lacked the funds to renovate or modernize their premises, but that post-war population shifts and housing development meant that audiences could no longer access the cinemas that were once within walking distance.

Not all neighbourhoods lost their audiences and smaller circuits increased their presence by purchasing cinemas rather than constructing

[129] Hodges and Smith, 'The Sheffield estate', p. 103.
[130] *The Star*, 3 Jan. 1958.
[131] *The Star*, 6 Feb. 1958.
[132] *The Star*, 28 Nov. 1958.
[133] *The Star*, 25 March 1961.

new ones. In December 1947, Newcastle-based chain Essoldo purchased the Forum, the Capitol and the Ecclesfield Cinema House for £250,000.[134] In 1955, Star Cinemas acquired majority shareholdings in nine cinemas and became Sheffield's largest cinema chain. It refitted these cinemas, installing CinemaScope screens and projection equipment.[135] Star was one of the fastest growing chains in the 1950s and, in 1962, Spraos commented that 'it is a chain of comparatively small cinemas and for that reason its expansion must have saved a few from permanent closure. Nevertheless it cannot be overlooked that it has also increased the already heavy weight of the chains in the cinema industry'.[136]

The Odeon

Journalists and commentators frequently reported that Sheffield's leisure infrastructure was underdeveloped in comparison to similarly-sized British cities. In 1951, a Jamaican visitor to Sheffield lamented that it was 'a city bereft of all night life, the younger set mostly, must turn to the cinema for relaxation – and the long queues I see in the evenings outside your cinemas suggest there is need in Sheffield for at least two modern motion picture houses'.[137] Exhibitors were aware of the demand for more cinemas in Sheffield city centre and Odeon had first received permission to build a centrally located cinema on Flat Street in 1933. Construction began in 1938, though was interrupted by the outbreak of the Second World War. In June 1954, new architectural plans for the cinema were completed and the Rank Organisation announced that construction would recommence in the next three months.[138] From March 1955, workmen cleared the steel girders on the original site and commenced construction of the new building.[139] In September, *The Star* included an artist's impression of the building and Roy Mason, district manager of the Circuits Management Association, stated that 'the decoration and interior will be something which has never been seen in a theatre before ... When this theatre is open, I know Sheffield will be proud of it'.[140]

Before the Odeon's opening, reports emphasized that its technology would differentiate it from existing cinemas. *The Star* claimed that the 2,300-seat Odeon would be the largest cinema in South Yorkshire and its fifty-foot

---

[134] *The Star*, 6 Dec. 1947.
[135] *The Star*, 29 March 1955.
[136] J. Spraos, *The Decline of the Cinema: an Economist's Report* (London, 1962), p. 103.
[137] *The Star*, 6 July 1951.
[138] *The Star*, 28 June 1954.
[139] *The Star*, 28 March 1955.
[140] *The Star*, 6 Sept. 1955.

Figure 3.3. Interior of Odeon, Sheffield, July 1956 (Picture Sheffield, Sheffield City Council Archives and Local Studies Service).

screen the largest in the north of England (see Figure 3.3). It claimed further that 'the shape of the auditorium is unique. It will be deeply curved and will accommodate any type of picture and any type of sound will be possible. Modernistic architecture is being used for the front entrance. Glass walls will be featured'.[141] After the cinema's completion, *Kine Weekly* noted the contrast with Sheffield's existing cinemas, stating that 'the new theatre is a departure from conventional design. Internally, clean, simple lines, warm colour schemes, contemporary lighting treatment and considerable areas of close-carpeting create a comfort-with-a-modern-look atmosphere'.[142] *The Star* even claimed that it was 'the most modern cinema in the country ... the number of seats has been reduced to give more "leg room", and there are many novel facilities for patrons' comfort'.[143] The *Sheffield Telegraph* added that 'sound engineers have put all their knowledge and experience into making the

[141] *The Star*, 8 Dec. 1955.
[142] *Kinematograph Weekly*, 12 July 1956.
[143] *The Star*, 16 July 1956.

theatre acoustically perfect'. It claimed that the high definition screen threw all available light into the seating area, ensured maximum picture clarity and provided good viewing conditions from anywhere in the auditorium.[144]

On 16 July 1956, the Odeon's opening night featured a screening of *Reach for the Sky* (UK, 1956) five days after its London premiere. There were 1,800 tickets available to members of the public with prices ranging from 2*s* 6*d* to 3*s* 6*d*. The Dagenham Girl Pipers marched across Sheffield from the Gaumont to the Odeon, where state trumpeters from the York and Lancaster Regiment sounded a fanfare for the arriving guests.[145] The demand for tickets was so great that they were limited to two per person and applications were received from as far away as South Africa.[146] John Davis, managing director of the Rank Organisation, attended the opening with his wife Dinah Sheridan.[147] He used his speech to counter the emergence of television and assert the strength of the cinema exhibition industry: 'At this time if you read press reports and listen to some people, you may get the impression that the future of the industry is somewhat doubtful. We have our problems. We do not deny it, but we know that this industry will continue to satisfy 23 million people who visit cinemas every week in this country'.[148] Deputy Lord Mayor Alderman J. Curtis highlighted the changes he envisioned in Sheffield cinema exhibition. He 'appealed that the city should have a higher place on the list of provincial releases so that films were not shown two years after lesser-known towns like Pudsey, Oswaldtwistle and Chorlton-cum-Hardy'.[149] In the 1950s, press reports had frequently commented on Sheffield's low place in the list of releases and his comments 'were greeted with deafening applause'.[150]

The Odeon's luxury interior and facilities, alongside its access to first-run films, drew patrons away its city centre rivals. Sheldon Hall claims that its arrival was as much responsible as television for the Gaumont's declining admissions in the mid-to-late 1950s.[151] While it is clear that there was demand for a new first-run cinema in Sheffield city centre, declining audiences meant that the Odeon placed greater emphasis on ancillary revenue, such as sales of sweets, chocolate, ice cream and cigarettes. *Kine Sales and Catering Review* commented that 'great care was given to the design'

[144] *Sheffield Telegraph*, 17 July 1956.
[145] *The Star*, 20 June 1956.
[146] *The Star*, 9 July 1956.
[147] *The Star*, 14 July 1956.
[148] *Kinematograph Weekly*, 19 July 1956.
[149] *Kinematograph Weekly*, 19 July 1956.
[150] *The Star*, 17 July 1956.
[151] S. Hall, 'Going to the Gaumont', *Picture House*, xlii (2018), 50–67, at p. 65.

of its two sales kiosks 'so that they formed an integral part of the foyer'.[152] In 1956, 224 UK cinemas closed and the Odeon was one of only fourteen new cinemas that opened.[153] In September 1956, *The Economist* reported that while it was increasingly making more money from manufacturing, it 'would be a gross exaggeration to suggest that the Rank Organisation is edging sideways out of the film business. But there is no doubt which side of its activities is developing fastest, and this is not films'. Cinemas were increasingly expensive to develop and the commercial space they occupied could be used often for more profitable purposes. The report highlighted that the majority of Rank cinemas were purchased before the war and 'since 1939 the cost of building a cinema has risen about four and a half times'.[154] Despite Rank's rationalization programme of cinema closures, it opened new cinemas on sites that the company already owned and in areas where it held a large presence.

Cinema closures in Sheffield

In 1952, the Scala was the first cinema to shut its doors in post-war Sheffield. The cause of this closure was neither the decline in post-war cinema attendance nor the rise in television ownership. It was purchased by Sheffield University, whose bursar stated that while it intended to demolish the cinema, '[d]ifficulties in regard to licences for building and material would not permit this, so it was intended to use part of the cinema buildings for academic purposes'.[155] From the introduction of ITV in November 1956 to the end of 1957, four Sheffield cinemas closed down. The Weston Picture Palace was located in inner-city Sheffield, close to the University. Mrs A. Burrows, secretary of Hallamshire Cinemas Ltd., stated that '[t]here has been so much demolition work and rehousing in the area that the people just aren't here any longer. Patrons who have been coming here for years are now in Parson Cross and other housing estates'.[156] By the end of 1957, the Victory, the Darnall Cinema and the Woodhouse Picture Palace had all closed. Arnold Favell claimed that high levels of taxation meant that some suburban cinemas were losing money and *The Star* proposed that 'only an immediate relief in Entertainment Tax can prevent the closing of more Sheffield suburban cinemas in 1958'. It added that '[t]elevision is not entirely to blame for the falling support ... Extra costs on every side of the industry

[152] *Kine Sales and Catering Review*, 23 Aug. 1956.
[153] *Kinematograph Year Book 1958* (London, 1958), p. 509.
[154] *The Economist*, 15 Sept. 1956.
[155] *The Star*, 16 June 1952.
[156] *The Star*, 1 Jan. 1957.

have led to increased admission prices'.[157] From February to March 1958, the Tinsley Picture Palace, the Don Picture Palace and the Hillsborough Kinema House all shut their doors. *The Star* claimed that the closure of the Tinsley Picture Palace was 'not the direct result of the entertainments tax burden' and that the premises were to become a motor auction. The cinema's director, J. E. L. Wadsworth, hinted that cinema sites might be profitably used for other purposes and added that 'I would like to make it clear that we are not going out of business because we are losing money. We are not making much, but we are not losing'. His brother, cinema manager L. V. Wadsworth, protested against Entertainment Tax and stated that 'TV has made some difference but without this vicious tax many cinemas need not close down'.[158] In March 1959, the Don Picture Palace was reopened as Progress House, the new premises of the Bradford Woollen Company. While the interior was converted into a 'brand new, streamlined fashion house and warehouse', the little changed exterior was a 'reminder of the days when cinemas were themselves threats to radio and the theatre'.[159]

In February 1959, the Carlton, the Chantrey Picture House, the Darnall Picture Palace and the Wincobank Picture Palace all closed down. The Carlton had served the newly built Arbourthorne Estate since 1938 and was the youngest cinema to close in the period under review. The large majority of Sheffield cinemas that closed before 1965 were constructed prior to the 1930s. Manager W. H. Brown said that 'many youngsters could now afford to go into the city for cinema entertainment and as a result only the old "faithfuls" remained'. He added that, as the large circuits had greater booking power, the 'independent suburban cinema is being crushed out of existence and it is a great loss to the community'. Exhibitors were clearly aware that their counterparts in other areas of the country were also struggling. Sydney Jackson, northern divisional organizer for NATKE, compared Sheffield cinema closures to those in other cities: 'Leeds had lost 10 cinemas in the last two years. The pattern of entertainment is changing and people want better and bigger pictures in more comfortable surroundings'.[160]

The Star reported that television and taxes were the chief causes of recent closures and lamented that 'for the first time in more than 20 years, there are now a number of unemployed projectionists'. Wilfred Sedgwick, chief projectionist at a city cinema, stated that 'soon thousands will be out of work unless something is done to draw the public from the TV set – if it is

---

[157] *The Star*, 10 Jan. 1958.
[158] *The Star*, 15 Feb. 1958.
[159] *The Star*, 10 March 1959.
[160] *The Star*, 20 Feb. 1959.

the TV set that is causing declining audiences'.[161] Several readers responded to this article. 'Sprocket', for instance cited a range of factors and implied that there was public demand for more city centre cinemas:

> I don't think TV is the sole cause of falling attendances. Many of the pictures shown in the locals leave a lot to be desired. Some which are re-booked as supposed reissues are the original copies, generally cut and carved beyond recognition. The good attendance at the city cinemas where good pictures are generally shown prove that the cinema is not dead ... Some of the trouble can be put down to the fact that in some cases profits made in the past have been taken out in the form of dividends, and nothing put back into the business in the form of improvements, or comfort, as an inducement for the patrons to attend. I know of some locals where the same seating is still in use which was first put in about 40 years ago.[162]

The failure to upgrade or renovate cinemas meant that they no longer retained their status as 'picture palaces'. Patrons were not simply paying to see the film and increasingly demanded the higher standards of comfort that newer cinemas offered.

Five more cinemas closed in 1959: the Heeley Green Picture House, the Unity, the Roxy, the Globe and the Norfolk Picture House. In November 1959, the Kinematograph Renters' Society forced the Norfolk Picture House to abandon a scheme offering half-price tickets on Monday and Thursday as it broke the terms of its film hire contract. The manager claimed that he was forced to offer the deal as '[t]he Corporation have wrecked the area near the cinema' and slum clearance led to the loss of patrons.[163] The attempts to turn Heeley Green Picture House into a theatre show the range of potential uses for defunct cinemas. In February 1959, *The Star* reported that 'Sheffield Amateur Theatre Project's quest for a building to house amateur drama and music groups has ended in success' and its representatives had voted in favour of purchasing the Heeley Green Picture House.[164] Despite a fundraising campaign and promise of financial support from the city council this plan did not come to fruition. The costs of the project increased and the City Council were no longer able to provide financial assistance.[165] From April 1961 to July 1962, it briefly reopened as the Tudor cinema and was later used as a bingo hall.[166]

---

[161] *The Star*, 26 Feb 1959.

[162] *The Star*, 6 March 1959.

[163] *The Star*, 10 Nov. 1959.

[164] *Kinematograph Weekly*, 9 Feb 1958.

[165] *The Star*, 14 Sept. 1959; *The Star*, 24 Apr. 1960.

[166] P. Tuffrey, *South Yorkshire's Cinemas and Theatres* (Stroud, 2011), p. 120.

Despite the abolition of Entertainment Tax in April, more cinemas closed in 1960, such as the Crookes Picture Palace, the Phoenix and the Park. Poor attendance led to the closure of the Crookes cinema. Manager A. Burrows stated that 'the audiences have simply drifted away'.[167] The impact of cinema closures was generational. While younger cinema-goers were able to travel into the city centre once their local neighbourhood cinema closed down, for those with families and children, financial constraints often prevented these trips. Andrew and Carol Palmer had their first child in 1958 and Andrew claimed that: 'When we had a young family from when we first got married, you couldn't afford to go. You couldn't afford to go. I mean, I used to go to work and I used to pay my wages over to Carol and I'd just got enough money to go to work for rest of the week'.[168] David Ludlam, born in 1930, stated that before the introduction of television, the cinema was his main form of entertainment. After he got married in 1956, he claimed that 'we certainly didn't go to the cinema going into the fifties, having got married and pennies were tight … I'd go along to the pub instead, that was nearer'.[169] The solo nature of these pub visits indicates the gendered impact of cinema closures and its influence on separate leisure patterns. Though female pub-going increased in the post-war years, it remained a predominantly male institution. Claire Langhamer has claimed that leisure patterns in marriage were diverse, yet the 'notion that men earned leisure while women facilitated it framed gendered experiences of leisure within a marriage'.[170] Married women tended to engage in more informal leisure activities as they lacked the financial resources to go to the cinema and there was a greater expectation that spare money should be spent on the household. Trips to local cinemas were convenient and cheap. But when these cinemas closed, trips to the city centre were more time consuming and often prohibitively expensive.

In January 1961, *The Star* reported that forty-one cinemas had closed 'in and around Sheffield' in the past four years and Arnold Favell stated that 'the drop in attendances made it impossible for some of the very small cinemas to function'.[171] Other commentators noted that while inner-city and suburban cinemas were closing, city centre cinemas were increasing their trade. In March 1961, Anthony Tweedale asked '[h]ow many times have you walked into a darkened cinema on the outskirts of Sheffield and discovered, when the lights have gone up, that you, and a few rather lonely-

---

[167] *The Star*, 22 March 1960.

[168] Interview with Andrew and Carol Palmer (pseudonyms), Sheffield, 7 Aug. 2015.

[169] Interview with David Ludlam, Sheffield, 25 June 2014.

[170] C. Langhamer, *Women's Leisure in England* (Manchester, 2000), p. 152.

[171] *The Star*, 30 Jan. 1961.

looking individuals, are the only ones there?' His comments highlight the lack of incentives for investing in existing cinemas and the difficulty exhibitors faced in future planning:

> Only the prophets and the wise birds among the cinema-owners can visualise what will happen to their properties in, say, a month's time. The suburban house can't plan far ahead. It would be rather pointless and extravagant to do an auditorium over with a paint brush, only to be told it was going to be reduced to rubble.[172]

The decline of suburban cinemas was the result of the demise of cinema attendance as a regular habit. He claimed that while family films such as *Pollyanna* (US, 1960) did well in the suburbs, controversial 'X' rated films such as *Saturday Night and Sunday Morning* (UK, 1960) did better in the city centre. Big films such as *The Ten Commandments* (US, 1956) could also rely on extended runs in city centre cinemas, 'exhausting their selling-power long before they appear in the suburbs'. He claimed that suburban cinema managers were 'wizards of a kind' who have no choice but to show worn copies of old films in dishevelled buildings. He added that '[w]hen the last of the suburban halls is finally knocked flat, and you see a petrol pump standing in its place, or a smoking heap of old bricks, I hope you won't blame the films or the cinemas.'[173]

ABC

By 1961 UK cinema attendance had fallen to 449 million, less than a third of its post-war peak. In 1959 and 1960, net cinema closures totalled 425 and 396 respectively.[174] Despite this, ABC opened a new city centre cinema in 1961, showing that large exhibitors consolidated their interests in fewer sites and placed greater emphasis on first-run luxury cinemas that were better able to compete with the attractions of television and rival leisure activities. The circuit had no presence in Sheffield since it relinquished its lease on the Hippodrome in 1948 and the opening of a new prestige cinema occurred at the same time as the company was converting many of its cinemas for other purposes. At its 1961 annual general meeting, chairman Sir Philip Warter stated that while twenty-six of the company's cinemas had closed in the previous year, it had opened bowling centres in Dagenham and Birmingham and was in the process of converting cinemas in Leytonstone

---

172 *The Star*, 25 March 1961.
173 *The Star*, 25 March 1961.
174 *The Kinematograph and Television Year Book 1966* (London, 1966), p. 450.

and Manchester.[175] In the same week as the Sheffield ABC opened, *Kine Weekly* announced that the Regal, Manchester was to be converted into a bowling alley and cinemas in Newcastle and Glasgow were to be converted into bingo halls.[176]

The new ABC cinema was ten years in the making. In January 1951, Sheffield estates surveyor W. H. Rothwell reported the lease of a city-centre site at the junction of Angel Street and Bank Street to a cinema company, which proposed to build a 2,200-seat cinema at a cost of £124,000.[177] In July 1953, Rothwell stated that 'Sheffield needed new kinemas in the city centre to replace those destroyed in the war' and that they 'were also needed to bring Sheffield up to standard in this section of the entertainment world'.[178] In 1956, ABC announced plans to build at least five new cinemas, including a '2,000-seater at Sheffield'.[179] By October 1958, Alderman J. W. Sterland, chairman of the Town Planning Committee, told *The Star* that the new ABC was due for completion in January 1960: 'all details were now almost completed and that within a short time A.B.C would begin building the cinema at the corner of Bank Street and Angel Street'.[180] The opening of the new Odeon cinema and news of the forthcoming ABC cinema generated concerns among exhibitors that too much of Sheffield's exhibition industry was held in the hands of a small number of large exhibitors. Sheffield CEA members postulated that the arrival of the ABC would affect suburban cinemas (where losses were already greater than first-run city centre cinemas), damage the business of other city centre cinemas, lead to a greater reliance on second-run films and have an adverse impact on valuation rating appeals. Jack Reiss proposed that 'a delegation should be formed to see the appropriate authority and point out that the city was adequately served with cinemas, that another cinema would be a disadvantage to ratepayers, and to ask about second thoughts about the permission to build'.[181] In February 1959, a spokesman for ABC stated that 'despite the recent closing of suburban picture houses', they were 'definitely pushing ahead' with the new cinema.[182]

Construction work began in May 1960 and ABC's plans emphasized its comfort, 'decorative materials' and 'contemporary design in keeping with

---

[175] *The Economist*, 19 Aug. 1961.
[176] *Kinematograph Weekly*, 25 May 1961.
[177] *The Star*, 26 Jan. 1951.
[178] *Kinematograph Weekly*, 16 July 1953.
[179] *Kinematograph Weekly*, 10 May 1956.
[180] *The Star*, 11 Oct. 1958.
[181] *Kinematograph Weekly*, 30 Oct. 1958.
[182] *Kinematograph Weekly*, 20 Feb. 1959.

the most modern approach to cinema design'.[183] Reporter Anthony Tweedale stressed the benefits to Sheffield city centre and declared that 'the last word in luxury cinemas has materialised in our midst, the city's film fans have got what they deserved, and Sheffield IS a centre for picture palaces'. He even claimed that the cinema had 'warmed the hearts of A.B.C.'s rivals who are welcoming the new cinema as a further incentive to Sheffielders to spend their evenings and their pocket money in the quickly expanding city centre'.[184] Its opening night featured the world premiere of British comedy *Don't Bother to Knock* (UK, 1961) and personal appearances by Richard Todd, Nicole Maurey, June Thorburn and Dawn Beret. Todd claimed that '[i]f you need any evidence of the future we have in films, and in British film in particular, you have only to look around you at this simply marvellous cinema … We have several competitors, television, stately homes, bowling alleys … we think we can cope with them all'. Harold Slack, lord mayor of Sheffield, added that he was pleased that Sheffield was 'the only city in a wide area where two cinemas had been built since the war'.[185]

In a similar fashion to the Odeon, press reports highlighted the ABC's modern design and technological capabilities:

The space age for cinemas starts in Sheffield tomorrow with the opening of the streamlined, futuristic theatre which seems to have come straight from the pages of a science fiction magazine … Europe's most luxurious cinema – bowl shaped and gaudy as a dragonfly – might have been built with Flash Gordon in mind. Built at a cost of £200,000 the new A.B.C. Cinema in Angel Street is a garish prototype of what the cinema of the future will be. Other countries in Europe are expected to follow Sheffield's lead.[186]

The *Sheffield Telegraph* reported that '[t]he most advanced ideas and techniques of cinema design have been embodied in the project, resulting in a cinema which upholds the fine traditions of Associated British Cinemas and is a credit to the city'. It praised the sixty-foot 'mammoth screen' and claimed that the seating 'embodies all the latest improvements and has been designed to give spacious knee-room and easy access … features which are sadly lacking in so many cinemas up and down the country'.[187] *Ideal Kinema* declared that '[a]dvanced ideas in design and décor, combined with functional efficiency, make the new ABC, Sheffield, one of the most

[183] *The Star*, 6 Apr. 1960.
[184] *The Star*, 17 May 1961.
[185] *Sheffield Telegraph*, 19 May 1961.
[186] *The Star*, 17 May 1961.
[187] *Sheffield Telegraph*, 18 May 1961.

notable of additions to the Associated British Cinemas circuit'.[188] These press reports used similar hyperbolic language to ABC's souvenir brochure and it is difficult to accept this praise at face value. The fact that newspapers were a key source of information for cinema-goers meant that they made significant amounts of money from advertising revenue and it was in the interests of the local press to promote the benefits of new cinemas.

In 1962, reporter Anthony Tweedale praised the Odeon and the ABC, stating that they were 'not white elephants, rather the opposite. Prudent, imaginative, long-sighted officials in London have discovered that the only way to induce families and couples to pay five shillings to see a film is to offer them luxury'.[189] Robert Heathcote was born in 1950 and many of his local neighbourhood cinemas closed in childhood. He stated that the attraction of the ABC and the Odeon cinemas was not just the improved surroundings and better technology, but also the access to first-run films: 'As soon as a top film come out, it was on their chain ... and when you're a young person you wanted to go and see a film as soon as it came out'.[190] These cinemas were more expensive and in 1961, evening prices at the ABC ranged from 3s to 5s. On Saturday, reduced prices of 1s 6d and 2s were available for children under fourteen. Other interviewees revealed that they were content to remain in their local neighbourhood cinemas. Ernest Walker was born in 1947 and his comments show that city centre cinemas were often inaccessible to adolescents: 'As I got towards my teens I would have been going to cinemas less and less. And invariably, because the local cinemas were closing down, you went more and more into the city centre'. However, 'when the local cinemas closed down, you know, it weren't just that easy to go into town and go to a cinema. Apart from the fact that they probably cost a little bit more money anyway'.[191]

Further closures

The ABC's arrival exacerbated cinema closures in Sheffield, and only two days after its opening, Star Cinemas sold the Regal Cinema in Attercliffe: 'It is believed that the buyers intend to demolish the premises and redevelop the site for commercial use. A lot of money has been spent on the Regal in recent years'.[192] In 1959, the Cinema House was purchased by Mappin and Webb Ltd., but it closed in August 1961. A spokesman for the owners

---

[188] *Ideal Kinema*, 8 June 1961.
[189] *Sheffield Telegraph*, 24 May 1962.
[190] Interview with Robert Heathcoate, Sheffield, 30 July 2015.
[191] Interview with Ernest Walker (b. Sheffield), Belfast, 26 Nov. 2014.
[192] *The Star*, 20 May 1961.

stated that a 'lot of Sheffielders will be sorry to see it go, but that is the march of progress'.[193] In November 1960, Sheffield City Council purchased the Hippodrome under a compulsory order and planned to demolish the building as part of the Moorhead improvement scheme. In June 1961, *The Star* reported that the Corporation planned to purchase Sheffield's oldest cinema, the Union Street Picture Palace, for £60,000 and demolish it to provide further space for the same scheme.[194]

Tweedale was the only commentator to consider the architectural heritage of cinema buildings and reported that before the end of the following year Sheffield would have lost its three oldest cinemas: the Hippodrome, the Palace and the Cinema House.[195] In September 1961, *Star* reader Brian Parkin complained that, 'with the closure of several city centre cinemas, smaller towns such as Rotherham and Chesterfield will be its equal soon in entertainments'. He believed that the closure of the Cinema House was already leading to greater queues outside other cinemas and they 'are forming again where none existed before'. He claimed that the people of Sheffield 'deserve good entertainment in their own city. They should get it and get it without the futility of that so called game Bingo. Sheffield must replace the Hippodrome and Palace when they have to go'.[196] The Hippodrome, however, did not close until March 1963 and the Picture Palace remained open until October 1964.

Several cinemas were closed because their sites and buildings could be put to a more profitable use. In September 1961, the Sunbeam closed due to 'lack of patronage' and the board of directors received 'an offer from a firm interested in building a petrol station on the site'.[197] Later that month, reports of the Woodseats Palace's closure highlighted the geographical differences in cinema closures and claimed that there were only three cinemas on the southern side of the city. Derek Eckart, director of Star Associated Holdings said that the cinema 'has been having a prosperous time, but we have been offered a tempting sum for development'.[198] In January 1962, *The Star* reported that the Paragon Cinema was to close: 'The proprietors, it is understood, have been offered a price for the building by a firm of investors'.[199]

[193] *The Star*, 31 July 1961.
[194] *The Star*, 12 June 1961.
[195] *The Star*, 17 June 1961.
[196] *The Star*, 15 Sept. 1961.
[197] *The Star*, 2 Sept. 1961.
[198] *The Star*, 20 Sept. 1961.
[199] *The Star*, 30 Jan. 1962.

In the early 1960s, many British cinemas were converted into bingo halls or bowling alleys. In October 1961, Kenneth Kerner saved the Roscoe from closure, 're-modernized' the building and introduced bingo sessions on Wednesday evenings.[200] This venture, however, lasted only until April 1962. While many owners found that bingo was more profitable than cinema exhibition, they often retained their Saturday morning matinees. Many adolescent cinema-goers bemoaned the conversion of local cinemas. In 1963, local teenagers organized a protest march in response to news that the Manor cinema was to convert to bingo. Brenda Barnsley and Janice Rainsford collected 150 signatures and the latter stated that '[w]e go twice, sometimes three times a week to see films at the Manor. If it closes, our nearest cinema will be at Intake. There are already plenty of alternative places to play bingo'.[201] Their attempts to save the cinema failed and it reopened as the Manor Casino in July. Seventeen-year-old Barry Mark mounted a similar protest at the Plaza. The manager sated that 'the step had been taken regretfully, but unfortunately attendances had not been great enough to make the cinema a commercial proposition any more'.[202] In 1964, *The Star* reported that citizens were abandoning bingo and returning to the cinema. ABC manager Reg Helley said that '[p]eople are getting tired of what were novelties and are coming back to the cinema'.[203] Promotional activities were also key in attracting patrons away from bingo and Helley was announced as ABC's champion manager of 1964, receiving a cheque for £750.[204] In Sheffield, no cinemas were converted into bowling alleys, but some were demolished and replaced by new buildings. In December 1963, a new £250,000 ten-pin bowling alley was built on the site of the former Paragon cinema, Firth Park.[205] The head of Angallan Bowling stated that the new building was 'one of the few bowling centres in the country that has been built for that purpose. Converted cinemas are a thing of the past'.[206]

Several cinemas were refurbished and opened under different names. When these cinemas reopened they attempted to increase their box-office revenue by offering more specialized films and attracting niche audiences. In 1959, the News Theatre changed its name to the Cartoon Cinema. In January 1962, it was refurbished and renamed again, becoming the Classic. *The Star* claimed that it would be the city's repertory theatre and 'will show,

---

[200] *The Star*, 20 Sept. 1961.
[201] *The Star*, 15 July 1963.
[202] *The Star*, 3 Sept. 1963.
[203] *The Star*, 20 March 1964.
[204] *Kine Weekly*, 1 Apr. 1965.
[205] *The Star*, 12 Dec. 1963; *The Star*, 30 Jan. 1964.
[206] *The Star*, 1 Nov. 1962.

in the main, films of anything up to 30 years' vintage, which are considered classics of their kind'. *The Apartment* (US, 1960) was the first film shown at the cinema, followed by films such as *Wuthering Heights* (US, 1939), *The Robe* (US, 1953) and *Roman Holiday* (US, 1953). If films such as these were popular, reported *The Star*, 'they will branch out with more enterprising and unusual ideas – such as a Greta Garbo season'.[207] Following the cinema's opening, Tweedale claimed that it was the 'the best news Sheffield film fans have had for many years … it promises to bring back one of the most revered old terms in the trade – the film fan. The person who "goes to the flicks," who makes a habit of it – reserves, perhaps, every Wednesday night for the pictures'.[208]

In August 1962, the Wicker underwent refurbishment and reopened as Studio 7. It aimed to show films 'off the beaten track' and Bernard Rains, regional controller of Star Cinemas stated that '[w]e have long thought Sheffield was neglected so far as good international films were concerned. The Wicker has had a certain type of draw over the years. We certainly don't expect to show many nude films at the new cinema'.[209] In October 1962, Studio 7's opening ceremony featured an appearance by the lord mayor of Sheffield, Alderman P. C. J. Kirkman. *Kine Weekly* reported that the first film screened was *Il Tetto* (Italy, 1956. English title: *The Roof*), 'a Titanus film, with Italian dialogue and English sub-titles – setting the pattern of films to be shown at the cinema, which will specialise in films of an international character'.[210] Following the opening, *The Star* reported that '[o]nce upon a time (about ten days ago, in fact) nice people approached The Wicker with the furtive anxiety of a distressed gentlewoman entering a pawnshop … Nice people need tremble no more, for the Wicker was closed a week last Saturday'. The report commented on the cinema's changing audience profile:

> Since 1955, when the management had to ban youngsters wearing Edwardian clothes from the cinema, the audience has changed from being predominantly teenage to being predominantly adult … As Studio 7, the cinema will have to live down a past marred by mediocrity and create an appreciative audience for good, but demanding films.[211]

In response to declining audiences and the increased need for comfort in cinemas, the seating capacity was decreased to seven hundred to create

---

[207] *The Star*, 4 Dec. 1961.
[208] *The Star*, 13 Jan. 1962.
[209] *The Star*, 29 Aug. 1962.
[210] *Kinematograph Weekly*, 25 Oct. 1962.
[211] *The Star*, 11 Oct. 1962.

more room and it was reported that 'intimate, comfortable and attractive surroundings make the theme of this "off-beat" film centre'. *The Star* emphasized the modernist nature of the new exterior, which included neon signs and an aluminium facade.[212] In December 1962, *Ideal Kinema* commented that of 'particular interest is the practice of using aluminium sheet or curtain walling systems to re-face existing buildings, to give them a "face lift" in fact. This can be done with buildings such as cinemas that are still structurally sound but which require a more modern and brighter appearance'.[213]

Conclusion

In 1945, cinemas were a visible presence in local neighbourhoods and town centres across the United Kingdom, forming an important part of the topography in industrial cities such as Belfast and Sheffield. Declining audiences naturally led to cinema closures and while many of these premises were repurposed, investors found that it was often more profitable to demolish old cinemas and construct new buildings, such as bowling alleys and shops. By 1965 changing leisure habits and urban redevelopment meant that the place of cinemas in the built environment altered dramatically. Beyond providing us with an insight into the diverse reasons for cinema closures, such as dilapidated buildings and rising fixed costs, newspapers reports in Belfast and Sheffield show how these changes were perceived and understood by cinema owners, employees and patrons.

Large operators such as ABC and Rank were better placed than their independent counterparts to cope with the decline in cinema admissions and increased their market share from the 1950s onwards. The preceding analysis showed that they varied their strategies in different UK cities, displaying sensitivity to regional markets and adapting to local conditions. Slum clearance and population shifts physically removed audiences from their local neighbourhood cinemas. Margaret Dickinson and Sarah Street observed that independent cinemas were trapped in a vicious circle: 'as their takings decreased they became less able to modernise their cinemas, which became less attractive so that takings decreased further'.[214] Though this statement is undoubtedly true, their research excluded Northern Ireland and this chapter nuances their findings by showing how small chains and independent exhibitors built a relatively high number of cinemas in inner-

---

[212] *The Star*, 15 Oct. 1962.

[213] *Kinematograph Weekly*, 6 Dec. 1962.

[214] M. Dickinson and S. Street, *Cinema and State: the Film Industry and the British Government 1927–84* (London, 1985), p. 228.

city and suburban areas of Belfast in the mid 1950s. These case studies of two industrial cities, focusing on the relationship between cinema and the built environment, suggest that cinema-going experiences should be understood not only in relation to the wider social and economic changes discussed in the previous chapter, but also the priorities of cinema exhibitors, commercial developers and local councils.

4. Cinema exhibition, programming and audience preferences in Belfast

In May 1945, the *Belfast Telegraph* reported that 'the average patron may not be aware that no matter whether a cinema makes money or loses it, anything from 40 to 45 per cent of every shilling taken at the box office does not go into the cinema's coffers but is handed over to the Minister of Finance in entertainment tax'.[1] The fact that levies from cinema admissions constituted the lion's share of total Entertainment Tax (referred to as Entertainments Duty by the Northern Ireland Ministry of Finance) reflects both the popularity of cinema-going and its fiscal importance to the Northern Ireland Government (see Table 4.1). Entertainments Duty was one of its few revenue generating powers, but it was a consistent thorn in the side of Belfast exhibitors. In his study of film exhibition and distribution in Ireland, Kevin Rockett outlined the policies of the Northern Ireland Government, changes in the rates of duty and the responses of cinema exhibitors.[2] Here, however, the records of Entertainments Duty kept by the Ministry of Finance are used to investigate cinema exhibition, programming practices and audience preferences in post-war Belfast.[3] Box-office data and records of individual cinemas are surprisingly rare and the creative use of taxation returns shows one way to overcome this paucity of primary source material. The detailed quantitative analysis presented here expands the geographical range of several historians who have used box-office figures and cinema listings to assess the cinema-going habits of particular UK communities.[4] It also builds on the work of contemporary statisticians and economists

---

[1] *Belfast Telegraph*, 7 May 1945.

[2] K. Rockett with E. Rockett, *Film Exhibition and Distribution in Ireland, 1909–2010* (Dublin, 2011), pp. 125–40.

[3] PRONI, FIN/16/6/A-D, Ministry of Finance records of Entertainments Duty.

[4] For instance, see J. Sedgwick, *Popular Filmgoing in 1930s Britain: a Choice of Pleasures* (Exeter, 2000); S. Harper, 'A lower middle-class taste community in the 1930s: admissions figures at the Regent cinema, Portsmouth, UK', *Historical Journal of Film, Radio and Television*, xxiv (2004), 565–87; 'Fragmentation and crisis: 1940s admission figures at the Regent Cinema, Portsmouth, UK', *Historical Journal of Film, Radio and Television*, xxvi (2006), 361–94; R. James, 'Cinema-going in a port town, 1914–1951: film booking patterns at the Queens Cinema, Portsmouth', *Urban History*, xl (2013), 315–35.

who compiled data on audiences and exhibition in Great Britain, but who excluded Northern Ireland from their analysis.[5]

Table 4.1. Entertainments Duty receipts in Northern Ireland, 1949–60.

Financial year	Cinema (£)	Others (£)	Total (£)
1949–50	605,798	57,736	663,534
1950–1	607,495	58,129	665,624
1951–2	656,063	52,711	708,774
1952–3	644,041	54,505	698,545
1953–4	643,685	51,998	695,684
1954–5	648,484	44,712	693,196
1955–6	603,704	36,909	640,613
1956–7	640,246	35,846	676,092
1957–8	528,521	5,268	533,789
1958–9	284,216		284,216
1959–60	199,610		199,610
April–Dec. 1960	103,311		103,311

Note: In 1951, other contributions came from theatres, boxing matches, wrestling, greyhound racing, ice skating, speedway and zoo admissions. In 1957, Northern Ireland finance minister Terence O'Neill removed Entertainments Duty from live theatre and sport and freed cinema admissions up to 9*d* from taxation. In 1958 O'Neill announced significant further reductions in Entertainments Duty and tickets priced up to 1*s* 1*d* were freed from taxation. In Northern Ireland, Entertainments Duty was abolished in 1961.

Sources: Northern Ireland Ministry of Finance, *Digest of Statistics, Northern Ireland*, no. 1–15 (Belfast, 1954–61); PRONI, FIN/15/6/A/9, Ministry of Finance, increase in certain rates of duty, 1951.

The records contain statistics kept by the Ministry of Finance, details of alterations in the rates of Entertainments Duty and the weekly returns of most Northern Ireland cinemas. These allow for an investigation into the relationship between box-office revenue and Entertainments Duty during a period of rapidly declining attendances. The availability of weekly returns dictates the timeframe of this study as they are available only for the

---

[5] For instance, see H. E. Browning and A. A. Sorrell, 'Cinemas and cinema-going in Great Britain', *Journal of the Royal Statistical Society*, cvxii (1954), 133–70; Political and Economic Planning, *The British Film Industry* (1952); Political and Economic Planning, *The British Film Industry 1958* (London, 1958), pp. 132–70.

financial years ending March 1948, 1953, 1956 and 1961 (hereafter 1948–9, 1952–3, 1956–7 and 1960–1). The weekly returns were kept for financial purposes and show only dutiable admissions. As the minimum threshold for the payment of Entertainments Duty changed throughout the period under review the records provide a more accurate picture of attendance at cinemas that charged higher prices. In 1956–7, for example, the 56,784 admissions recorded at the Arcadian reflect its low ticket prices rather than its actual attendance figures.

The Ministry of Finance went to great lengths to ensure cinemas provided accurate data. The returns forms show that cinemas were inspected weekly and the *Belfast Telegraph* assured its readers that the Ministry of Finance 'takes good care to see that a careful check is kept on all cinema returns and that the money due for entertainments tax is paid promptly'. It added that 'patrons of any place of entertainment may not know that they can be called upon by any official of the Ministry to produce their half of the admission ticket'.[6] In 1946, the Northern Ireland CEA reminded its members 'that the patron must retain his half-ticket in case an entertainment tax inspector asked to see it'.[7] The threat of prosecution also encouraged exhibitors to provide accurate returns and, in 1948, entertainment promoter Cecil Greenwood was fined £20 for failure to pay the full amount of duty.[8] One drawback of the weekly returns is that they do not record the films shown by cinemas. By combining them with programme listings published in the *Belfast Telegraph* it is possible to examine programming practices and the changing nature of exhibition in the period under review. In his analysis of the film-booking patterns at the Queen's Cinema, Portsmouth, Robert James argued that, even without data to indicate which films were most popular, film preferences gleaned from booking patterns 'can be used as indicators of the popular *mentalities* and social attitudes' of a particular community.[9] By using the evidence provided by the Entertainments Duty summaries, it is possible to combine film listings and box-office data to investigate audience preferences and show the relative popularity of films in Belfast cinemas. These sources are supplemented by local newspapers, trade journals and oral history testimony that show how films were marketed, distributed and consumed in Belfast.

Five cinemas have been selected for detailed investigation: the Broadway, the Regent, the Ritz, the Strand and the Troxy (see Table 4.2). The choice of these five cinemas is designed to examine the differences between city

6   *Belfast Telegraph*, 7 May 1945.
7   *Kinematograph Weekly*, 31 Jan. 1946.
8   *Belfast Telegraph*, 13 Sept. 1948.
9   James, 'Cinema-going in a port town', p. 316.

centre cinemas and their inner-city and suburban counterparts, and to assess whether Belfast's sectarian divide influenced audience preferences and cinema-going habits. The cinemas were located in different geographical areas of Belfast, catered for audiences with different religious and political identities, and served patrons with different levels of disposable income. The Regent, opened originally in 1911 as the Picture House, was located centrally on Royal Avenue. Before the construction of the 1930s 'picture palaces' such as the Ritz, it was one of the most upmarket Belfast cinemas and it was the first cinema to exhibit sound pictures when it screened *The Singing Fool* (US, 1928) in 1929. In 1947, local cinema chain Curran Theatres purchased the Picture House, renovated the building and reopened it as the Regent. This meant Curran Theatres owned eleven cinemas in Northern Ireland, including five in Belfast: the Apollo, the Astoria, the Broadway, the Regal and the Capitol. Kevin Rockett stated that Curran cinemas attracted a largely lower middle-class audience and *Kine Weekly* claimed that its venues catered for 'black-coated workers' such as civil servants and bank clerks.[10] In 1948, the 850-seat Regent had its own café, and evening prices ranged from 1s 9d to 3s 6d.[11] It acted as Curran's first-run city centre cinema and had first preference on films distributed by Columbia. In December 1956, the Rank Organisation purchased the Curran chain and the Regent remained Odeon's first-run cinema until it purchased the Royal Hippodrome in November 1960.[12] The 1,380-seat Broadway was located on the largely nationalist and working-class Falls Road in west Belfast. It was one of Curran's second-run cinemas and screened many films exhibited previously at the Regent. Local cinema historian James Doherty described it as 'beyond comparison to any other cinema on the road' and its higher status was reflected in its evening prices, which, in 1948, ranged from 10d to 2s 3d.[13] In contrast, the highest priced tickets at the three other Falls Road cinemas – the Arcadian, the Clonard and the Diamond – cost 9d, 1s 6d and 8d respectively.

[10] Rockett, *Film Exhibition*, p. 82; *Kinematograph Weekly*, 13 Jan. 1944.
[11] *Kinematograph Year Book 1948* (London, 1948), p. 446.
[12] M. Open, *Fading Lights, Silver Screen: a History of Belfast Cinemas* (Antrim, 1985), pp. 25–6; Rockett, *Film Exhibition*, p. 124.
[13] J. Doherty, *Standing Room Only: Memories of Belfast Cinemas* (Belfast, 1997), p. 52; *Kinematograph Year Book 1948* (London, 1948), p. 446.

Table 4.2. Revenue, taxation and admissions in selected Belfast cinemas, 1948–61.

	Gross box-office revenue (£)	Entertainments Duty payments (£)	% of gross revenue paid as Entertainments Duty	Dutiable admissions
1948–9				
Broadway	36,286	11,657	32.1	
Regent	44,495	17,898	40.2	
Ritz	129,611	51,152	39.5	
Strand	36,076	12,598	34.9	
Troxy	30,336	9,407	31.0	
1952–3				
Broadway	32,855	9,892	30.1	489,899
Regent	48,631	19,529	40.2	473,564
Ritz	156,302	64,409	41.2	1,252,019
Strand	42,491	13,698	32.2	534,144
Troxy	28,504	7,884	27.7	507,432
1956–7				
Broadway	31,555	8,695	27.6	455,119
Regent	51,220	18,563	36.2	443,273
Ritz	152,943	59,681	39.0	1,107,646
Strand	38,384	11,898	31.0	480,431
Troxy	29,228	7,721	26.4	434,107
1960–1				
Broadway	19,524	1,725	8.8	218,309
Regent	46,234	8,207	17.8	353,958
Troxy	8,040	866	10.8	144,114

Notes: The weekly returns detail the daily box-office revenue generated by cinemas with Entertainments Duty and net revenue (gross revenue from admissions minus Entertainments Duty) listed separately. The number of admissions is absent from the records for 1948–9, though in later years they contain weekly breakdowns of the number of tickets sold within each price category. In 1960–1, records for the Ritz and the Strand in 1960–1 are incomplete and are not included.

Source: PRONI, FIN/15/6/C/1–143, Entertainments Duty weekly returns, 1948–61.

The Ritz and the Strand were operated by ABC, which took control of the Union Cinemas chain in October 1938.[14] The Ritz opened in 1936 and was a first-run cinema which had first preference on films distributed by Warner Brothers and MGM. Its 2,219 seating capacity made it Belfast's largest cinema and, in 1952–3, its 1,252,019 recorded admissions were higher than any other of the city's cinemas. Its prices were the highest of the five cinemas and, in April 1952, evening tickets ranged from 2*s* to 5*s* 6*d*. *Kine Weekly* believed that 'everything about the Ritz, from its imposing exterior to the comfort of its seats and efficient and excellent acoustics, spells the Modern Efficient Super. The result is that four pay boxes hum so loudly as that huge aircraft factory not so many miles away'.[15] Interviewees also highlighted the cinema's upmarket nature, describing it as 'totally different' to other cinemas in Belfast.[16] The 1,166-seat Strand opened in 1935 on Holywood Road, in the predominantly unionist area of Ballymacarett, east Belfast. Its architect, John McBride Neill, also designed the Alpha, the Apollo, the Picturedrome, the Majestic, the Curzon, the Troxy and the Lido. James Doherty described the cinema as '"junior" to Ulster's premier cinema, the Ritz'. He recalled that '[t]he downtown quality films were handed down only three or four weeks later and for the many (most) who could not afford the expensive Ritz, they could be certain to see the new releases at the Strand'.[17] The 1,164-seat Troxy opened on 24 October 1936 and was an independent, second-run cinema that exhibited many films screened previously at the Ritz and the Strand. The cinema's location on Shore Road, between two residential properties, made it geographically the farthest from the city centre of the five cinemas. It was also the cheapest, and in April 1952, evening prices ranged from 9*d* to 2*s*. In 1944, *Kine Weekly* stated that the cinema was patronized by the 'better middle-class residential type'.[18] Eric Lennox, projectionist at the cinema in the late 1940s and early 1950s described it as 'a respectable cinema' in comparison to local 'fleapits', such as the Duncairn.[19]

1948–9: attendance patterns

The post-war restriction of consumer goods meant that money continued to pour into commercial leisure activities. Richard Farmer stated that 'the

[14] Rockett, *Film Exhibition*, p. 76.
[15] *Kinematograph Weekly*, 13 Jan. 1944.
[16] Interview with Noel Spence, Comber, Co. Down, 26 March 2014.
[17] Doherty, *Standing Room Only*, p. 43.
[18] *Kinematograph Weekly*, 13 Jan. 1944.
[19] Interview with Eric Lennox, Belfast, 2 May 2014.

age of austerity was marked less by poverty than paucity; there was money to be spent, but there was little to spend it on' and exhibitors were well placed to take advantage of millions of habitual cinema-goers.[20] From 1948 to 1949, however, UK attendances fell by 6 per cent from 1,514 million to 1,430 million. The decline in cinema attendance was less severe in Northern Ireland and the total number of recorded admissions fell by 3 per cent from 32.98 million in 1948 to 31.94 million in 1949.[21] While the 1948–9 weekly returns do not provide admissions data, they do record daily box-office revenue and this allows us to assess the relative earning potential of cinemas and the financial success of particular films. In March 1948, tickets exceeding 3d were subject to Entertainments Duty and this includes all tickets sold by the five cinemas. Table 4.2 shows that the Ritz's gross revenue of £129,611 was significantly higher than the Regent, which generated only £44,495. Both cinemas, however, paid a similar proportion of their revenue in the form of Entertainments Duty (39 per cent and 40 per cent respectively). The Broadway, the Strand and the Troxy generated less money from admissions but paid a smaller proportion of their revenue in Entertainments Duty (32 per cent, 35 per cent and 31 per cent respectively). The weekly returns do not record details of ancillary income from food, drink and cigarette sales. In 1951, Browning and Sorrell estimated that the average value of sales for each admission was 2.5d and this amount increased with the size of the cinema.[22] The Ritz and the Regent also generated further revenue from their restaurants. The returns do not record outgoings such as wages, repairs and film hire. The latter formed a significant part of cinema expenditure and, in 1950, the Federation of British Film Makers calculated that film hire constituted 35 per cent of box-office revenue, less Entertainments Duty.[23]

In 1950, 74 per cent of cinemas in England, Scotland and Wales showed double feature programmes.[24] They were the norm at all five cinemas and programmes also often included newsreels, cartoons, interest films and trailers. Larger cinemas, such as the Ritz, also featured organ performances from Stanley Wyllie, who regularly performed on the BBC Home Service.

In 1952, less than 0.5 per cent of UK cinemas kept their programmes unchanged for longer than a week. One quarter screened one programme

[20] R Farmer, *Cinemas and Cinema-Going in Wartime Britain: the Utility Dream Palace* (Manchester, 2016), p. 240.
[21] PRONI, FIN/15/6/A/12, Ministry of Finance, reduction in rate of Entertainments Duty, 9 June 1958.
[22] Browning and Sorrell, 'Cinemas and cinema-going in Great Britain', pp. 162–3.
[23] S. Harper and V. Porter, *British Cinema of the 1950s: the Decline of Deference* (Oxford, 2003), p. 7.
[24] Browning and Sorrell, 'Cinemas and cinema-going in Great Britain', p. 144.

a week and 60 per cent screened two programmes.[25] In first-run city centre cinemas such as the Regent and the Ritz, programmes changed on a weekly basis and were exhibited for at least six days from Monday to Saturday. In 1950, 23 per cent of cinemas in Great Britain showed one programme a week and 62 per cent showed two programmes a week.[26] In 1948–9, the Regent altered its programme on the fewest occasions and exhibited thirty-seven separate programmes. Twenty-four features were screened for a week, eleven first features were screened for a fortnight and two films had extended runs: *The Assassin* (US, 1947) was exhibited for three weeks and *The Swordsman* (US, 1947) was exhibited for four weeks. The Ritz, meanwhile, screened forty-five separate programmes and seven first features – including *Johnny Belinda* (US, 1948), *My Wild Irish Rose* (US, 1947) and *Spring in Park Lane* (UK, 1948) – were screened for two weeks. In second-run cinemas there was a greater emphasis on renewal and in most weeks the Broadway, the Strand and the Troxy changed their programmes on Monday and Thursday. The Troxy changed its programme most frequently and screened 100 separate programmes. Neither the Broadway, the Strand nor the Troxy screened any film for a period longer than a week.

The fact that Curran Theatres operated both the Regent and the Broadway meant that they screened many of the same films, and films that were successful at the former were generally also successful at the latter. In 1948–9, seventeenth-century Scottish swashbuckler *The Swordsman* (US, 1948) was the highest grossing film at the Regent. It played for four weeks from 30 August 1948 and generated £3,801 in box-office revenue. The Broadway then screened it in the week beginning 6 December, where it was the fourth highest grossing film. ABC controlled three Belfast cinemas and many films exhibited at the Ritz were subsequently shown in the Majestic and the Strand. While the Troxy was independently owned, it screened many films previously exhibited at ABC cinemas. *My Wild Irish Rose*, for example, performed well at the Ritz, the Strand and the Troxy. As it moved down the chain of distribution it generated less revenue and was screened for a shorter period of time, allowing the distributor to maximize revenue. In 1948–9, it was the most successful film at the Ritz and yielded £7,321 in the two weeks beginning 20 December 1948. It was also the most successful film at the Strand and yielded £986 in the week beginning 24 January. In March, it was still popular with inner-city and suburban audiences and generated £420 at the Troxy. This shows that cinema-goers with less disposable income, who lived farther away from Belfast city centre, were prepared to wait for a film

---

[25] Political and Economic Planning, *The British Film Industry* (London, 1952), pp. 201–2.
[26] Political and Economic Planning, *The British Film Industry* (London, 1952), pp 143–4.

to work its way down the chain of distribution. Noel Spence, for instance, recalled that 'we didn't go to the Ritz that often, quite honestly, because we couldn't afford it for a start, and secondly, we knew that the films they were playing as first runs, would, a few weeks later come, filter down to, either to Comber, or to some of the smaller suburban [Belfast] cinemas'.[27]

American first features predominated in all five cinemas and the proportion exhibited ranged from 57 per cent at the Ritz to 83 per cent at the Troxy. Cinemas in Northern Ireland were excluded from the British film quotas imposed on exhibitors in England, Scotland and Wales from 1927, which required distributors and exhibitors to take an increasing quota of British productions. In December 1946, William Wilton told the Northern Ireland senate that he was 'amazed at the number of American films shown in Belfast in proportion to British pictures. In England it was necessary to show 25 per cent. of British films, but in Belfast any American rubbish could be screened'. Minister of Commerce Sir Roland Nugent, however, observed 'that the British film had, by its own merits, won an increasing popularity in Northern Ireland' and believed that many cinemas exceeded the British quota.[28] In reality, many British cinemas failed to meet the film quota and Sue Harper and Vincent Porter argued that it 'only really worked by consent, since the Board of Trade was unable to exert much real pressure on exhibitors'. In the year ending September 1952, there were only ten convictions of the 1,043 cinemas which failed to comply with the quota.[29] The number of cinemas defaulting on the first feature quota fell to 431 in 1957.[30]

The Troxy's ten highest grossing first features were American productions and the best performing British film – a 1947 re-release of *Sanders of the River* (UK, 1935) – was only the eighteenth highest-grossing first feature. The success or failure of other films had as much to do with the weather as the film itself. *The Courtneys of Curzon Street* (UK, 1947) was exhibited for three days from 17 May and generated only £145 in box-office revenue. This was the lowest figure of any programme and less than half the average of £303. This is surprising, given that the film is estimated to be the seventeenth most popular film of all time in the UK, with an overall attendance of 15.9 million.[31] On 18 May, the *Northern Whig* reported on the unusually hot temperatures in Belfast and this clearly drew patrons away from the

---

[27] Interview with Noel Spence, Comber, Co. Down, 26 March 2014.
[28] *Kinematograph Weekly*, 19 Dec. 1946.
[29] Harper and Porter, *British Cinema of the 1950s*, p. 7.
[30] Political and Economic Planning, *The British Film Industry 1958* (London, 1958), p. 162.
[31] *The Ultimate Film: the UK's 100 Most Popular Films* (London, 2005), ed. R. Gilbey, pp. 71–2.

cinema.[32] All five cinemas performed poorly from 17 to 19 May and the Broadway's screening of *Helzapoppin* (US, 1941) generated only £107.

In 1948–9, the Ritz screened nineteen British first features and three of its ten highest-grossing first features at the Ritz were British productions: *Spring in Park Lane* (UK, 1948), *My Brother Jonathan* (UK, 1948) and *An Ideal Husband* (UK, 1947). Upper-class farce *Spring in Park Lane*, starring Anna Neagle, was the most successful of these and generated £6,372 in the two weeks beginning 3 January 1949. The success of this film is unsurprising given that it is recorded as having the fifth highest attendance figures (20.5 million) of any film ever exhibited in the UK.[33] Weekly returns do not show whether tickets were purchased by men or women, but Mark Glancy claimed that the film's success, alongside other 'woman's pictures', such as *The Wicked Lady* and *The Seventh Veil*, 'testifies to the importance of women as cinema-goers in the 1940s ... and also to the appeal of films that addressed – however obliquely – the wartime upheavals in class and gender relations'.[34]

Why did the Ritz exhibit such a high proportion of British first features? The first reason is that it was controlled by ABC and, in 1948–9, the three major British circuits achieved 48 per cent of British first features. Meanwhile, 77 per cent of cinemas which defaulted on the quota were owned independently.[35] Large chains had first access to the best British films. It is not necessarily that British films were unpopular in Belfast, but that independent cinemas found that there were not enough good British films to screen. The second reason is the August 1947 introduction of a 75 per cent *ad valorem* tax on US-imported films and the subsequent boycott of the British market by Hollywood film companies.[36] Most Northern Ireland exhibitors were not immediately concerned by the American film duty as only four first-run cinemas were affected directly. The *Irish Independent* reported that as 'agents in Belfast carry advance stocks of films for six to twelve months' new showings, no immediate shortage of films from Hollywood is feared'. A spokesman for the Belfast cinema industry stated that '[t]here are a large number of top-of-the-bill pictures still to

---

[32] *Northern Whig*, 18 May 1948.

[33] *The Ultimate Film*, pp. 24–9.

[34] M. Glancy, *Hollywood and the Americanization of Britain: From the 1920s to the Present* (London, 2014), pp 36–7.

[35] *The Economist*, 25 Feb. 1950.

[36] For further information, see I. Jarvie, 'British trade policy versus Hollywood, 1947–1948: "food before flicks"?', *Historical Journal of Film, Radio and Television*, vi (1986), 19–41; M. Dickinson and S. Street, *Cinema and State: the Film Industry and the British Government 1927–84* (London, 1985), pp. 170–89.

be exhibited in Northern Ireland'.[37] *Kine Weekly* reported that, as cinemas were not subject to the British film quota, 'most exhibitors are well into 1948 and some into 1949 in their bookings. By that time they say, in effect, the position will have remedied itself'.[38] As the boycott continued, Belfast exhibitors displayed greater concern. In February 1948, the *Belfast Telegraph* reported that 'American companies, who maintain offices, film dumps and repair depots, having no films to offer are planning to close down … Other companies have reduced their staff and are to review their position in the near future'.[39] The cinemas themselves fared better and it reported that:

> Ulster's film bookings as far as first run houses are concerned are six months after their English screening, except in a few cases, and this gives us a temporary relief. As some Belfast centre houses are able to run a film for two or three weeks they do not need such a big supply. Two of Belfast's first houses belong to big British circuits who have the first call on the outputs of British studios, and with an occasional re-issue they will manage to make ends meet.[40]

The Ritz was one of these cinemas and in 1948 it screened a large number of British films and American reissues. From March to September 1948, it exhibited *Mrs. Miniver* (US, 1942), *Broadway Melody of 1940* (US, 1940), *Northwest Passage* (US, 1940) and *City for Conquest* (US, 1940). In April 1948, *Kine Weekly* reported that the revocation of the duty:

> resulted in a headache for many Ulster exhibitors … Fearing a shortage of film product, they rushed to book any available box-office product, and not a few date-books are pencilled in as far as two years ahead. Now the crisis is over they have no dates free for any of the new American product which will be available in July. Renters are being asked by not a few exhibitors to release them from their contracts.[41]

The Ritz was clearly able to return to its normal exhibition practices. From October 1948 to March 1949, all films exhibited at the Ritz were produced in either 1947 or 1948 and the proportion of American films increased.

In 1948–9, all five cinemas booked few films produced outside either the US or the UK, and those that were exhibited tended to be particularly unpopular. From 8 to 11 December 1948, the Regent screened *A Cage of Nightingales* (France, 1946, Original Title: *La Cage aux rossignols*). The

---

[37] *Irish Independent*, 11 Aug. 1947.
[38] *Kinematograph Weekly*, 21 Aug. 1947.
[39] *Belfast Telegraph*, 13 Feb. 1948.
[40] *Belfast Telegraph*, 18 Feb. 1948.
[41] *Kinematograph Weekly*, 15 Apr. 1948.

Monthly Film Bulletin described the film as 'a touching and sentimental film, relieved by excellent moments of comedy'. It also, however, praised the school set as 'grim and genuine; the singing in the dingy classrooms is as beautiful as the sunlit countryside that the boys are never allowed to see'.[42] Both subtitled and dubbed versions of the film were released in the UK and even though the cinema emphasized the 'English dialogue' of the film in advertisements, it performed particularly badly.[43] In 1948–9, it was the least successful film at the Regent and generated only £445 in box-office revenue, well below the average of £870. There were other outlets for foreign language films and, in April 1951, the *Belfast Telegraph* noted the large crowds at the Mayfair for a Belfast Institute Film Society midnight matinee of Jacques Tati's comedy *Jour de fête* (France, 1949).[44] In October 1951, the formation of the Queen's University Film Society provided another forum for foreign language films. Its first show at the University's Whitla Hall featured *Sylvie et la Fantome* (France, 1946) and *Romantici a Venezia* (Italy, 1948). The programme 'was well received by an audience of upwards of 600' and the society's membership reached 858 by the end of its first season.[45] In 1954, membership was capped at 1,200 and there was a 'considerable waiting-list'. Programme secretary K. R. Shimeld used reaction sheets to infer that the most popular films it had screened were both French productions: *Kermesse Heroique* (France, 1935) and *Les Enfants du Paradis* (France, 1945).[46]

In Belfast, going to the pictures was a popular activity on public holidays, including Christmas Day. In 1946, Northern Ireland CEA members stated that 'while a Christmas Day might not be profitable to exhibitors in Great Britain, it was a really profitable day in Ulster'.[47] In 1948–9, it was the highest grossing day at the Regent and it generated £311. In 1948, the *Northern Whig* reported that 'Northern Ireland cinemas controlled by the big British circuits will again be closed on Christmas day this year in accordance with the holiday agreement across the Channel'.[48] While the Strand and the Ritz closed on Christmas Day, they performed well on preceding and subsequent days. *My Wild Irish Rose* was the second highest grossing film at the Ritz, where it screened for two weeks from 20 December 1948 and generated £7,321 in box-office revenue. On 12 July, a public holiday in Northern Ireland, all cinemas did good business and this day witnessed the

---

[42] *Monthly Film Bulletin*, xiii, no. 12 (1946), 172–3.
[43] *Belfast Telegraph*, 6 Dec. 1948.
[44] *Belfast Telegraph*, 19 Apr. 1951.
[45] *Belfast Telegraph*, 25 Oct. 1951; 29 May 1952.
[46] *Irish News*, 14 June 1954.
[47] *Kinematograph Weekly*, 26 Dec. 1946.
[48] *Northern Whig*, 16 Dec. 1948.

sixth highest daily gross box-office revenue at the Broadway, the fifth at the Ritz, and the seventh at the Strand and the Troxy.

The day of the week was a key determinant of attendance. Despite their varying locations, programming and patronage, the revenue created by these cinemas was spread across the week in a similar manner. Saturday screenings were the greatest revenue generators. In 1948–9, the proportion of total revenue taken on Saturday ranged from 22 per cent at the Ritz, to 25 per cent at the Troxy. While it appears that Saturday was the most popular day for attendance, it is possible patrons were willing to spend more money on the more expensive seats at Saturday screenings. Monday was the second most lucrative day for all five cinemas, demonstrating that patrons were keen to view a new film at the first possible opportunity. The Regent and the Ritz changed their programmes on Mondays, but never on Thursdays. The Broadway, the Strand and the Troxy often changed their programmes on both a Monday and a Thursday. The proportion of box-office revenue generated by cinemas on Thursdays was similar across all five cinemas. It ranged only from 13.96 per cent at the Ritz, to 14.31 per cent at the Troxy. Even where new programmes were exhibited on Thursday, patrons preferred to attend Saturday screenings. Across all five cinemas, box-office revenue remained relatively constant during the week and increased sharply on Saturday. This indicates that cinema attendance was linked to the rhythms of daily life, with a core of people who attended habitually during the week, alongside an additional number of patrons, likely to have been children and young workers, who attended on Saturdays only. Belfast cinemas closed on Sunday and this may have generated increased demand for cinema attendance on other days. In the UK, there was wide variation in the levels of Sunday opening and admissions. The strength of nonconformist traditions in Scotland meant that, in 1951, only one in twelve cinemas opened and Sunday admissions were less than 1 per cent of total admissions. In the south of England, Sunday admissions were greater and constituted 12 per cent of total admissions.[49]

Ireland on the silver screen

One of the challenges for new cinema historians is to incorporate film texts into an analysis of the social experience of cinema-going without resorting to an assessment of visual aesthetics and style. According to Daniel Biltereyst et al., studies of film programming and exhibition offer an opportunity to show that 'there is no antagonism between new cinema historiography

---

[49] Browning and Sorrell, 'Cinemas and cinema-going in Great Britain', p. 147.

and the examination of films'.[50] By investigating the exhibition and consumption of *Captain Boycott* (UK, 1947) and *The Quiet Man* (US, 1952), it is possible to reveal the popularity of Irish-themed films in Belfast, demonstrate methodological problems in the study of audience preferences and highlight the danger in assuming that the main feature was the primary attraction for audiences. British historical drama *Captain Boycott* depicted the defeat of Captain Charles Boycott in the Irish Land War of the 1880s. It starred Cecil Parker as Captain Boycott, Robert Donat as Charles Parnell and Stewart Granger as Hugh Davin. On 1 September 1947, *Captain Boycott*'s world premiere was held at the Gaumont Haymarket in London.[51] The film reached Belfast's Classic, a first-run city centre cinema, on 1 December and was such a success that it was retained for a second week.[52] It is likely that the supporting feature – a Technicolor film of the royal wedding of Princess Elizabeth and Philip Mountbatten – also contributed to its success. There is no evidence to suggest that this combination of Irish historical nationalism and contemporary British royalty led to controversy in Belfast cinemas, and it is possible that the support feature constituted the main attraction. In 1948–9, *Captain Boycott* was the highest grossing film at the Broadway and, in the week beginning 29 March 1948, it generated £1,190 in box-office revenue, £449 greater than the next highest grossing film that year. It is likely that patrons at the Broadway were attracted to a film that depicted historical events in Ireland, and one that focused on Irish politics and identity. Despite its content, it held broad appeal and a *Belfast Telegraph*'s review stated that if 'you go in search of entertainment, putting your political views with your hat under your seat, you will find this film grand value for money'.[53] The Broadway booked *Captain Boycott* because they believed it would attract patrons to their cinema. Nevertheless, there are a range of factors that contributed to its success and the first feature was not necessarily the main attraction. The supporting feature was the film of the World Flyweight Championship boxing fight between Rinty Monaghan and Jackie Patterson that took place at Belfast's King's Hall on 23 March 1948. Monaghan lived in Little Corporation Street, north Belfast, and had popular appeal in the area. Following the fight, the *Belfast Telegraph* reported that 'all the streets in the dock area had bonfires. Crowds paraded up and down the streets running between York Street and Little Corporation Street dancing.

---

[50] D. Biltereyst, R. Maltby and P. Meers, 'Programming, popularity and film: Introduction', in *The Routledge Companion to New Cinema History*, ed. D. Biltereyst, R. Maltby and P. Meers (Abingdon, 2019), pp. 269–70.

[51] *The Times*, 30 July 1947.

[52] *Kinematograph Weekly*, 18 Dec. 1947.

[53] *Belfast Telegraph*, 29 Nov. 1947.

Singing. Shouting'.[54] The fact that tickets for the fight itself ranged from £2 2s to £10 10s meant that this film presented a more affordable alternative for most spectators.[55] While the fight was broadcast live on the BBC Light Programme, the cinema provided the only opportunity to view footage of the contest. Monaghan attended a preview of the film at the Regent and, in April, was presented with his World Flyweight Championship belt at a reception in its restaurant.[56] The film was screened at all Curran cinemas from Monday 29 March.[57] Belfast docker-turned-poet/writer John Campbell recalled watching footage of the fight at the Alhambra: 'A cheer went up when the referee raised Rinty's hand and he grabbed a microphone with his free hand to belt out *A Brokenhearted Clown*. The cinema bar was full that night, as it often was when fights were shown'.[58] The timing of its exhibition was also crucial to its success. In 1948, Easter Monday fell on 29 March and it was the highest grossing day at the Broadway and the Troxy. In Belfast, Easter was traditionally a popular time for cinema-going and programmes during this week were popular in all five cinemas. The main feature's Irish theme, local interest in Rinty Monaghan and the fact that Easter was a popular time for cinema attendance all contributed to the success of *Captain Boycott* at the Broadway. This example demonstrates the difficulty of disentangling the number of factors that attracted patrons to the Broadway during this particular week.

On 6 June 1952, the world premiere of *The Quiet Man* (US, 1952) was held simultaneously in Dublin and London. This film depicts an imagined and idealized version of Ireland and follows the return of American émigré Sean Thornton (John Wayne) to his native Galway village, where he falls for Mary Kate Danaher (Maureen O'Hara).[59] On 18 August, it was screened privately at the Ritz to a 'specially invited audience of shop assistants, bus conductors, housewives, factory workers and others'. The *Belfast Telegraph* described it as 'one of the most refreshing films with an Irish setting to reach the screen for a long time' and predicted that it 'should enjoy a longer-than-average run'.[60] Reviewer Harris Deans stated the film was 'joyous entertainment for those who don't take their nationality too seriously. It is

---

[54] *Belfast Telegraph*, 24 March 1948.

[55] *Belfast Telegraph*, 22 March 1948.

[56] *Belfast Telegraph*, 27 March 1948; *Northern Whig*, 28 Apr. 1948.

[57] *Belfast Telegraph*, 27 March 1948; *Belfast Telegraph*, 29 March 1948.

[58] J. Campbell, 'Movie-house memories', *Causeway: Cultural Traditions Journal*, i (1994), 9–14, at p. 11.

[59] A. Frazier, *Hollywood Irish: John Ford, Abbey Actors and the Irish Revival in Hollywood* (Dublin, 2011), pp. 205–38; L. Gibbons, *The Quiet Man* (Cork, 2002); D. MacHale, *The Complete Guide to The Quiet Man* (Belfast, 2000).

[60] *Belfast Telegraph*, 14 Aug. 1952.

seldom I have heard such happy laughter in a cinema as at the Press showing of John Ford's film'.[61] It formed part of the Ritz's regular programme for five weeks from 18 August 1952. Table 4.3 shows that it was by far the most successful film in 1952–3 and the sale of 195,485 tickets generated £23,617 in box-office revenue. The *Northern Whig* reported that while the record run in a Belfast cinema was a seven-week screening of *Gone with the Wind*, it had two daily screenings while the *The Quiet Man* had four.[62]

Table 4.3. Ten highest-grossing films at the Ritz, 7 April 1952 to 28 March 1953.

Date	Main feature	Gross revenue (£)	Admissions	Days screened
18/08/52	*The Quiet Man* (US, 1952)	23,617	195,485	30
14/04/52	*The African Queen* (US/UK, 1952)	6,588	52,098	12
02/02/53	*Because You're Mine* (US, 1952)	6,583	52,067	12
05/01/53	*The Sound Barrier* (UK, 1952)	6,352	48,795	13
13/10/52	*Ivanhoe* (US/UK, 1952)	6,072	47,896	12
02/03/53	*The Crimson Pirate* (US, 1952)	5,048	40,087	13
29/12/52	*Jack and the Beanstalk* (US, 1952)	4,029	35,344	6
14/07/52	*On Moonlight Bay* (US, 1952)	4,028	33,148	6
22/12/52	*Lovely To Look At* (US, 1952)	3,683	26,743	6
05/05/52	*A Streetcar Named Desire* (US, 1952)	3,342	27,140	6

Source: PRONI, FIN/16/6/C/1/64, Entertainments Duty weekly returns.

The nature of attendance for *The Quiet Man* was exceptional. In 1952–3, no other film was screened for a period longer than two weeks and when films were screened for two weeks, they usually sold significantly fewer tickets during their second week of exhibition. For instance, *The African Queen* (US/UK, 1952) sold 33,014 tickets in its first week of exhibition and 19,084 in its second. Attendances for *The Quiet Man* remained steady for the first three weeks of exhibition with 41,554, 42,727 and 40,510 admissions respectively. Only in the last two weeks of exhibition did admissions fall to 34,861 and 35,833 respectively. During its fourth week, *The Quiet Man* was supported by *Irish Symphony* and a fashion display of Irish linen organized by the Irish Fashion Guild, which involved 'a team of mannequins, drawn from a Belfast agency, [who] presented 43 models in 20 minutes', accompanied by music

[61] *Belfast Telegraph*, 23 Aug. 1952.
[62] *Northern Whig*, 19 Sept. 1952.

from the Ritz organist Stanley Wylie.[63] On 15 September, cinema listings emphasized *The Quiet Man*'s sustained popularity and one advertisement read: 'definitely last week, 155,000 people must be right. It is your last opportunity to see this happy wonderful picture'.[64]

Large attendance figures during a single week of exhibition do not indicate that a film was well received by those who attended. Patrons attended films for many reasons, and a large number of admissions may have been the result of a successful marketing campaign or the appearance of a particular star. Its leading man, John Wayne, was a particular draw and in 1951 was the highest grossing western star in UK cinemas.[65] The sustained interest in *The Quiet Man* though, and the fact that attendances remained stable until its fourth week of exhibition, indicates that the film received a highly positive reception. Table 4.4 shows that the number of admissions in all Belfast cinemas totalled at least 310,000 and it is likely that many of residents paid to see the film on several occasions.[66] John Campbell attested to its cultural impact:

> Perhaps we were naïve to identify with the characters and plots then ... Male cinema goers squared their shoulders and swelled their chests as they identified with John Wayne when he hauled Maureen O'Hara across meadow and field in the scene which culminated in an angry and bloody confrontation with her 'broth of a boyo' brother, Victor McLaglan, who had been foolish enough to cast aspersions on John's masculinity.[67]

The film performed well during subsequent exhibition in Belfast cinemas. The Strand exhibited the film for two weeks from 27 October and, in 1952–3, it was the only film to be shown for a period longer than a week. It was the most successful film of the year and the sale of 26,643 tickets generated £2,076 in box-office revenue. This also indicates that this Irish-themed film was popular in predominantly unionist areas of Belfast. It became the second highest grossing first feature at the Troxy, where it screened for six days from 1 December 1952 and sold 11,813 tickets. While *Kine Weekly* included *The Quiet Man* in their annual survey of the fifteen highest grossing films, the strong performance in these cinemas indicates that it was disproportionately popular in Belfast.[68]

---

[63] *Belfast Telegraph*, 2 Sept. 1952.
[64] *Belfast Telegraph*, 15 Sept. 1952.
[65] *The 1952–3 Motion Picture and Television Almanac* (New York, 1952), p. 924.
[66] *The Ulster Year Book: the Official Year Book of Northern Ireland* (Belfast, 1953), p. 35.
[67] Campbell, 'Movie-house memories', p. 11.
[68] *The Times*, 18 Dec. 1952.

Table 4.4. Exhibition of *The Quiet Man* in Belfast.

Date	Cinema	Gross revenue (£)	Dutiable admissions	Days screened
18/08/52	Ritz	23,617	195,485	30
27/10/52	Strand	2,076	26,643	12
27/10/52	Majestic	2,079	25,644	12
01/12/52	Troxy	680	11,813	6
08/12/52	Picturedrome	647	11,107	6
15/12/52	Alhambra	199	3,263	6
05/01/53	Stadium	407	6,995	3
08/01/53	Curzon	466	6,814	3
08/01/53	Forum	404	7,688	3
02/02/53	Windsor	323	4,632	3
09/02/53	Coliseum	59	1,563	3
09/03/53	Savoy	229	4,491	3
16/03/53	Clonard	193	5,091	3
30/03/53	Duncairn	—	—	3
23/04/53	Park	—	—	3

Source: PRONI, FIN/15/6/C/34–74, Entertainments Duty weekly returns, 1952–3.

Further Irish-themed films were popular with Belfast audiences throughout the period under review. 'Thousands besieged the Classic' at its first showing of Belfast-set *Odd Man Out* (UK, 1947) and the audience's reaction 'seemed to promise a profitable future for the production', reported the *Irish Independent*.[69] This was the first major film to deal with the conflict in Northern Ireland, featuring James Mason as a member of an 'illegal organisation' shot during an armed robbery. The presence of the Royal Ulster Constabulary at the film's premiere prevented it from becoming a Republican rallying point and no major incidents were recorded.[70] John Ford's previous film, *Rio Grande* (US, 1950), was more controversial than the *The Quiet Man* and city centre managers had to display sensitivity to Belfast's political divisions. In 1952, Royal Hippodrome manager Basil Lapworth 'saw trouble brewing' and removed part of the reel containing

[69] *Irish Independent*, 4 March 1947.
[70] K. J. Donnelly, 'The policing of cinema: troubled film exhibition in Northern Ireland', *Historical Journal of Film, Radio and* Television, xx (2000), 385–96.

footage of the nationalist ballad *The Bold Fenian Men*.[71] *Captain Boycott* held long-lasting appeal and, in 1956, the Regent and the Broadway exhibited it as the supporting feature for *The March Hare* (UK, 1956), advertising it as 'an excellent all-Irish programme'. In January 1958, *Kine Weekly* reported that *The Story of Esther Costello* (UK, 1957) was 'doing exceptional business' in its fourth week at the Regent and that 'added to its gripping content is the fact that part of it is set in Ireland'.[72] In July 1958, a double feature programme of *Rooney* (UK, 1958) and a reissue of Belfast-set *Jacqueline* (UK, 1956) did 'exceptional business last week at the Gaumont despite the fact that the weather was brilliant and most people were preparing for holidays'. It added that *Jacqueline*, which performed well in its first run, 'is still setting the box-offices jingling. Which just proves that there are horses for courses and that anything with a bit of Irish flavour is lapped up greedily in the North as well as the South'.[73] Other films with Belfast links were popular and, before the release of Titanic drama *A Night to Remember* (UK, 1958), one report suggested that 'since the Titanic was built in Belfast and since the film has many Ulster actors, cinema people are prophesying broken records with this Rank release'.[74] After its release, one reported stated it was 'doing first-class business at the Royal Hippodrome'.[75]

1952–3: changing habits

In 1952–3 the records of thirty-four Belfast cinemas reveal a total of 16.46 million admissions. As Belfast's population was 443,671, this equates to an average of thirty-eight cinemas admissions per head. Browning and Sorrell calculated that, in 1950, there were twenty-eight cinema admissions per head in Great Britain and thirty-seven admissions in towns with a population of over 100,000. Belfast's figure is similar to British cities such as Edinburgh (thirty-seven), Sheffield (thirty-nine) and Leicester (thirty-six).[76] In Great Britain, the average ticket price rose from approximately 1s 5d in 1949 to 1s 8d in 1952.[77] In 1952–3 the average ticket price in the five cinemas was 1s 9d and this ranged from 1s 2d at the Troxy to 2s 5d at the Ritz. The Ritz's comparatively high prices distort the figure for average ticket price and it is likely that the figure for all cinemas in Belfast was lower than the average calculated by Browning and Sorrell. It was only in 1960

---

[71] *Kinematograph Weekly*, 13 March 1952.
[72] *Kinematograph Weekly*, 23 Jan. 1958.
[73] *Kinematograph Weekly*, 17 July 1958.
[74] *Kinematograph Weekly*, 4 Sept. 1958.
[75] *Kinematograph Weekly*, 6 Nov. 1958.
[76] Browning and Sorrell, 'Cinemas and cinema-going in Great Britain', pp. 138–40.
[77] Browning and Sorrell, 'Cinemas and cinema-going in Great Britain', p. 134.

that price increases meant that prices in Northern Ireland became 'more or less comparable' with prices in similar areas in Great Britain.[78] In 1949, the Northern Ireland government raised the minimum threshold for the payment of Entertainments Duty from 3*d* to 5*d*. In September 1952, it raised it further to 7*d*, causing twenty-five Northern Ireland cinemas to alter their admission prices.[79] The Broadway, the Regent and the Ritz increased their most expensive ticket prices. The Ritz, for instance, increased its dress circle prices by 3*d* from 3*s* 9*d* to 4*s*.

In Belfast, the greatest number of admissions were recorded at the Ritz (1,252,019), the Gaumont (998,429) and the Royal Hippodrome (827,874). The lowest figure was recorded at the Arcadian (60,333), though it is likely that many of its admissions fell below the minimum threshold for Entertainments Duty payments and were not recorded. From 1948–9 to 1952–3, gross box-office revenue decreased at the Broadway and the Troxy, yet increased at the Regent, the Ritz and the Strand. The most significant increase was at the Ritz, where gross box-office revenue increased by 21 per cent from £129,610 to £156,302. Payments to Entertainment Duty, however, increased by 26 per cent from £51,151 to £64,409. In 1952–3, across the five cinemas, 34 per cent of gross revenue was spent on Entertainment Duty. Again, this figure varied widely between cinemas from 28 per cent at the Troxy to 41 per cent at the Ritz. The fact that Northern Ireland cinemas did not contribute to the British Film Production Fund (also known as the Eady Levy) provided some relief. In 1952, cinemas in Great Britain received gross takings of £109.9 million, paid £38.1 million in Entertainments Duty and a further £2.9 million to the British film production fund. This meant that they paid 37 per cent of gross takings in tax.[80]

In spite of anxieties about the price sensitivity of audiences, cinema proprietors risked charging higher prices for special performances. The Ritz held an annual St Patrick's Day charity midnight matinee, which often featured advance screenings, premieres and personal appearances of film stars. Prices were higher than at normal screenings and special late-night transport was arranged for patrons. In 1952, the Ritz held the Northern Ireland premiere of *The African Queen* in aid of the Cinematograph Trade Benevolent Fund. While normal evening prices ranged from 1*s* 10*d* to 3*s* 9*d*, prices for this screening ranged from 5*s* to 21*s*. The *Belfast Telegraph* reported that 'every seat was occupied' and the evening featured a personal appearance by film star Michael Denison and a 'stage show with local and

---

[78] *Kinematograph Weekly*, 18 Aug. 1960.

[79] Hansard (Northern Ireland), *Parliamentary Debates*, xxxvi (28 May 1952), col. 994; PRONI, FIN/15/6/A/1, alterations in full rates of Entertainments Duty.

[80] Browning and Sorrell, 'Cinemas and cinema-going in Great Britain', p. 34.

cross-Channel artists'.[81] The *African Queen* was then exhibited at the Ritz for two weeks from 14 April and the sale of 52,098 tickets generated £6,588. The 1953 midnight matinee featured the screening of *The Prisoner of Zenda*, the appearance of John McCallum and performances by comedian Jimmy O'Dea, the Dixilanders and the Metro Five.[82] ABC also organized New Year's Eve midnight matinees in the Majestic, the Ritz and the Strand. In 1952, for instance, the Strand's 'Grand Midnight Matinee' attracted a capacity crowd for *Annie Get Your Gun* (US, 1950), the Strandtown Silver Band and the finals of its amateur talent contest.

Though children's matinee screenings and programmes targeted at younger audiences generated less box-office revenue, they were an important part of the cinema programme. Browning and Sorrell estimated that attendances at special children's performances accounted for 4 per cent of all cinema admissions and about one-fifth of all children's admissions.[83] In 1946, the Gaumont-British Junior Club began at the Classic and, on 10 September 1949, over 2,000 children attended the first ABC minor's club matinees at the Strand and the Majestic.[84] Films were often accompanied by personal appearances and stage performances. In June 1952, Arthur Lucan demonstrated his intergenerational appeal, appearing onstage as his Irish washerwoman character Old Mother Riley, where he 'was given a tremendous reception by the kiddies before being besieged by their equally enthusiastic parents outside the theatre after the show'.[85] In August 1953, ventriloquist Edgar Bergen appeared with 'Charlie MCarthy'. The *ABC News* stated that children in care were invited from the Victoria Homes and Glendhu Hostel and 'a highlight of this enormously popular visit was the ceremony of making Charlie McCarthy an A.B.C. Minor. Charlie was presented with an A.B.C. Coronation Cap and Coronation Badge'.[86] The fact that the Strand paid no Entertainment Duty on children's matinee tickets means that they cost under 6*d*. In 1952–3, admissions to children's matinees generated £1,227 in box-office revenue and constituted 3 per cent of the total box-office revenue.

In 1952–3, the Ritz and the Strand opened on Christmas Day. Over the Christmas period, the Ritz targeted its programme at children and family audiences and, in the week beginning 29 December, it exhibited *Jack and the Beanstalk* (US, 1952), supported by the Roy Rogers western *Trigger*

[81] *Belfast Telegraph*, 18 March 1952.
[82] *Belfast Telegraph*, 18 March 1953.
[83] Browning and Sorrell, 'Cinemas and cinema-going in Great Britain', p. 147.
[84] *Irish Times Pictorial*, 28 Sept. 1946; *Belfast Telegraph*, 10 Sept. 1949.
[85] *Northern Whig*, 9 June 1952.
[86] *ABC News*, Aug. 1953, p. 2.

Junior (US, 1952). It was the seventh highest grossing programme of 1952–3. The sale of 866 children's matinee tickets was more than double the amount in any other week. Noel Spence was born in 1944 and recalled his first cinema-going experience:

> My Mother took us … to the Ritz in Belfast to see Abbott and Costello in *Jack and the Beanstalk* and the damage was done, you know, we were so absorbed by the whole experience. This huge big dark cinema and the giant and the colour pictures and the excitement, the music, and the atmosphere and the thrills, the whole – the film now, when you watch it now, is absolutely awful. But we were absolutely hooked then.[87]

Jean McVeigh was born in 1943 and recalled that trips to the cinema with her two brothers were 'always part of our Christmas activities'. She remembered that 'on Boxing Day they had a children's programme in the Ritz. The day after Christmas everybody was off school … I don't know if somebody took us, or whether we just went by ourselves'.[88]

The Regent hosted a variety of special children's screenings. On 18 October 1952, the BBC organized a private screening of *Alice in Wonderland* (US, 1951) and *Beaver Valley* (US, 1950) for its Junior Critic Circle. Patrons aged from eight to eighteen were asked for their views on the film, which were then broadcast on the Home Service's *Children's Hour*.[89] Other films were used for educational purposes and, on 25 October, the Regent held a private screening of Orson Welles's *Macbeth* (US, 1951) at which 'many teachers from local schools and colleges attended'.[90] It was then shown in the week beginning 4 November, which saw 12,132 admissions. The film's success was aided by the fact that special morning matinees for children were held at 10 am, with admissions priced 1s and 1s 6d.

Cinemas hosted multiple audiences and films aimed solely at adults were often successful. On 16 January 1951, the British Board of Film Censors (BBFC) wrote to the Belfast Corporation Police Committee and informed them of the new 'X' certificate 'to cover films which were wholly adult in theme or treatment and from which children under sixteen should be excluded'.[91] By July 1951, the BBFC had awarded an 'X' certificate to seventeen films.[92] However, in October the Northern Ireland Ministry of Home Affairs ruled that existing arrangements were satisfactory and 'that it

---

[87] Interview with Noel Spence, Comber, Co. Down, 26 March 2014.
[88] Interview with Terence and Jean McVeigh, Belfast, 2 Apr. 2014.
[89] *Belfast Telegraph*, 18 Oct. 1952.
[90] *Belfast Telegraph*, 25 Oct. 1952.
[91] Minutes of the Belfast Corporation Police Committee, 25 Jan. 1951, p. 128.
[92] Harper and Porter, *British Cinema of the 1950s*, p. 221.

was not intended to exhibit category "X" films in Northern Ireland'.[93] These comments were ill-informed and, in March 1952, the ABC district manager wrote to the Police Committee stating that *Murder Incorporated* (US, 1951) and *A Streetcar Named Desire* (US, 1952) were booked for exhibition at the Ritz, Majestic and Strand.[94] The Committee held private viewings of these films and granted permission for both to be shown under the conditions of the 'X' category certificate. This contrasted with the Irish Republic, where film censor Richard Hayes made twenty-seven cuts to *Streetcar*.[95] In the week beginning 5 May 1952, the Ritz exhibited *Streetcar* and the 27,140 viewers made it the ninth most successful film in 1952–3. In June 1952, the 24,435 admissions recorded for *Murder Incorporated* was almost identical to the weekly average of 24,445. Large cinema chains in Britain generally avoided screening 'X' certificated films and Steve Chibnall has argued that 'powerful exhibition circuits were suspicious of a certificate which would exclude much of their regular audience and thus reduce their ticket sales'.[96] Harper and Porter further noted that ABC 'relaxed its policy when it found that Warners' *Murder Incorporated* and *A Streetcar Named Desire* ... did better business in the big cities than elsewhere'.[97] In Belfast, these 'X' certificated films performed better in the Ritz than they did with suburban audiences at the Strand, where *A Streetcar Named Desire* and *Murder Incorporated* generated £292 and £386 respectively, well below the cinema's average of £443.

1956–7: declining fortunes

From 1953 to 1957, the introduction of television, population shifts, the rise in consumer culture and greater affluence meant that UK cinema admissions fell by 29 per cent from 1,285 million to 915 million.[98] In Northern Ireland decline was less precipitous and admissions fell by 15 per cent from 28,374,000 in 1953 to 24,123,000 in 1957.[99] Belfast cinemas fared better than Northern Ireland as a whole and recorded admissions fell by just 7 per cent

---

[93] Minutes of the Belfast Corporation Police Committee, 6 Oct. 1951, p. 185.

[94] McClay Library, minutes of the Belfast Corporation Police Committee, 6 March 1952, p. 210.

[95] K. Rockett, *Irish Film Censorship: a Cultural Journey from Silent Cinema to Internet Pornography* (Dublin, 2004), p. 132.

[96] S. Chibnall, 'From *The Snake Pit* to *The Garden of Eden*: a time of temptation for the board', in *Behind the Scenes at the BBFC: Film Classification from the Silver Screen to the Digital Age*, ed. E. Lamberti (London, 2012), pp. 29–52, at p. 35.

[97] Harper and Porter, *British Cinema of the 1950s*, pp. 221–2.

[98] *BFI Film and Television Handbook*, ed. E. Dyja (London, 2004), p. 39.

[99] PRONI, FIN/15/6/A/12, reduction in rate of Entertainments Duty, 9 June 1958.

(see Table 4.5). This meant that in Belfast the annual attendance per head of population of thirty-four was almost twice as high as the figure of eighteen for England, Scotland and Wales.[100] Cinema attendance declined unevenly across Belfast and the greatest proportional decline was experienced at the Ambassador, where admissions fell by 26 per cent from 386,583 to 287,213. At the Royal Hippodrome and the Crumlin Picture House, admissions even increased by 10 per cent and 8 per cent respectively. Of the two first-run city centre cinemas under review, the decline at the Ritz was far greater than at the Regent and admissions declined by 12 per cent and 6 per cent respectively. The Troxy suffered a greater decline than the Broadway or the Strand and admissions fell by 14 per cent. The extent of this decline, in part, is attributable to the opening of the Lido in March 1955, which was located less than a mile away from the Troxy, and operated by the same company, Troxy Cinemas Ltd.[101]

Table 4.5. Dutiable admissions at Belfast cinemas, 1952–3 and 1956–7.

Cinema	Financial year		Change (%)
	1952–3	1956–7	
Alhambra	138,394	122,718	-11.3
Ambassador	386,583	287,213	-25.7
Apollo	274,649	230,561	-16.0
Arcadian	60,333	56,874	-5.7
Astoria	449,698	404,897	-10.0
Broadway	489,899	455,119	-7.1
Capitol	481,115	463,796	-3.6
Castle	407,824	337,523	-17.2
Clonard	437,382	425,840	-2.6
Coliseum	167,107	133,710	-20.0
Crumlin Picture House	414,637	456,035	10.0
Curzon	572,815	548,811	-4.2
Duncairn Cinema	446,912	353,816	-20.8
Forum	600,568	507,970	-15.4
Gaumont	998,429	939,457	-5.9
Imperial	777,586	649,015	-16.5

[100] Political and Economic Planning, *The British Film Industry 1958* (London, 1958), p. 136.
[101] Open, *Fading Lights, Silver Screen*, p. 145.

Cinema	Financial year		Change (%)
	1952–3	*1956–7*	
Lido	—	354,857	—
Lyceum	323,647	286,623	-11.4
Majestic	537,035	498,971	-7.1
Mayfair Cinema	252,884	229,980	-9.1
New Princess	333,536	259,791	-22.1
Park Cinema	447,116	345,903	-22.6
Picturedrome	507,703	420,051	-17.3
Popular	437,102	343,632	-21.4
Regal	380,529	331,260	-13.0
Regent	473,564	443,273	-6.4
Ritz	1,252,019	1,107,646	-11.5
Royal Cinema	694,852	549,508	-20.9
Royal Hippodrome	827,874	890,504	7.6
Savoy	461,631	434,112	-6.0
Stadium	533,566	480,413	-10.0
Strand	534,144	480,431	-10.1
Tivoli	—	249,657	—
Troxy	507,432	434,107	-14.5
Willowfield	425,348	327,675	-23.0
Windsor	426,853	421,814	-1.2
Total	16,460,766	15,263,563	-7.3

Source: PRONI, FIN/15/6/C/1/34–110, Entertainments Duty weekly returns.

A direct comparison between the first-run Broadway and the second-run Regent shows the impact of changes in cinema attendance on different cinemas that were part of the same circuit. From 1952–3 to 1956–7, admissions at the Broadway fell by 7 per cent from 489,899 to 455,199. Increases in ticket prices meant that box-office revenue fell by only 4 per cent. Admissions at the Regent fell by 6 per cent from 473,564 to 443,273, yet gross box-office revenue increased by 5 per cent. Table 4.6 shows the tickets sold at the Broadway and the Regent in each seating category. It shows that from 1952–3 to 1956–7, the most significant decline in ticket sales occurred in the cheapest front stalls seats. The fact that admissions for balcony seats increased, despite falling attendances, demonstrates that while many former patrons were no longer attending the cinema, those who remained had greater amounts of disposable income and were willing to spend more on admission. The Regent charged much higher prices than the Broadway, and while this meant that it paid a larger proportion of its gross box-office revenue in Entertainments Duty, its net revenue was still much greater.

Table 4.6. Dutiable admissions at the Broadway and the Regent, 1952–61.

	Front stalls	Back stalls	Balcony	Transfers	Total
Regent					
1952–3	220,831	183,945	67,526	270	472,572
1956–7	156,932	213,188	73,153	600	443,273
1960–1	135,350	154,945	62,727	348	353,370
Broadway					
1952–3	227,563	192,165	75,523	138	492,389
1956–7	192,494	184,848	77,777	69	455,188
1960–1	38,218	140,159	40,772	2	219,151

Note: The minor variation in figures from Table 4.5 is due to the fact these figures are calculated from weekly returns that do not correspond exactly with end of year figures.

Source: PRONI, FIN/15/6/C/1/39, 63, 80, 100, 115, 133), Entertainments Duty weekly returns.

These changes allowed the Regent to increase its earning potential. For example, in the week beginning 6 August 1956, the Broadway screened *Safari* (UK/US, 1956), and yielded £711 from the sale of 10,083 tickets; 3,912 admissions were for the front stalls, 4,220 for the back stalls and 1,951 for the balcony. In the week beginning 16 July, the Regent screened *Picnic* (US, 1956) and yielded £1,145 from 10,011 admissions. The proportion of cinema-goers purchasing tickets in each price category was also broadly similar and it sold 3,459 admissions for the front stalls, 4,660 for the back stalls and 1,802 for the balcony. Despite almost identical ticket sales, the Regent paid £423 in Entertainments Duty compared to the Broadway's figure of £200.

Ticket prices at the Regent were far higher than at the Broadway, yet they incurred greater amounts of Entertainments Duty. In the Broadway, evening tickets ranged from 1s in the front stalls to 2s 6d in the balcony, and these tickets incurred 1.75d and 1s Entertainments Duty respectively. In the Regent, the equivalent tickets cost 1s 6d (5.5d) and 3s 6d (1s 5d). This again shows that cinemas which charged exponentially higher prices for their more expensive seats were better placed to take advantage of the changes in audience composition discussed in previous chapters.

The decline in US cinema admissions meant that Hollywood produced fewer films and the number of feature length films registered in the UK declined from 260 in 1950 to 200 in 1955, and then to 142 in 1960.[102] Consequently, many US distribution companies closed their provincial film offices. In October 1956, Paramount Film Services closed its Garfield Street office and transferred all dispatch arrangements to their Shankill Road depot.[103] In November, MGM closed its Northern Ireland office and stated that 'there are fewer films to handle and the general condition of the film industry demands economies'.[104] This meant that it became more difficult for cinemas further down the distribution chain to fill two double feature programmes every week – a 1958 report stated that many exhibitors 'feel that a film is often taken away from a cinema before it has drawn its maximum audience'.[105] Meanwhile, larger cinemas increasingly relied on a smaller number of event films that allowed them to generate greater amounts of box-office revenue from extended runs. The same report suggested that the problems involved in extended runs 'are indeed great, and it is easy enough for administrative apathy to regard them as too great'. There had been an increasing number of 'films being released outside the normal pattern and a substantial trend in this direction may have already started'.[106] The exhibition of *War and Peace* (US, 1956) at the Ritz in March 1957 provides an example of this trend. Attendance figures and box-office data exist only for the first of its three-week exhibition, though they demonstrate the potential for creating extra revenue through the policy of charging higher admission prices for certain films. In March 1957, evening prices at the Ritz ranged from 2s 4d in the front stalls to 4s 3d in the dress circle. For screenings of *War and Peace* 'special' raised prices were introduced which ranged from 2s 9d in front stalls to 5s 3d in the dress circle. 125 patrons paid as much as 6s to book circle reservations. In its first week of exhibition, the Ritz generated £3,940 from the sale of 22,385 admissions. These screenings were non-continuous and there were two separate performances at 2.50 and 7 pm. 16,740 tickets were sold for evening performances and 5,520 for matinee performances. The film was exhibited for a further two weeks, though from 25 March, the *Belfast Telegraph* advertised the film as '3¾ hours of entertainment at normal prices'.[107]

[102] Harper and Porter, *British Cinema of the 1950s*, p. 245.
[103] *Belfast Telegraph*, 4 Sept. 1956.
[104] *Belfast Telegraph*, 17 Oct. 1956.
[105] Political and Economic Planning, *The British Film Industry 1958* (London, 1958), p. 166.
[106] Political and Economic Planning, *The British Film Industry 1958*, p. 166.
[107] *Belfast Telegraph*, 25 March 1957.

Trade journals often foregrounded the weather as a key determinant of cinema attendance. On 5 July, for instance, *Kine Weekly* reported that the beginning of the holiday season 'was preceded by a spate of unusually good weather'.[108] In the week beginning 25 June, the Ritz recorded only 13,280 admissions. This was the second lowest figure in 1956–7 and well below the average of 20,899. On 26 July, *Kine Weekly* reported that a run of good weather meant that only three programmes attracted good crowds: *Picnic* (US, 1955) at the Regent, *The Court Jester* (US, 1955) at the Royal Hippodrome, and *The Man with the Golden Arm* (US, 1955) at the Imperial.[109] In 1956–7, *Picnic* screened for four weeks and was the second most successful film at the Regent, generating £4,528 from the sale of 39,567 admissions.

Public health concerns also had an impact on cinema attendance. In October 1957, the *Belfast Telegraph* claimed that, due to a recent global influenza epidemic, 'audiences in Belfast were down by between one third and a half, and that, in the larger cinemas, box-office revenue declined by up to £2,000 over the past four weeks'. It added that a 'few years ago a similar 'flu epidemic would not have had such a serious effect on the entertainment industry. But now with the counter attraction of television many people prefer to remain at home when there is a possibility of infection'.[110] In December 1957, *Kine Weekly* reported that attendances were still struggling after the influenza epidemic and exhibitors were 'hopeful that the approach of the Christmas season will see a swing back again to full houses and queues outside the cinema'.[111]

Long-term structural changes in employment also contributed to declining admissions:

> Shipbuilding, upon which a larger proportion of the Belfast population depends for livelihood, is in healthy condition, but has hit a bad patch and pay-offs in the aircraft industry, with the suggestion of more to come, have directly affected the entertainment industry. A major exhibitor said that the good pictures – well backed up with exploitation – were still playing a pretty tune at the box-offices. The proportionate fall-off was much worse with the poorer features.[112]

In January 1958, *Kine Weekly* reported that the 'holiday season brought the crowds back to Belfast cinemas after a period of several months during

---

[108] *Kinematograph Weekly*, 5 July 1956.
[109] *Kinematograph Weekly*, 26 July 1956.
[110] *Belfast Telegraph*, 19 Oct. 1957.
[111] *Kinematograph Weekly*, 5 Dec. 1957.
[112] *Kinematograph Weekly*, 5 Dec. 1957.

which receipts dropped badly'.[113] By June 1958, a cut in Entertainments Duty, the settlement of an eleven-week shipyard strike and the arrival of several 'good box-office pictures' meant that Belfast's cinema industry was in a healthier state.[114] *The Young Lions* (US, 1958), for instance 'gathered queues at the Belfast Imperial for five weeks and so justified George Lodge's "new look" policy in the cinema'.[115]

Alan Burton and Steve Chibnall have argued that, as cinema admissions declined, British cinema exhibitors intensified their promotional activities. Trade journals such as *Kine Weekly* encouraged exhibitors to compete for the most effective promotional campaigns and distributors issued campaign books suggesting ways for exhibitors to exploit films through the use of localized promotions with neighbouring businesses. They argue that 'foyer displays and front-of-house publicity became the most frequently used means of exploitation' as these added an experiential dimension to cinema-going. Street-stunts were also an important advertising tool, and, 'as with shop-window and foyer displays – certain themes and genres readily offered themselves for interpretation and exploitation'.[116] Promotional activity increased during the 1950s and the most outlandish promotional stunt was the appearance of 'Buck Alec' Robinson's lion to promote *A Lion is in the Streets* (US, 1953) at Belfast's Majestic. Patrons were assured they should not fear for their safety and were 'advised that rifles are not necessary. Certain precautions are being taken'.[117] Over 1,000 people came to see the lion and the *Northern Whig* reported that 'the more he growled and snarled, the more the young members of his audience enjoyed it, as they perched on parents' shoulders, hung from convenient lampposts, stood on nearby walls, sat on top of the furniture van or milled closely round the cage itself'.[118]

Strong promotional campaigns often led to high attendance figures and mitigated the impact of external factors on cinema attendance. In July 1956, Royal manager C. M. King stated that, despite the good weather, its first double horror bill in twelve months performed 'surprisingly well' and the use of a forty-five-foot poster outside the cinema helped to increase admissions.[119] In January 1957, *Kine Weekly* reported that Columbia's *Zarak* (UK, 1957) and MGM's *Guys and Dolls* (US, 1955), 'both heralded by plenty

---

[113] *Kinematograph Weekly*, 2 Jan. 1958.

[114] *Kinematograph Weekly*, 19 June 1958.

[115] *Kinematograph Weekly*, 17 July 1958.

[116] A. Burton and S. Chibnall, 'Promotional activities and showmanship in British film exhibition', *Journal of Popular British Cinema*, ii (1999), 83–99, at pp. 90–1.

[117] *Belfast Telegraph*, 23 July 1955.

[118] *The Northern Whig*, 26 July 1955.

[119] *Kinematograph Weekly*, 5 July 1956.

of publicity ... opened in Belfast to exceptional business' at the Regent and the Ritz respectively.[120] In 1956–7, *Guys and Dolls* was the third most popular film at the Ritz and *Zarak*, meanwhile, was the third most popular film at the Regent. Its manager, Frank Murray, was described as 'one of the most enterprising cinema managers in Belfast'. To promote *The Solid Gold Cadillac* (US, 1956), he arranged for a 1928 Cadillac to tour the city with posters claiming that 'this vintage Cadillac may make you smile, but "The Solid Gold Cadillac," a 22 carat comedy ... is guaranteed to make you laugh'.[121] The film performed well and in the two weeks beginning 12 November 1956 attracted 16,318 viewers. To promote *The Eddy Duchin Story* (US, 1956), Murray 'organised a singing and piano playing competition in conjunction with the Plaza ballroom'.[122] Newspaper listings advertised an Eddy Duchin wedding cake competition and asked pianists to 'enter for Eddy Duchin Piano Trophy at Plaza Ballroom'.[123] In the four weeks beginning 8 October, it sold 37,400 tickets and was the fourth best attended film of the year.

1960–1: changing exhibition

In 1960, the chancellor of the exchequer abolished Entertainment Tax in Great Britain. Despite pressure from cinema exhibitors, Northern Ireland finance minister Terence O'Neill did not follow suit and, in May 1960, stated that 'the first £20 of duty payable by a cinema in any week will be remitted, so that a small cinema which does not reach £20 of duty in a week will pay no tax at all and the bigger cinemas will be relieved at the rate of £1,040 a year'.[124] He claimed that large city centres were still performing well and that 'the concession is aimed specifically at helping the cinema which is in the greatest difficulty'.[125]

These changes in the rates of Entertainments Duty mean that many admissions were no longer documented and the records for 1960–1 provide a less reliable indication of audience preferences. They are most accurate for the large city centre cinemas that charged higher prices. Box-office data for the Ritz is incomplete and covers only the weeks from 21 March 1960 to 23 April 1960, 30 May 1960 to 2 July 1960, and 20 March 1961 to 27 May 1961. Nonetheless, they provide a rough indication of the decline in admissions. In the five weeks beginning 19 March 1956, admissions totalled

---

[120] *Kinematograph Weekly*, 24 Jan. 1957.
[121] *Kinematograph Weekly*, 6 Dec. 1956.
[122] *Kinematograph Weekly*, 6 Dec. 1956.
[123] *Belfast Telegraph*, 8 Oct. 1956.
[124] Hansard (Northern Ireland), *Parliamentary Debates*, xlvi (24 May 1960), cols. 1703–4.
[125] Hansard (NI), xlvi (25 May 1960), cols. 1766–8.

103,297. This number fell to 70,562 in the five weeks beginning 21 March 1960. Its city centre rivals experienced similar declines and admissions at the Gaumont fell from 939,457 to 676,938. The records for the Broadway and the Regent are extent for the period from 21 March 1960 to the abolition of Entertainments Duty on 27 May 1961. At the Regent, the same price categories are recorded in 1956–7 and 1960–1 and admissions fell from 443,273 to 353,958. From 1956–7 to 1960–1 recorded admissions at the Broadway fell from 455,119 to 218,309. The fact that matinee tickets from the Troxy's 1960–1 records are excluded mean that the 67 per cent decline in attendance is exaggerated.

Although attendances were in decline, cinemas were still able to generate large amounts of revenue from individual films. In March 1958, *Kine Weekly* reported on the excellent performance of Columbia's *Bridge on the River Kwai* (UK/US, 1957): 'It is collecting handsome queues outside the Belfast Gaumont every day'. The film was helped by positive media coverage and its selection as film of the week by BBC Northern Ireland.[126] Even smaller inner-city cinemas reported record attendances and, in January 1959, Crumlin Picture House manager H. W. Bell claimed that *Rock-a-Bye Baby* (US, 1958) broke five records in a single week: '[b]est ever six-day take; the best ever Monday, Tuesday and Wednesday take; best Thursday, Friday and Saturday take; best individual day and best attendance for a six-day film'.[127] In 1960, reporter Martin Wallace stated that while city centre centres were still doing good business from films with wide appeal such as *Gigi* (US, 1958), *South Pacific* (US, 1958) and *The Nun's Story* (US, 1959), 'it is difficult to say what makes a success – and safe to say that only a few films hit the jackpot'.[128]

A case study of *Ben-Hur* (US, 1959) demonstrates that large cinemas increasingly relied on longer runs, separate screenings and advanced seat booking. On 21 March 1961, 'clergymen of all denominations' attended a preview of *Ben-Hur* at the Ritz and members of the press were then entertained by MGM's Richard Hawkins and ABC executive Stanley Mills. The *Belfast Telegraph* informed readers that the film 'begins with an extended season there with a gala premiere on April 10 … Booking has already begun for the film, which will be shown daily with matinees on Mondays, Wednesdays and Saturdays. Arrangements have been made to accept party bookings of 50 to 2,100 patrons'.[129] Prices were increased for *Ben-Hur* and reserved seats ranged from 5s in the front stalls to 10s 6d in

[126] *Kinematograph Weekly*, 20 March 1958.
[127] *Kinematograph Weekly*, 22 Jan. 1959.
[128] *Belfast Telegraph*, 5 Oct. 1960.
[129] *Belfast Telegraph*, 21 March 1961.

the front circle. Normal prices were 2s 6d in the front stalls and 4s 6d in the front circle. These price increases did not deter patrons and the films was exhibited for nine weeks. During its first seven weeks of exhibition, it generated £24,394 from the sale of 71,575 tickets. Evening performances were substantially more popular than their matinee counterparts. On 17 April, for instance, the Ritz generated £200 from the matinee and £713 for evening exhibition. Attendances decreased significantly during its exhibition. In the week beginning 10 April, 12,324 admissions were recorded and this fell to 6,374 in its seventh week of exhibition. The emphasis on greater amounts of box-office revenue from a smaller number of films continued and, in March 1962, *The Young Ones* (UK, 1961) set a new box-office record at the Ritz in its first week of exhibition. This beat the previous record, set for *This is the Army* (US, 1943) in the Second World War.[130] Both large chains also adopted more flexible booking patterns. In November 1961, Odeon (NI) introduced a 'run by results' policy where a film was booked for a specific length of time that was extended if it was successful. In October 1962, managing director R. V. C. Eveleigh claimed that this new policy led to an 88 per cent increase in box-office revenues.[131] In March 1962, ABC introduced occasional first-run films at the Strand and the Majestic and *Kine Weekly* believed that the 'two main circuits, Odeon and ABC are now both broadening their service to the public'.[132]

These exhibition strategies contrasted with the smaller exhibitors who struggled to provide two double feature programmes every week. In 1960–1, the Broadway targeted a younger family audience by exhibiting *Darby O'Gill and the Little People* (US, 1959) at both Christmas and Easter. In the three days beginning 26 December 1960, it was the highest grossing film of the year and yielded £565. The Broadway brought the same film back on Easter Monday and generated a further £321 in box-office revenue. The Broadway filled its schedule with a greater number of foreign language films, and, according to Harper and Porter, many suburban second and third-run cinemas at the end of the distribution chain resorted to continental films to fill their booking schedules.[133] In 1960–1, the Broadway screened a range of European films, including *Babette Goes to War* (France, 1959), *Tamango* (France/Italy, 1957), *Paris, Palace Hotel* (France/Italy, 1956) and *Battle Inferno* (Germany, 1959).

The Troxy responded to the absence of good films by returning to cinema's music hall roots with stage shows and cine-variety. It advertised

---

[130] *Kinematograph Weekly*, 1 March 1962.
[131] *Kinematograph Weekly*, 25 Oct. 1962.
[132] *Kinematograph Weekly*, 22 March 1962.
[133] Harper and Porter, *British Cinema of the 1950s*, p. 246.

performances by hypnotist Edwin Heath and illusionist Mandrake, and hosted 'international wrestling' with 'stars of TV'. From February to March, comedian Frank Carson presented a 'discoveries of 1961' talent competition and the finals were held at a St Patrick's Day Midnight Matinee. On Friday 14 April, 675 patrons then attended 'Late Nite Cine Variety' featuring Carson and the prizewinners. In December 1961, 'a shortage of top-class films' led the Troxy to stage a Christmas pantomime of *Little Red Riding Hood*. The *Belfast Telegraph* commented that it was 'a brave and pleasing effort … and one which obviously delighted the very young in last night's audience'.[134] In January 1962, it reported that the Lido was following the Troxy and 'experimenting with live presentations to combat the lean days of attendance'. Manager John McKeown stated that if the show was a success he would consider cutting films on Tuesday night and replacing them with live variety shows.[135] The Troxy also resorted to nudist films, for example screening *The Nudist Story* (UK, 1960) in February 1961. In October 1962, *Kine Weekly* claimed that the Troxy was 'instrumental in introducing nudist films to the Ulster public'. It added that, while *West End Jungle* (UK, 1961) was playing at the Troxy, 'the Belfast public is no longer as easily led by an X certificate or by a nudist poster, and some observers say that the demand for sensational films, particularly of the nude variety, is already on the wane'.[136] From 1964, the Troxy hosted theatre productions presented by the Lyric Opera Company and the Ulster Theatre Company. This diverse programme could not save the cinema from the general decline in admissions. It finally closed in September 1965 and a month later reopened as the Grove Theatre.[137]

Conclusion

In his 1961 Budget statement, O'Neill responded to pressure from cinema exhibitors and abolished Entertainments Duty on all films. Following its abolition, the Ministry of Finance no longer kept records of cinema admissions in Northern Ireland. This was a source of concern for exhibitors and, in 1962, *Kine Weekly* reported that the 'Northern Ireland cinema trade is following closely present efforts aimed at encouraging the Ulster government to publish a wider range of research statistics on the Province. A number of commentators have felt the need for annual or even more frequent figures on the state of the cinema industry'.[138] It is fortunate then

[134] *Belfast Telegraph*, 27 Dec. 1961.
[135] *Belfast Telegraph*, 6 Jan. 1962.
[136] *Kinematograph Weekly*, 18 Oct. 1961.
[137] *Belfast Telegraph*, 12 Sept. 1965.
[138] *Kinematograph Weekly*, 25 Oct. 1962.

that the implementation of Entertainments Duty leaves a paper trail of attendance data from 1948 to 1961. Given the popularity of cinema-going, records of individual cinemas are surprisingly rare and the weekly returns provide a set of empirical data that facilitates in-depth scrutiny of the changing nature of cinema-going in the period, showing the struggles of exhibitors and the reasons behind audience engagement. By combining these records with programme listings we can establish the practices of Belfast exhibitors and the popularity of certain films. A clear benefit of the detailed qualitative evidence provided by oral testimonies, newspapers and trade journals is that it shows how receptive exhibitors were to local social and economic conditions.

These findings expand our understanding of cinema attendance across the UK and challenge existing ideas about audience tastes. For instance, in their study of British cinema of the 1950s, Harper and Porter claimed that the 'stratification of taste by region, which had been such an important feature of the 1930s and 1940s, disappeared completely in the 1950s'.[139] The popularity of Irish-themed films such as *The Quiet Man* or *Captain Boycott*, which in some way depicted audiences sense of their own identity, directly challenges Harper and Porter's statement and suggests the continuation of place-specific audience preferences within the UK into the 1960s. At the same time, declines in cinema attendance and the consequent shift in cinema-going from a ritual practice to one of occasional attractions should be placed in a broader international context. John Sedgwick, for instance, has shown that in the US there was a greater focus on big-budget films that were more attractive to increasingly younger and more selective audiences with greater amounts of disposable income.[140] Hollywood retained its dominant position by producing big-budget spectaculars, such as *War and Peace* or *Ben-Hur*, which disproportionately benefited the proprietors of the larger and more expensive cinemas in Belfast, such as the Ritz. These proprietors, however, had to attract a shrinking audience base while satisfying local tastes and negotiating a more stringent system of taxation than the rest of the UK.

---

[139] Harper and Porter, *British Cinema of the 1950s*, p. 264.
[140] J. Sedgwick, 'Product differentiation at the movies: Hollywood, 1946 to 1965', *The Journal of Economic History*, lxii (2002), pp. 676–705.

5. Film exhibition in post-war Sheffield

In 1954, H. E. Browning and A. A. Sorrell presented their findings on cinemas and cinema-going in Great Britain to the Royal Statistical Society. Their wide-ranging paper brought Simon Rowson's 1934 findings up to date, covering topics such as admissions, box-office revenue, venues, programming and audiences. Their statistical survey also provides a snapshot of cinema exhibition in cities across England, Scotland and Wales, including Sheffield. In 1951, its fifty cinemas held seating for 51,000 patrons and yielded £1,277,000 from the sale of 20.07 million recorded admissions. Sheffield's thirty-nine admissions per person was higher than the figure of twenty-eight for Great Britain as a whole and was similar to industrial cities such as Bradford (forty-one), Salford (thirty-nine) and Stoke-on-Trent (thirty-eight). It was just under the figure of forty for Yorkshire towns with a population of over 100,000.[1] These generalized findings, however, tell us little about the programming and audiences of individual cinemas.[2] Despite the large number of venues in operation across the UK, the records that survive are fragmented and vary in scope, chronology and detail. Cinema historians have creatively used programming listings and attendance figures to assess cinema-going habits and film preferences in a variety of locations across the United Kingdom. Sheldon Hall's detailed analysis of booking policies and audience tastes at the Sheffield Gaumont from 1947 to 1958 combined quantitative data provided by attendance figures and box-office takings with qualitative information on audience reaction provided by the cinema manager.[3] Here, close scrutiny of two Sheffield cinemas, the Rex and the Cartoon (later the Classic), alongside the free film screenings organized by Sheffield libraries, builds on Hall's study by enabling us to assess major changes in cinema exhibition in close detail across the period from 1945 to 1965. Though the use of quantitative data does not provide watertight evidence of audience tastes, it is important for cinema historians to find imaginative ways to analyse cinema listings and box-office figures.

---

[1] H. E. Browning and A. A. Sorrell, 'Cinemas and cinema-going in Great Britain', *Journal of the Royal Statistical Society*, cvxii, no. 2 (1954), 133–70, at p. 138.

[2] See Appendix 2 for further details of all Sheffield cinema open in the period under review.

[3] S. Hall, 'Going to the Gaumont', *Picture House*, xlii (2018), 50–67.

'Film exhibition in post-war Sheffield', in S. Manning, *Cinemas and Cinema-Going in the United Kingdom: Decades of Decline, 1945–65* (London, 2020), pp. 163–91. License: CC-BY-NC-ND 4.0.

As Sue Harper has recently suggested, a 'set of popularity figures, if carefully interpreted, can give us unparalleled access to the audience's mindscape'.[4]

The Rex Cinema, 1945–65

The 1,350-seat Rex Cinema opened in July 1939. It was a large suburban cinema located three miles south-east of Sheffield city centre, adjacent to two recent housing developments (see Figures 5.1 and 5.2). One report stated that it was built to meet the 'entertainment needs of the people of Intake and for the rapidly developing areas in the vicinity, such as Frecheville, Richmond and Gleadless'.[5] It was the last pre-war suburban cinema in Sheffield to close, surviving until December 1982.[6] In 1945, evening ticket prices ranged from 10*d* in the front stalls to 1*s* 9*d* in the circle and, by 1965, prices had increased to 2*s* 9*d* and 3*s* 6*d* respectively.[7] The Rex normally changed its programme on Monday and Thursday, though a small minority of programmes were kept for an entire week. Matinee performances of the normal programme were held on Monday and Thursday, and in September 1958, the cinema introduced a 6*d* Saturday morning family matinee. It was in a minority of Sheffield cinemas that closed on Sundays in the period under review. The records of the Rex Cinema cover the entire period of its existence, though this chapter focuses on the period from 1945 to 1965, assessing box-office revenue, ancillary income and expenditure on tax and film hire.[8] It then looks at patterns of attendance and examines box-office successes and failures at the Rex. The absence of admissions figures, alongside variations in taxation and admission prices, makes it difficult to assess the relative popularity of films in the period under review. However, it is possible to provide a detailed analysis of the box-office success of particular films by combining these records with cinema listings published in *The Star*.

Across the UK, significant increases in ticket prices meant that the decline in box-office revenue was less drastic than the fall in admissions. In 1946, the sale of 1.635 billion admissions yielded £121 million in gross box-

---

[4] S. Harper, '"It is time we went out to meet them": empathy and historical distance', *Participations*, xvi (2019), 687–97, at p. 692.

[5] *Sheffield Daily Telegraph*, 24 July 1939.

[6] C. Shaw and C. Stacey, 'A century of cinema', in *Aspects of Sheffield 2: Discovering Local History*, ed. M. Jones (Barnsley, 1999), pp. 182–200, at p. 199.

[7] Sheffield City Archives, MD7333/2/2, Rex Cinema (Sheffield) Limited, minute books, 8 Feb. 1961; Sheffield City Archives, MD7333/2/2, Rex Cinema (Sheffield) Limited, minute books, 14 Dec. 1965.

[8] The records are largely financial and contain profit and loss accounts, financial reports, payments and receipts ledgers that detail the cinemas' revenue and expenditure. These are supplemented by the minutes of monthly shareholder meetings, which provide qualitative information on the cinema's operation.

Figure 5.1. Rex Cinema (centre) and surrounding area, Intake, Sheffield, 1951 (Ordnance Survey, National Grid 1:2500. © Crown Copyright and Landmark Information Group Limited 2016. All rights reserved. 1951).

Figure 5.2. Rex Cinema, Sheffield, c.1943–5 (Picture Sheffield, Sheffield City Council Archives and Local Studies Service).

office revenue.[9] In 1950, these figures declined to 1.395 billion and £105.2 million respectively.[10] As Table 5.1 shows, in 1946 the Rex yielded £34,795 in gross box-office revenue and this amount fell by 7 per cent to £32,361 in the following year. In the next two years, gross box-office revenue remained relatively stable and then increased to £34,947 in 1950. In July 1951, Sheffield CEA members voted in favour of price increases and, from 5 August, the Rex changed its prices to 1s, 1s 6d and 1s 9d.[11] The fact that 1951–2 was the peak year for gross box-office revenue is attributable partly to these price changes. In Great Britain, gross box-office revenue fell precipitously from £104.2 million in 1956 to £61.7 million in 1965.[12] The Rex followed similar trends and revenue fell from £34,018 in 1956 to £12,975 in 1965. It witnessed its most significant decline from 1957 to 1958 and revenue fell by 20.67 per cent from £30,089 to £23,870. At the 1958 annual general meeting, chairman T. W. Ward stated that average weekly attendances had dropped by 3,000 in the year and added that, while reduced rates of Entertainment Tax provided some relief, there was still a significant fall in net profit. The decline in attendance was exacerbated further by the fact that its nearest rival, the Manor, was taken over by the Star circuit.[13]

As a private limited company, the net profit and the dividends paid to the Rex's shareholders at the end of each financial year provide an indication of the company's success or failure. Net profit fell from its peak of £3,626 in 1948 to £430 in 1963 and in the same period the shareholder dividend fell from 45 per cent to just 5 per cent. Despite the decline in gross box-office revenue and net profit, the Rex still performed better than many other Sheffield cinemas. From 1957 to 1964, twenty-six cinemas closed down, which were most commonly older and smaller cinemas located in inner-city working-class areas. The Rex's relative youth and upmarket status meant that it was well placed to deal with the changes in the cinema exhibition industry. The Manor, meanwhile, closed in 1963 and reopened as the Manor Casino. The cinema started showing films on a part-time basis in November and closed finally in 1964. This reduced competition is the likely cause of the sudden increase in revenue at the Rex from £12,423 in 1963 to £15,656 in 1964.

[9] P. Swann, *The Hollywood Feature Film in Postwar Britain* (London, 1987), p. 36.

[10] Central Statistical Office, *Annual abstract of statistics 1954*, no. 91 (London, 1954), p. 73.

[11] *Kinematograph Weekly*, 12 July 1951; Sheffield City Archives, MD7333/2/1, Rex Cinema (Sheffield) Limited minute books, 25 July 1951.

[12] Central Statistical Office, *Annual Abstract of Statistics 1966*, no. 103 (London, 1966), p. 81.

[13] Sheffield City Archives, MD7333/2/2, Rex Cinema (Sheffield) Limited, minute books, 26 Nov. 1958.

Table 5.1. Selected revenue and expenditure at the Rex Cinema, Sheffield, 1945–64.

Year (Aug. to July)	Income			Expenditure				Profit		Retail price index (RPI)	
	Gross box-office revenue (£)	Net box-office revenue (£)	Total receipts (£)	Tax (£)	British Film Production Fund (£)	Film hire (£)	Wages (£)	Net profit (£)	Shareholder dividend (%)	RPI (Jan. 1974 = 100)	Annual change in RPI
1945–6	34,795	24,440		10,355		8,995	1,873	2,327	35		
1946–7	32,361	22,670		9,691		8,520	2,196	3,169	40		
1947–8	32,831	22,985		9,846		8,554	2,481	3,626	45	33.3	
1948–9	32,767	22,959		9,809		8,185	2,710	3,326	40	34.4	3.3
1949–50	34,947	23,895	40,976	11,052		9,131	2,915	2,984	40	35.1	2.0
1950–1	34,146	23,695	40,166	9,918	533	9,727	2,972	2,662	35	38.7	10.3
1951–2	37,340	25,052	44,222	10,984	1,305	9,894	3,378	2,787	35	40.5	4.7
1952–3	35,725	24,101	45,487	10,375	1,248	8,851	3,210	3,233	40	41.5	2.5
1953–4	35,890	24,486	47,108	10,155	1,249	8,613	3,382	3,271	40	42.3	1.9
1954–5	33,504	23,969	44,969	8,725	811	9,569	3,609	3,144	40	43.7	3.3
1955–6	34,018	24,263	45,881	8,931	824	9,060	3,669	3,275	37.5	45.8	4.8
1956–7	30,089	21,705	41,001	7,686	698	7,514	3,918	2,431	27.5	47.3	3.3
1957–8	23,870	18,534	32,148	4,463	873	6,517	4,127	1,427	15	48.7	3.0
1958–9	19,394	17,495	26,858	1,068	831	6,023	4,094	2,639	20	49.2	1.0
1959–60	16,028	14,355	23,297	952	721	5,380	3,918	1,256	12.5	49.8	1.2
1960–1	15,905	13,936	22,442	1,135	833	5,310	3,898	1,142	10	51.2	2.8
1961–2	13,836	12,161	20,205	901	774	4,638	3,981	903	7.5	53.0	3.5
1962–3	12,423	11,722	18,277		701	3,939	3,974	430	5	54.0	1.9
1963–4	15,656	14,667	22,090		989	4,971	3,961	1,272	7.5	55.8	3.3

Sources: Sheffield City Archives, MD7333/3/1, Rex Cinema (Sheffield) Limited, account ledger; MD7333/4/1–2, payments ledgers; MD7333/5/1–2, receipts ledgers; MD7333/7/7–26, published accounts profit and loss account and balance sheets; R. Middleton, *The British Economy since 1945* (Basingstoke, 2000), p. 149.

The consumption of food and drink was a central part of the cinema-going experience, and for exhibitors provided an important source of ancillary income. The Rex sold chocolate, cigarettes and ice cream, and the growth in sales of these items reflects greater amounts of disposable income and the shift towards a more consumer-oriented society. Figure 5.3 shows that in 1946, the Rex generated only £106 in net profit from the sale of £692 worth of chocolate and cigarettes. In the Second World War, food rationing and price controls led to a ban on luxury foods, and ice cream was absent from cinemas between September 1942 and March 1945.[14] When ice cream returned at the Rex, it soon generated greater amounts of revenue than chocolate. By 1951, *The Economist* claimed that British output of ice cream was three to four times higher than before the war, claiming that only the lack of household refrigerators prevented further consumption.[15] The introduction of sweets rationing in July 1942 limited the sale of chocolate and these restrictions lasted until February 1953. *Kine Weekly* reported that with the end of sweets rationing, exhibitors stood to lose thousands of pounds due to confectionary's much lower profit margin than ice cream.[16] In 1954, the estimated profit margins of ice cream, sweets and tobacco were 50 per cent, 30 per cent and 9 per cent respectively.[17] The end of rationing had an immediate impact and from January to March 1953, the Rex's chocolate sales increased from £324 to £596. Annual sales increased by 67 per cent from £2,826 in 1952 to £4,714 in 1953 and reached their peak in 1954. From 1955, chocolate sales decreased and sales of ice cream fared much better, which may have been a result of better promotion and marketing.[18]

Combined sales of chocolate, ice cream and cigarettes peaked in 1955–6 when the Rex made £3,079 in net profit from them. Although cigarettes were never rationed, sales increased dramatically from £930 in 1951–2 to £2,456 in 1952–3. From 1956 onwards, the concurrent decline in sales of all items and box-office revenue indicates that the Rex was attracting fewer patrons. As attendances fell, these ancillary sales were key to the profitability of cinemas. In 1957, *The Economist* reported that while Britain's cinema earned a profit of £2.5 million from the exhibition of films, they earned £7.5 million from showing advertisements and selling ice-cream.[19] Sales of ancillary items declined faster than box-office revenue. From 1956

---

[14]   R. Farmer, *Cinemas and Cinema-Going in Wartime Britain: the Utility Dream Palace* (Manchester, 2016), p. 71.

[15]   *The Economist*, 6 Jan. 1951.

[16]   *Kinematograph Weekly*, 29 Jan. 1953.

[17]   *The Economist*, 6 Feb. 1954.

[18]   *Kinematograph Weekly*, 17 Dec. 1953.

[19]   *The Economist*, 16 Feb. 1957.

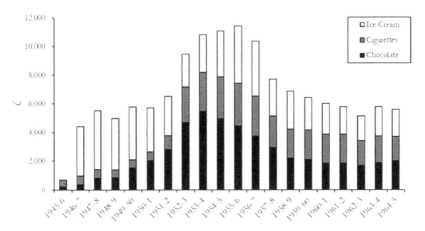

Figure 5.3. Gross revenue of ancillary items at the Rex Cinema,
Sheffield, 1945–65 (Source: Sheffield City Archives, MD7333/5/1,
Rex Cinema (Sheffield) Limited, receipts ledger).

to 1962, net box-office revenue fell by 50 per cent from £24,263 to £12,117.
The decline in sales of ancillary items was more precipitous and in the same
period net profits fell by 61 per cent from £3,069 to £1,192. While this
may suggest that they were less important to the cinema's profitability, this
depends on the extent that expenses are attributed to film exhibition or to
the cinema as a whole.

In the previous chapter, the records of Entertainments Duty provided no
indication of further expenditure for cinemas in Northern Ireland. The Rex's
payments register, however, provides a detailed account of expenditure such
as Entertainment Tax, film hire, wages, advertising, utility bills and repairs.
Entertainment Tax was the greatest form of expenditure at the Rex. In
1950–1, fifty Sheffield cinemas paid £127,000 (33 per cent) of their £421,000
gross takings in the form of Entertainment Tax. In the same year, the Rex
paid 29 per cent of its revenue in the form of Entertainment Tax, lower
than the UK average. In 1951, the average price of admission in Sheffield was
15.3d and tickets at the Rex cost 12d, 18d and 21d.[20] In August 1950, *The Star*
reported that cinemas seats were cheaper in Yorkshire than in other regions
and argued that one reason for lower ticket prices was that single-feature
programmes were more common in the north than they were in London.
It claimed that:

[20] Browning and Sorrell, 'Cinemas and cinema-going in Great Britain', p. 138.

Experience in Sheffield has shown that suburban cinemas find it hard to show two double-feature programmes in an evening because of the time factor. Mr D.D. Craig, president of the Sheffield Cinematograph Exhibitors' Association, told 'The Star' that the earliest practicable time for starting was 6 p.m. normally, and the licence expired at 11 p.m. Allowing an interval for 'clearing the house' this did not give a lot of time to present two full length feature films, twice'.[21]

Payments in Entertainment Tax fell from their peak of £11,052 to £7,685 in 1957. In 1958, significant concessions were made to Entertainment Tax and payments at the Rex fell to £1,068 in 1958–9. Despite the abolition of Entertainment Tax in April 1960, the cinema recorded tax on the sale of cinema tickets until April 1962.

The Rex's profitability was also hit by the introduction of the British Film Production Fund (also known as the Eady Levy) in 1950, whereby cinemas voluntarily contributed ¼d of every ticket sold in exchange for changes in the rate of Entertainment Tax. In 1951, the levy increased to ¾d for tickets priced above 1s and the rate changed at various times throughout the 1950s. The 1957 Cinematograph Films Act established the British Film Fund Agency and introduced a statutory levy. The Rex first paid into the fund in September 1951 and payments fell from £1,305 in 1951–2 to £701 in 1962–3.

After the payment of Entertainment Tax film hire was the greatest form of expenditure. Second features and newsreels were generally hired at a flat rate. For first features, the exhibitor paid an agreed percentage of his net box-office receipts to the distributor. This percentage was agreed on a sliding scale and the cinema paid a greater proportion of its box-office revenue for well-attended films.[22] From 1946 to 1956, the Rex's expenditure on film hire remained relatively stable and ranged from £8,185 in 1948–9 to £9,894 in 1951–2. Significant reductions in box-office revenue correspond to lower expenditure on film hire and payments decreased from £7,514 in 1957 to £4,638 in 1962. The Rex consistently spent a greater proportion of its revenue on film hire than the national average. After the abolition of Entertainment Tax, this proportion increased at the Rex, but decreased across British cinemas as a whole.

In 1950–1, when Browning and Sorrell calculated that Sheffield cinemas paid 36 per cent of their net takings on film hire, the Rex paid 41 per cent of its net takings on this form of expenditure. This was the highest proportion in the period under review.[23] The fact that the Rex was an independently owned cinema meant that it paid more on film hire than cinemas in large

[21] The Star, 18 Aug. 1950.
[22] Browning and Sorrell, 'Cinemas and cinema-going in Great Britain', pp. 156–7; Political and Economic Planning, The British Film Industry (London, 1952), pp. 209–10.
[23] Browning and Sorrell, 'Cinemas and cinema-going in Great Britain', p. 138.

circuits such as ABC, Gaumont and Odeon. In 1950, W. C. Harte, booking manager at the Rotherham Hippodrome countered claims that films were 'sold to the highest bidder as soon as they leave the hands of the producer'.[24] He explained that:

> The reason that the large circuits get priority on new films is because of their greater bargaining power, due to the number of cinemas they control, and at which they can give a first run showing. If you had access to their figures over 12 months, you would find, possibly much to your astonishment, that the price paid over that period was on the average, much lower than that paid by the independent cinemas.[25]

Film hire payments were a consistent source of concern for Sheffield exhibitors. In July 1953, Sheffield CEA 'reiterated a previous minute that 50 per cent. should be the maximum film-hire rate' and Harold Gent suggested that distributors had used the increased rates for 3D film *House of Wax* (US, 1953) and Technicolor epic *Quo Vadis* (US, 1951) as an opportunity to increase film rentals in general. L. Clegg added that '[o]nce renters got in the thin end of the wedge exhibitors would be fighting a hopeless battle'.[26] The introduction of CinemaScope in March 1955 explains the sharp increase in film hire payments from 1954 to 1955.

Wage payments formed a significant part of the UK cinema owners' expenditure and, in 1950, the average cinema employed nineteen staff.[27] Browning and Sorrell calculated that in the first quarter of 1952, cinemas in Great Britain paid £4,188,000 in wages and that cinemas with between 1,251 and 1,500 seats paid an average of £1 in wages per seat.[28] In the same period, the Rex spent £1,068 in wages, which means that it paid 15s 10d in wages per seat. Browning and Sorrell added that there was wide regional diversity and the northern region displayed the lowest wage levels. Wage payments increased dramatically from £1,873 in 1946 to £3,918 in 1957. As attendances declined, expenditure on wages remained relatively stable and declined slightly from £4,127 in 1958 to £3,961 in 1964. The records do not show the wages of individual staff, though board minutes reveal that that cinema manager Tony Ward's weekly wage increased from £12 10s in May 1954 to £14 in July 1956.[29] The cinema ledgers also reveal the range of expenses required to successfully run a cinema. In 1956, for example, the Rex spent

[24] *The Star,* 14 Jan. 1950.
[25] *The Star,* 17 Jan. 1950.
[26] *Kinematograph Weekly,* 30 July 1953.
[27] Political and Economic Planning, *The British Film Industry* (London, 1952), pp. 217–18.
[28] Browning and Sorrell, 'Cinemas and cinema-going in Great Britain', pp. 159–60.
[29] Sheffield City Archives, MD7333/2/2, Rex Cinema (Sheffield) Minute Books, 12 May 1954; 16 July 1956.

£833 on rates, £412 on billposting and posters, £259 on advertising, £315 on electricity and gas, £350 on coke, and £325 on repairs and renewals. There were also significant one-off investments, such as the £1,550 paid for the installation of a new CinemaScope screen in 1955.

The day of the week was a key determinant of attendance at the Rex. From August 1945 to July 1960, Saturday screenings were collectively the greatest revenue generators and provided 21 per cent of gross box-office revenue. The highest grossing Saturday was 2 February 1957, when British drama *A Town Like Alice* (UK, 1956) yielded £198. Monday and Thursday – the days when new programmes were shown – were the next most profitable days at the Rex contributing 19 per cent and 18 per cent of gross box-office revenue respectively. Despite the popularity of Saturday screenings, the forty highest grossing days from 1945 to 1960 were on either Monday (twenty-seven) or Thursday (thirteen). Monday 6 August 1951 was the highest grossing single day at the Rex, when *Father's Little Dividend* (US, 1951) generated £288. The extra matinee screenings on Monday and Thursday helped the Rex to generate extra revenue, and if these are excluded, thirty-three of the forty highest grossing days were Saturdays. The highest box-office revenue for a matinee performance was recorded on Monday 6 August 1956 when the screening of *River of No Return* (US, 1954) generated £98.

Patterns of attendance varied and there were distinct changes in the way that patrons used their leisure time. In 1946, Monday screenings were the greatest revenue generators and yielded 21 per cent of box-office revenue. Combined takings from Friday and Saturday screenings comprised 35 per cent of box-office revenue. Wednesday was consistently the worst performing day and the proportion of box-office revenue varied only between 12 per cent in 1950 and 10 per cent in 1953. From 1947 to 1957, Monday was the second most profitable day at the cinema. From 1957 to 1960, when gross box-office revenue fell by 47 per cent, Monday takings suffered more than any other day of the week and fell by 55 per cent. By 1960, Monday was only the fourth most profitable day. These statistics help to identify changing social habits, showing that by the late 1950s, the day on which a film was released was less important to overall box-office revenue, and there was an increased preference for Friday and Saturday screenings. By 1952, they contributed 38 per cent of box-office revenue, and by 1960, this figure increased to 43 per cent. In 1958, Friday and Saturday screenings generated £4,730 and £4,735 respectively. In the following year, Friday revenue fell to £3,564, yet the introduction of a Saturday morning family matinee in September 1958 led Saturday revenue to decline only slightly to £4,532. In 1959, the Rex generated £910 from its Saturday morning screenings. During his research from 1959 to 1960, M. P. Carter found that 'Friday night was *the* night for the cinema come rain, come shine, irrespective of the film, on the same day and at the same time these children went to the cinema, usually to the same place'.[30] The increased importance of Friday screenings suggests a younger audience in the late 1950s, who perhaps spent their other nights participating in alternative leisure pursuits.

Cinema attendance at the Rex was seasonal and the periods from March to May and from August to October were the most profitable. While these records do not reveal intergenerational differences in cinema attendance, Carter found that the '[a]ttendance of some children was affected by the time of the year – some who went every week in the winter seldom or never went in the summer'. He added, however, that 'changes of interest, "getting fed up" with going or with not going, and changes of friends were as important as seasonal changes' accounting for fluctuations in attendance.[31] Adverse weather also interrupted patterns of attendance. The Rex's receipts suggest that unusually cold weather had a detrimental impact and the notoriously harsh winter of 1946–7 caused attendances to decline.

The Rex often generated greater amounts of box-office revenue on public holidays, such as Whitsuntide. In 1946, for instance, Whit Monday was the second highest grossing day via the screening of *The Road to Utopia* (US, 1946). While the Rex closed on Christmas Day, screenings in the proceeding days were popular. In the three days beginning 27 December 1945, the Rex screened *Hollywood Canteen* (US, 1944). It generated £448 in box-office revenue and was the fifth highest grossing film of 1945–6. New Year's Day and Easter Monday were both popular days for cinema attendance. In 1950–1, the Rex screened *The Blue Lamp* (UK, 1950) from 1–3 January. It was the most successful film of the year and New Year's Day was the highest grossing day in 1950–1. The second highest was the Easter Monday exhibition of *Top Hat* (US, 1935). In 1952–3, the New Year's Day exhibition of *Singin' in the Rain* (US, 1952) was the second highest grossing day and was beaten only by the Easter Monday exhibition of *The Desert Hawk* (US, 1950).

The Rex changed its programme on Monday and Thursday. It retained a small number of films for an entire week and no programme was exhibited for longer than six days. In 1953–4, only two programmes were retained for a week and these were the highest grossing features: *Hans Christian Anderson* (£794) and *Rob Roy* (£728). In the same period, however, the highest grossing week yielded £967 and this demonstrates the benefits to the Rex of continuously changing its programme. Table 5.2 shows that between

---

[30] M. P. Carter, *Home, School and Work: a Study of the Education and Employment of Young People in Britain* (Oxford, 1962), p. 297.
[31] Carter, *Home, School and Work:*, pp. 296–7.

1945 and 1960, the second highest grossing film was *Elizabeth is Queen* (UK, 1953), which offers further evidence of the popularity of coronation films across Sheffield. Extra matinee performances were held on Tuesday and Wednesday and it generated £794 during its six-day exhibition. *Father's Little Dividend* (US, 1951) was the most successful film screened over a three-day period and generated £636 in box-office revenue. It was the sequel to *Father of the Bride* (US, 1950), which was the eighth most profitable film in 1950–1, and the success of the former may have encouraged patrons to attend the latter. Its box-office success is also attributable to the fact that it was screened in August, which was generally the Rex's most profitable month. These figures also ignore the fact that many successful films were brought back for further exhibition. *The Dam Busters* (UK, 1956), for instance, was exhibited for a second time from 2 July 1956 and generated £359. Its total revenue from six days of exhibition was £938, far greater than that of *Hans Christian Anderson*. In this instance, the tastes of the Rex's patrons for British war films matched the national trend as in 1955, *The Dam Busters* was the highest grossing film in Britain.[32] Even though most films screened at the Rex were American productions, five of the ten highest grossing films were British and one was a US/UK co-production. Table 5.3 shows the most successful programmes at the Rex in each year from 1945–6 to 1959–60. In 1948, Sheffield exhibitor H. S. Watson stated that 'most British films were not wanted by the public and the box-office showed the fact'.[33] In 1948–9, however, *Holiday Camp* (UK, 1947) was the most popular film of the year and four of the ten highest grossing films were UK productions. From 1955–6 to 1958–9 the most successful films were either British comedies or war films.

The Rex's programming was affected by national legislation and the policies of the British government. In 1948, following the abolition of the *ad valorem* film duty, the Board of Trade applied a 45 per cent quota on exhibition of British films. In July 1948, Sheffield CEA members agreed to write to the Board of Trade and contact their local MPs to protest against its implementation. One exhibitor stated that 'we must bombard the Board of Trade from every conceivable angle so as to let them know we mean business'.[34] On 13 July 1948, the company secretary told the Rex's board members that the cinema had applied to the Board of Trade for relaxation of the quota and had also sent a letter to two MPs.[35] In August, the CEA

[32] *Motion Picture Herald*, 7 Jan. 1956.
[33] *Kinematograph Weekly*, 8 July 1948.
[34] *Kinematograph Weekly*, 8 July 1948.
[35] Sheffield City Archives, MD7333/2/1, Rex Cinema (Sheffield) Limited, minute books 13 July 1948.

Table 5.2. Ten highest-grossing main features at the
Rex Cinema, August 1945–July 1960.

Date	Main feature	Gross revenue (£)	Days screened
Mon. 30/11/53	*Hans Christian Anderson* (US, 1952)	794	6
Mon. 15/06/53	*Elizabeth is Queen* (UK, 1953	791	6
Mon. 05/07/54	*Rob Roy* (US/UK, 1954)	728	6
Mon. 28/03/55	*Black Shield of Falworth* (US, 1954)	671	6
Mon. 28/07/58	*Dunkirk* (UK, 1958)	669	6
Mon. 06/08/51	*Father's Little Dividend* (US, 1951)	636	3
Mon. 23/08/54	*Doctor in the House* (UK, 1954)	603	3
Mon. 17/06/57	*Doctor at Large* (UK, 1957)	580	6
Thurs. 05/01/56	*The Dam Busters* (UK, 1955)	579	3
Thurs. 29/07/54	*Quo Vadis* (US, 1951)	578	3

Source: Sheffield City Archives, MD7333/5/1, Rex Cinema (Sheffield) Limited, Receipts Ledger.

Table 5.3. Most successful programmes at the Rex Cinema
by year (August to July), 1945–6 to 1959–60.

Year	Date	Main feature	Gross revenue (£)	Days screened
1945–6	Mon. 06/08/45	*Dark Victory* (US, 1939)	518	3
1946–7	Thurs. 10/10/46	*Adventure* (US, 1946)	507	3
1947–8	Mon. 04/08/47	*Blue Skies* (US, 1946)	506	3
1948–9	Thurs. 05/08/48	*Holiday Camp* (UK, 1947)	478	3
1949–50	Thurs. 15/09/49	*Johnny Belinda* (US, 1948)	538	3
1950–1	Mon. 01/01/51	*The Blue Lamp* (UK, 1950)	555	3
1951–2	Mon. 06/08/51	*Father's Little Dividend* (US, 1951)	636	3
1952–3	Mon. 15/06/53	*Elizabeth is Queen* (UK, 1953)	791	3
1953–4	Mon. 30/11/53	*Hans Christian Andersen* (US, 1952)	794	6
1954–5	Mon. 28/03/55	*Black Shield of Falworth* (US, 1954)	671	6
1955–6	Thurs. 05/01/56	*The Dam Busters* (UK, 1955)	579	3
1956–7	Mon. 17/06/57	*Doctor at Large* (UK, 1957)	580	6
1957–8	Mon. 28/07/58	*Dunkirk* (UK, 1958)	669	6
1958–9	Thurs. 02/04/59	*The Square Peg* (UK, 1958)	482	3
1959–60	Mon. 28/09/59	*Rio Bravo* (US, 1959)	500	6

Source: Sheffield City Archives, MD7333/5/1), Rex Cinema (Sheffield) Limited, Receipts Ledger.

secretary wrote to Harold Wilson, the president of the Board of Trade, to ask for quota concessions and stated that:

> In an industrial area like Sheffield it is only the films of outstanding merit which attract a good attendance, and the great majority of British films are quite unacceptable to our audiences. Even the best of films, either British or American, can only gainfully be shown once or, at the most, twice in each district and over a period of years.[36]

Quota relief was granted on the basis of local competition and, in October, it was reported that the Rex's quota had been fixed at a reduced rate of 20 per cent in the year ending September 1949.[37] In Great Britain, the Rex was one of 1,327 cinemas granted partial relief from the quota. A further 305 were fully exempted and 800 applications were rejected.[38] The Rex was more fortunate than many other Sheffield exhibitors and, in November, the claims of fifteen cinemas were rejected and several exhibitors received no reply from the Board of Trade.[39] However, Harper and Porter stated than even when cinemas failed to fulfil their quota requirements prosecutions were few and far between. The quota worked largely by consent and the Board of Trade were unable to force the hands of exhibitors.[40]

In 1949, the national quota decreased to 40 per cent and the Rex's quota increased to 27 per cent in the year ending September 1950.[41] In 1950, the national quota was reduced to 30 per cent. The Rex's quota returned to 20 per cent for the year ending 30 September 1951 and remained at that level until September 1959.[42] In October 1959, the Board of Trade stated that no relief could be given for the upcoming year.[43] The cinema received relief the following year and the quota for the year ending September 1961 was fixed at 22.5 per cent.[44] The fact that the Rex continually applied for a reduction in

[36] *Kinematograph Weekly*, 5 Aug. 1948.

[37] Sheffield City Archives, MD7333/2/1, Rex Cinema (Sheffield) Limited, minute books, 13 Oct. 1948.

[38] M. Dickinson and S. Street, *Cinema and State: the Film Industry and the British Government 1927–84* (London, 1985), p. 197.

[39] *Kinematograph Weeky*, 4 Nov. 1948.

[40] S. Harper and V. Porter, *British Cinema of the 1950s: the Decline of Deference* (Oxford, 2003), p. 6–7.

[41] Sheffield City Archives, MD7333/2/1, Rex Cinema (Sheffield) Limited, minute books, 9 Nov. 1949.

[42] Sheffield CityArchives, MD7333/2/1, Rex Cinema (Sheffield) Limited, minute books, 12 July 1950, 25 July 1951, 23 July 1952, 19 Aug. 1953; MD7333/2/2, Rex Cinema (Sheffield) Limited, minute books, 14 July 1954, 27 July 1955, 22 Aug. 1956, 14 Aug. 1957.

[43] Sheffield City Archives, MD7333/2/2, Rex Cinema (Sheffield) Limited, minute books, 14 Oct. 1959.

[44] Sheffield City Archives, MD7333/2/2, Rex Cinema (Sheffield) Limited, minute books, 12 Sept. 1960.

its quota indicates that it preferred to screen a greater number of American features. From 1945–6 to 1948–9, the number of British first features that the cinema exhibited increased from fifteen to twenty-seven. The US film boycott had little impact at the Rex and there was no significant increase in the number of British films exhibited in 1948. The high number of films in 1949 and 1950 is most likely attributable to the 27 per cent quota imposed in the year ending September 1950.

British comedies were popular with patrons at the Rex and the *Doctor* series, starring Dirk Bogarde, did particularly well. In 2005, the British Film Institute estimated that *Doctor in the House* was the thirty-sixth best attended film in UK history, with 12.2 million admissions.[45] In 1954, *Kine Weekly*'s annual survey suggested it was the most popular film of the year. This success was matched at the Rex and, in August 1954, it yielded £603. In October, it generated a further £528 and its total gross box-office revenue of £1,130 was far higher than any other individual film. Its sequels were also popular at the Rex and, in March 1956, *Doctor at Sea* (UK, 1955) generated £426 from its three-day exhibition. It was also the third-highest grossing film in Britain in 1955 with Dirk Bogarde the highest grossing star.[46] In June 1957, *Doctor at Large* (UK, 1957) generated £580 from six days exhibition, and in April 1960, returned as a supporting feature to *Man of the Moment* (UK, 1955). In 1960, Easter Monday fell on 18 April and this comedy double feature was the sixth most popular programme at the Rex. The *Doctor* films were also popular at the Gaumont and in 1954 and 1957, *Doctor in the House* and *Doctor at Large* were its most its most popular films respectively.[47] The popularity of the *Doctor* films provides some indication of the kinds of patrons that the Rex attracted. Harper and Porter observed that these films appealed to both occasional cinema-goers and regular patrons, stating that

> The seductive message they offered was that in the new meritocratic Britain all you needed to become a new professional was integrity, modesty, application, and a sense of humour. But this mild social radicalism was underpinned by a sexual conservatism, which permitted viewers to enjoy the image of themselves being socially adventurous while being sexually comfortable.[48]

Other British comedies were popular at the Rex, particularly those starring Norman Wisdom. In June 1954, *Trouble in Store* (UK, 1953) generated £538 in box-office revenue and was the year's fourth highest grossing film. In November, it was exhibited again and generated a further £298. In 1955,

[45] *The Ultimate Film: the UK's 100 Most Popular Films* (London, 2005), ed. R. Gilbey, pp. 138–9.

[46] *Motion Picture Herald*, 7 Jan. 1956.

[47] A. Eyles, *Gaumont British Cinemas* (London, 1996), p. 193.

[48] Harper and Porter, *British Cinema of the 1950s*, p. 256.

Motion Picture Herald claimed that Norman Wisdom was the 'sensation' of its end of year poll of British exhibitors. After only one film he was the third-highest grossing British star and the 'fact that he's been a television personality for several years was no detriment'.[49] This was reinforced in the oral history interviews. Mike Higginbottom recalled that 'I remember Norman Wisdom, which we thought was hysterical. I mean we thought he was an absolute hoot, couldn't get enough. Which I think was the popular view, he was big bucks in the British film industry in the fifties'.[50] From 1956 to 1958, the Rex also screened *Man of the Moment* (UK, 1955), *Up in the World* (UK, 1956) and *Just my Luck* (UK, 1957). In 1958–9, *The Square Peg* was the most successful film at the Rex and was brought back for a second time.

In Belfast, films with a local connection, such as *Odd Man Out, Jacqueline* and *A Night to Remember*, were particularly popular. At the Rex, the evidence that films with a local connection generated increased revenue is mixed. There were very few films that represented aspects of Sheffield, though when there was, the cinema exploited it in their advertising. In November 1949, the Rex screened *The Case of Charles Peace* (UK, 1949), the story of the Victorian Sheffield criminal hanged for murder. It was the tenth highest grossing film of that year and generated £453. Other films, however, do not show a direct correlation between a local connection and increased box-office success. In July 1951, the cinema screened *When You Come Home* (UK, 1947) and advertised it as 'good clean Yorkshire fun' starring Frank Randle. The film generated only £282 in box-office revenue, well below the average of £327 per film in 1951. In February 1959, it exhibited *Tread Softly Stranger* (UK, 1958). Harper and Porter described the film as a clumsy melodrama, yet claim that it performed well at the box office.[51] In their advertisement for the film, the Rex boasted that it was 'Sheffield and district's own film taken against the fiery background of Steel'.[52] Despite this, the film generated only £165, well below the average of £184 per film in 1959. This points to a segregation of tastes within Sheffield. Perhaps the Rex's patrons, located on the edge of the city were trying to get away from Sheffield. At the city centre Gaumont, Sheldon Hall observed that local factors drew audiences to the cinema who, for instance, were attracted by the topic of *Steel Town* (US, 1952).[53]

[49] *Motion Picture Herald*, 1 Jan. 1955.
[50] Interview with Mike Higginbottom, Sheffield, 20 Aug. 2015.
[51] Harper and Porter, *British Cinema of the 1950s*, p. 164.
[52] *The Star*, 19 Feb. 1959.
[53] Hall, 'Going to the Gaumont', pp. 65.

Cartoon/Classic Cinema, 1961–4

In 1945, the Electra Palace closed for alterations and reopened as the Sheffield News Theatre, screening a variety of 'news, documentary, travel and educational films'.[54] In 1947, the cinema held a capacity of 491 and screened continuous programmes throughout the week with prices ranging from 10*d* to 1*s* 6*d*. It was operated by Capital and Provincial News Theatres, who in 1946 ran six news theatres: four in London, one in Liverpool and one in Sheffield.[55] These specialized cinemas were relatively rare outside of London and, in 1951, Rowntree and Lavers observed that while news items used to constitute the majority of the programme, 'animated cartoons, travel films, and films on matters of general interest such as sports, fashions, and domestic economy, make up the balance'.[56] The fact that the News Theatre changed its names to the Cartoon Cinema in 1959 reflects these developments.[57] In 1961, *The Economist* adopted a patronizing tone, stating that news and cartoon cinemas 'serve a well-defined demand: to while away the idle hours which beset unintellectual people in large cities, whether waiting for trains, avoiding the rush hour or simply lonely in their lunch-breaks'.[58] Figure 5.4 suggests the importance of the itinerant audience, showing the cinema's location next to a major tram terminus. The oral history testimony also shows it was attended by city centre workers. 'Occasionally on a wet day at lunchtime, we'd pop down to the News Theatre and see that for an hour with a sticky bun or a sandwich', recalled David Ludlam.[59]

The Cartoon Cinema's admissions fell steeply during the second half of 1961, from 30,677 in August to 20,850 in December. In January 1962, the cinema was renovated (see Figure 5.5), the seating capacity reduced to 484 and reopened as the Classic Cinema, replacing the variety programme with screenings of older feature films.[60] This trend occurred across the county and by 1963, Capital and Provincial Theatres operated eighteen of their twenty-eight cinemas under the Classic moniker.[61] The day book of the Cartoon Cinema runs from April 1961 to January 1962 and contains information on programming, weather, admissions (subdivided by price category), daily returns and weekly Levy payments. A separate day book

---

[54] R. Ward, *In Memory of Sheffield's Cinemas* (Sheffield, 1988), p. 47; *The Star,* 14 June 1945.
[55] *Kinematograph Year Book 1946* (London, 1946), p. 365.
[56] S. Rowntree and G. R. Lavers, *English Life and Leisure: a Social Study* (London, 1951), pp. 251–2.
[57] *Kinematograph Year Book 1959* (London, 1959), p. 330.
[58] *The Economist*, 24 June 1961.
[59] Interview with David Ludlam, Sheffield, 25 June 2014.
[60] P. Tuffrey, *South Yorkshire's Cinemas and Theatres* (Stroud, 2011), p. 94.
[61] *Kinematograph and Television Year Book 1963* (London, 1963), p. 222.

Figure 5.4. Cartoon Cinema, Fitzalan Square, Sheffield, c.1959–60 (Picture Sheffield, Sheffield City Council Archives and Local Studies Service).

for the Classic contains information on programming, daily admissions, daily gross revenue, weekly Levy payments and net profit until November 1964. The fact that both day books contain daily weather reports indicate its importance to exhibitors and its impact on cinema attendance. In 1961, *The Economist* noted that the audience in news and cartoon cinemas was 'drawn indiscriminately from the amorphous crowds outside. A shower of rain will bring in coatless hundreds, a fog will fill them for the whole twelve hours of their daily opening, [and] winter winds will drive the most respectable to a taste for this slightly disreputable … entertainment'.[62]

From April 1961 to January 1962, the Cartoon Cinema changed its programme on Sunday and Thursday, which included a range of items including news, pictorials, cartoons, short comedy features, sports footage and serials. In the week beginning 23 April, for instance, it screened *Loopy De Loop*, *Donald Duck*, *Sylvester*, *Dutch Flowers*, *Look at Life*, *Tom and Jerry* and *Royal Review*. Although the Cartoon Cinema released new programmes on Sunday, Figure 5.6 shows that it was the least popular day for attendance. Mondays were more popular and attendances then declined on Tuesday and Wednesday. The release of a new programme led

[62] *The Economist*, 24 June 1961.

180

Figure 5.5. Classic Cinema, Fitzalan Square, Sheffield, 1963 (Picture Sheffield, Sheffield City Council Archives and Local Studies Service).

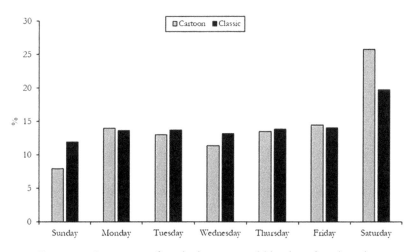

Figure 5.6. Percentage of total admissions sold by day of week at the Cartoon Cinema, April 1961–January 1962 and the Classic Cinema, January 1962–November 1964 (source: Cinema Theatre Association Archive, day book of the Sheffield Cartoon Cinema and Classic Cinema).

to increased attendances on Thursday and admissions increased further on Friday and Saturday. Saturday was by far the most popular day with 26 per cent of admissions. From January to July 1962 the Classic exhibited single feature programmes and in August switched to a two-feature programme. It changed its programme weekly and had no separate Sunday programme. Following the conversion, Saturday remained the most popular day for attendance, though admissions were distributed more evenly during the rest of the week. Sundays were far more popular at the Classic than they were at the Cartoon Cinema. The highest grossing day at the Classic was for the screening of *Wuthering Heights* (US, 1939) on Saturday 10 February 1962, when it generated £270 from the sale of 1,528 admissions. It is possible that the success of this pre-war film had something to do with its mythologized Yorkshire setting. Seven of the ten highest grossing days were Saturdays and the three highest grossing Saturdays were all in January and February 1962.

Fixed programmes and greater admission prices at the Classic meant that it was able to generate far greater amounts of revenue than the Cartoon Cinema. From 23 April 1961 to 13 January 1962, the average ticket price at the Cartoon Cinema was 1s 7d and it generated £15,635 (202,147 admissions). In its final week of operation it yielded £419 in gross box-office revenue (5,351 admissions). In the Classic's first week of operation, it yielded £1,030 (6,013 admissions). From 15 January to 31 December 1962, the average ticket price at the Classic was 3s 6d and it generated £40,211 (235,102 admissions). Table 5.4 displays admissions and revenue during six-monthly intervals from July 1961 to June 1964. From April 1961 to January 1962, the Cartoon Cinema yielded a daily average of £59 (763 admissions). In contrast, from 15 January 1962 to 14 November 1964, the Classic yielded a daily average of £110 (645 admissions). This demonstrates that, by charging increased prices for extended programmes, the cinema was able to generate exponentially greater revenue despite the fact that attendance declined significantly. In May 1962, *The Star* reported that:

> The Classic Cinema is proving in Sheffield that the condition of the industry is not so critical that it can't revive itself with regular doses of vintage films, to show they still look a lot better in their natural surroundings — and possibly prove films are neither better nor worse than they were. The best thing about this recovery is that it seems to be happening with dignity. There are surprisingly few gimmicks.[63]

---

[63] *Sheffield Telegraph*, 23 May 1962.

Table 5.4. Gross box-office revenue and admissions at
the Sheffield Cartoon/Classic Cinema, 1961–4.

Six months ending	Admissions	Gross box-office revenue (£)
December 1961	139,799	10,772
June 1961	123,843	20,075
December 1962	123,428	21,066
June 1963	122,454	20,791
December 1963	123,334	20,536
June 1964	118,454	20,505

Source: Cinema Theatre Association Archive, day book of the Sheffield Cartoon/Classic
Cinema, Sheffield.

The Cartoon's average weekly attendance was 5,320 with admissions
ranging from 3,146 in the week beginning 25 June 1961 to 7,828 in the
week beginning 21 May 1961. The fact that the latter was Whitsuntide week
led admissions to increase by 74 per cent from the previous programme.
New Year was also a motivator for attendance and in the week beginning 31
December the Cartoon cinema sold the fifth highest number of admissions.
The correlation between public holidays and increased cinema attendance
lasted well into the 1960s. In 1964, Easter Sunday fell on 29 March and in
this week the Classic sold 8,290 admissions to *King Solomon's Mines* (US,
1950), making it the best attended week in the period under review (see
Table 5.5). This film was as big an attraction as it was in 1951, when it was
the third-highest grossing film at the British box-office.[64] The programme
was clearly a key determinant of attendance and Table 5.5 shows the ten
highest weekly attendances at the Classic. *King Solomon's Mines* (US, 1950),
The Dam Busters (UK, 1955) and *Doctor at Large* (UK, 1957) were popular in
their original screenings at the Rex and *Fancy Pants* (US, 1950) was the third
highest grossing film at the Gaumont in 1950.

Sheffield Library Theatre and branch libraries, 1947–62

A significant minority of Sheffield cinema-goers complained at the lack of
screening of films produced outside either America or Britain. In 1948, one
Star reader complained that 'while mediocre American and British films are
regularly shown on the screens of Sheffield cinemas, no space can apparently
be found for the masterpieces produced by French and Italian studios'.[65]
Groups such as the Sheffield Film Society and the City Films Kine Society,

[64] *The 1952–3 Motion Picture and Television Almanac* (New York, 1952), p. 924.
[65] *The Star*, 15 Sept. 1948.

Table 5.5. Ten highest weekly attendances, Classic
Cinema, January 1962–November 1964.

Week beginning Sunday	First feature	Second feature	Admissions	Gross revenue (£)	Levy (£)
29/03/64	King Solomon's Mines (US, 1950)	Tarzan, the Ape Man (US, 1959)	8,290	1,536	129
05/08/62	Carlton Browne of the F.O. (UK, 1959)	The Tall Men (US, 1955)	7,446	1,308	108
04/02/62	Wuthering Heights (US, 1939)		7,034	1,191	97
24/02/63	The Dam Busters (UK, 1955)	The Flame of Araby (US, 1952)	6,893	1,201	98
21/06/64	Freaks (US, 1932)	The Green Mare's Nest (France/Italy, 1959)	6,798	1,143	93
29/12/63	Sergeants 3 (US, 1962)	Morgan the Pirate (US, 1961)	6,727	1,149	94
12/08/62	Two Way Stretch (UK, 1960)	Laughter in Paradise (UK, 1951)	6,615	1,129	92
11/08/63	G.I. Blues (US, 1960)	Fancy Pants (US, 1950)	6,615	1,137	93
14/04/63	Doctor at Large (UK, 1957)	Hercules (Italy, 1957)	6,528	1,138	93
25/08/63	Journey to the Center of the Earth (US, 1959)	The Misadventures of Buster Keaton (US, 1950)	6,346	1,073	87

Source: Cinema Theatre Association, day book of the Sheffield Classic Cinema, Sheffield.

provided a forum for the exhibition of foreign language films. In 1959, student newspaper *Darts* claimed that these 'save the city from being a cinematic desert'.[66] The membership of Sheffield Film Society increased from 358 in 1954 to 550 in 1958 and society secretary B. D. Laitner commented that while the society had 'quite a good cross section of the community – school teachers, business and professional people and students', they wished to attract more young members.[67] In June 1950, the Sheffield University Film Unit began screenings in Graves Hall and *Darts* reported that its purpose was 'to present in an atmosphere totally different from the bustle and push

[66] *Darts*, 5 March 1959.
[67] *The Star*, 29 Sept. 1954; 20 Jan. 1956; 19 Sept. 1957; 9 Sept. 1958.

of the ordinary commercial cinema, film classics that would otherwise not receive a showing in this benighted city'.[68] By 1962, the screenings were so popular that 2s tickets for *Hiroshima Mon Amour* (France/Japan, 1959) were reportedly sold on the black market for 7s 6d.[69]

Another forum for the dissemination of foreign language and alternative films was the screenings held at the Library Theatre. The published minutes of Sheffield City Council detail the film shows arranged by the Libraries, Art Galleries and Museums Committee between 1947 and 1962, and record programme and attendance of film screenings (see Figure 5.7). They complement the records of commercial cinemas such as the Rex and the Cartoon/Classic by showing the nature of alternative film exhibition in Sheffield and demonstrating that there was a demand for foreign language films and programmes aimed at younger audiences. The Library Theatre is located in the basement of Sheffield City Library and first held film screenings in November 1936.[70] In 1951, *Kelly's Directory of Sheffield and Rotherham* recorded that the 390-seat Library Theatre (see Figure 5.8) 'is equipped by Arc cinema projectors and the libraries provide each winter a series of film weeks showing adult feature films, foreign films and documentaries. Saturday feature films for children are also shown. Total attendances reach 22,000 yearly'.[71] In April 1961, the Libraries Committee submitted plans for alterations to the Library Theatre. After renovations costing £10,000, it reopened in December with a reduced capacity of 268.[72] Film screenings were held from December to March 1962, though, following further renovations, film exhibition was stopped as a cost-saving measure.[73] From 1948, film screenings were also held in various branch libraries, such as Park, Hillsborough and Walkley.

In September 1947, 'the City Librarian submitted a proposal that free displays of films of an educational nature should be held one evening per month in the Library Theatre'. In his proposal, 'he stated that suitable films were available through the Central Film Library, and that the services of the Central Office of Information were available in connection with Exhibition of this nature'.[74] The purpose of these shows was 'to impart knowledge and stimulate interest in various subjects by documentaries; to arouse interest in literature through films based on good novels and plays; and to raise the

[68] *Darts*, 11 Nov. 1950.

[69] *The Star*, 17 March 1961.

[70] R. Harman and J. Minnis, *Pevsner Architectural Guides: Sheffield* (London, 2003), p. 101.

[71] *Kelly's Directory of Sheffield and Rotherham and Suburbs, 1951* (Sheffield, 1951), p. lxxiv.

[72] *The Star*, 8 Dec. 1961.

[73] Cinema Theatre Association Archive, Clifford Shaw, The Library Theatre.

[74] Sheffield Local Studies Library, minutes of Sheffield City Council Libraries, Art Galleries and Museums Committee, Sept. 1947, p. 533.

general standard of taste by films of outstanding merit, including some of the best foreign films'.[75] On Wednesday 12 November 1947, 376 patrons attended a series of documentary screenings on the subject of commonwealth and empire.[76] From November 1947 to April 1948, the Library Theatre hosted a further seven midweek documentary screenings and 2,629 citizens watched films on themes such as 'Industrial Britain', 'Educating the Young' and 'Secrets of Nature'. In May 1948, 'the City Librarian was directed to arrange a draft programme for fortnightly shows to be held during next winter including, if possible, a number of films in foreign languages'.[77] From October 1948, screenings were held fortnightly and there were two showings of each programme. Separate screenings were organized for adults and children. Attendance normally declined in the second screening and, for instance, a programme titled 'Fur and Feather' attracted 400 patrons in its first showing and only 242 in its second. In the week beginning 7 March 1949, the library held separate screenings for adults and grammar school children of its first foreign language feature film, *Une Femme Disparaît* (Switzerland, 1944).

In 1950, the library introduced 'film weeks' and Clifford Shaw explained that '[o]n Mondays and Tuesdays there were programmes of documentary shorts; on Wednesdays and Thursdays there was a foreign language feature, while on Fridays and Saturdays there was an English speaking film based on a literary work ... in addition to the performances on Friday and Saturday evening there was a Saturday matinee'.[78] In June 1950, the city librarian explained that while the film shows at the Library Theatre were devoted to feature films 'to be shown three times (one morning, two afternoons) on six Saturdays during the Winter', screenings at branch libraries consisted of six 'monthly showings of documentaries with a cartoon where one can be obtained'. They added further that tickets were to 'be issued through the Children's Libraries and Children's Corners to children using the libraries and that no adults [were] to be admitted to these performances'.[79] On 25 September 1950, it was confirmed that the film programme for both children and adults 'was submitted and approved' and that instructions

---

[75] Sheffield City Archives, CA990/48, Sheffield City Council, Libraries, Archives and Information Files, correspondence and papers regarding Library Theatre.

[76] Sheffield Local Studies Library, minutes of Sheffield City Council Libraries, Art Galleries and Museums Committee, 15 Dec. 1947, p. 79.

[77] Sheffield Local Studies Library, minutes of Sheffield City Council Libraries, Art Galleries and Museums Committee, 24 May 1948, p. 358.

[78] Cinema Theatre Association Archive, Clifford Shaw, The Library Theatre.

[79] Sheffield Local Studies Library, minutes of Sheffield City Council Libraries, Art Galleries and Museums Committee, 19 June 1950, p. 88.

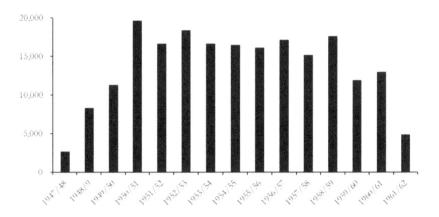

Figure 5.7. Annual attendance of film screenings at the Library Theatre, Sheffield (source: Sheffield Local Studies Library, minutes of Sheffield City Council Libraries, Art Galleries and Museums Committee, 1947–62).

Figure 5.8. Film screening at the Library Theatre, Sheffield, November 1950 (Picture Sheffield, Sheffield City Council Archives and Local Studies Service).

'were given for a copy of the programme to be forwarded to each member of the Council'.[80] In October 1950, the Library Theatre screened three films for adults: *This Modern Age* (UK, 1946–50), *Monsieur Vincent* (France, 1947) and *Henry V* (UK, 1944). *This Modern Age* was the least popular of these and 690 admissions were recorded at five screenings. *Henry V* attracted the most patrons and 1,096 admissions were recorded for three screenings. This film was also successful at the Regent, when manager Frank Bradley arranged viewings for 12,000 schoolchildren.[81]

Monsieur Vincent was screened only twice and attracted 778 patrons. However, its average attendance of 389 was higher than that of 365 for *Henry V*. In October, the screening of *Treasure Island* (US/UK, 1950) was almost as popular and 1,093 admissions for three screenings were recorded. During the 1950–51 season, 13,060 admissions were recorded for fifty-nine adult screenings of eighteen separate programmes. For children, 5,211 admissions were recorded for eighteen screenings of six separate programmes. While the Central Library offered a broader service for adults, the service for children was better attended in terms of individual screenings. In 1949–50, the library produced a 3*d* printed programme. For the 1951–52 season of films, they printed 2,500 printed programmes, including 500 complimentary copies. On 3 October 1951, the chairman reported that, from 11 to 27 September it sold 803 copies. He stated that the previous year '3,500 copies were printed and 2,959 sold. Receipts from sales covered approximately half the printing costs'. [82] As the service expanded, its operating costs increased. In 1949–50, the library paid only £40 on film hire, £10 in projectionist's fees and £15 in steward's fees. By 1955–6, it paid £293 on film hire and £123 on operations.[83]

In 1948, screenings were introduced at Hillsborough, Firth Park, Walkley and Woodhouse. In October 1949, *The Star* reported that:

> [m]ore film shows for adults and children will be given in Sheffield libraries during the winter. This year, shows are being given as before at Firth Park, Hillsborough, Walkley and Woodhouse junior libraries, and for the first time at the Park Junior Library and the new Ecclesall branch. When building is completed they will also be shown at the new Attercliffe junior library and the proposed branch at Southey.[84]

[80] Sheffield Local Studies Library, minutes of Sheffield City Council Libraries, Art Galleries and Museums Committee, 25 Sept. 1950, p. 232.

[81] *Motion Picture Herald*, 31 Aug. 1946.

[82] Sheffield Local Studies Library, Sheffield City Council Meeting, Chairman's Notes – Libraries Committee, 3 Oct. 1951.

[83] Sheffield City Archives, CA990/48, Sheffield City Council, Libraries, Archives and Information Files, correspondence and papers regarding Library Theatre.

[84] *The Star*, 18 Oct. 1949.

Screenings at Attercliffe, Southey and Upperthorpe were introduced in October 1950. In October 1958, screenings were introduced at Broomhill, and in November 1959, at Manor and Highfield. The largest recorded attendance at any of the branch libraries was 133, at the November 1959 screening of *Hamlet* (UK, 1948) at Firth Park.

As the service expanded, attendances increased significantly. In 1947–8, 2,629 were recorded at eight screenings. The following year, this increased to 10,215 admissions at fifty-seven screenings, and in 1949–50, 14,173 were recorded at seventy-seven screenings. 1950–1 was the peak year for attendance and 24,314 admissions were recorded at 131 screenings. Even at their most popular, library screenings drew much smaller audiences than their commercial counterparts due to the library theatres' small seating capacity, the nature of the films screened, and the infrequent nature of exhibition.

In 1950–51, the average attendances for adult and children's screenings were 221 and 290 respectively. Screenings for children at nine branch libraries contributed a further 4,666 admissions. Of the 22,937 admissions recorded during the 1950–51 season of film screenings, 9,877 (43 per cent) were for children, and 13,060 (57 per cent) were for adult screenings. In each month, the three separate adult programmes were normally a series of documentaries, a foreign language film and a feature film adaptation of a novel. In December 1950, the Library Theatre screened *The Blue Angel* (Germany, 1930), David Lean's adaptation of *Great Expectations* (UK, 1946) and a series of documentaries on the theme of 'inventions and discoveries'. While feature films were screened either two or three times, documentaries were screened five times and tended to have smaller numbers in attendance. In 1950–1, while the average attendance at individual documentary screenings was 131, the equivalent figure for feature films was 315. Of these, the twelve screenings of foreign language films attracted 3,786 patrons at an average attendance of 316 per screening. The foreign language films were proportionally as popular as the literary adaptations and the latter attracted 5,347 to seventeen separate screenings, with an average attendance of 315. During 1950–1, adult documentaries were attended by 3,927 people, foreign films were attended by 3,786 people, feature films were attended by 5,347 people and children's films were attended by 5,211 people.

In 1951, the format for adult screenings remained and an extra documentary screening for children was introduced. This format remained largely intact for the duration of the free film screenings the library offered until 1962. In August 1954, the Library Committee altered the age limits 'in respect of the admission of children to Film Shows at Branch Libraries and at the Central Library'. For children's film shows the minimum age of admission was lowered from nine to seven years. For documentary film shows, they proposed changing the current rule – no children under fourteen to be admitted unless accompanied by an adult – to no restrictions except those applied by the BBFC. Many screenings, however, were unaffected as they noted that the 'present minimum age limit of 16 years in respect of the admission of children to foreign and feature films at the Central Library Theatre will continue to apply'.[85] The latter changed in July 1959 when the Libraries Sub-Committee decided 'that the present regulations governing the admission of children to Film Shows at the Central Library Theatre be varied to provide for the admission to foreign and feature films carrying "U" or "A" Certificates, of children aged 11 to 16 years accompanied by adults'.[86]

Though the Library Theatre ceased film exhibition in 1962, the library service continued branch library screenings during the period under review. Other cinemas filled the vacuum left by the library screenings and from 1964 the Abbeydale cinema hosted the Sheffield Film Society. The group's secretary stated that the society was set up to show outstanding films, believing that 'some cinemas in Sheffield underestimate the taste of their customers'. [87] In February 1964, it screened *The Pelicans* (Romania, 1962, original title: *Printre Pelicani*), *Just for Fun* (USA, 1963) and *Knife in the Water* (Poland, 1962, original title: *Noz w Wodzie*).[88] In 1965, the British Film Institute's John Huntley praised the strength of alternative film exhibition in Sheffield. He claimed that the city was left out of plans for a national film theatre as '[w]ith a Classic Cinema, a university film society and a good city film society you are better off at this level than many cities'.[89]

Conclusion

One key feature of recent scholarship in new cinema history has been the desire to integrate quantitative and qualitative methods. The detailed analysis of three venues presented here helps to narrow this gap by connecting the social experience of cinema-going discussed in previous chapters to box-office data and audience figures that show the constraints placed upon exhibitors and the ways they adapted to cater for their patrons. These findings magnify changes in cinema-going behaviour that are often written about in more generalized ways and throw the trends they refer to into sharp relief. The Rex was defined by its status as an independent upmarket

---

[85] Sheffield Local Studies Library, minutes of Sheffield City Council Libraries, Art Galleries and Museums Committee, 16 Aug. 1954, p. 200.

[86] Sheffield Local Studies Library, minutes of Sheffield City Council Libraries, Art Galleries and Museums Committee, Libraries Sub-Committee, 14 July 1959, p. 264.

[87] *The Star*, 3 Oct. 1964.

[88] Programme of the Sheffield Film Society, Feb. 1964. Courtesy of Margaret O'Brien.

[89] *The Star*, 2 Apr. 1965.

suburban cinema. The post-war slump in cinema audiences affected its profitability, but it fared better than many of its local rivals, managing to negotiate the challenges of increased expenditure without significantly altering its exhibition model. The Cartoon Cinema, meanwhile, found that upgrading its premises and replacing its variety programme with screenings of reissues and classic films led to far greater revenue. The screenings organized at the Library Theatre and other branch libraries show the benefits of looking beyond conventional cinemas to assess films with little commercial potential. Children's screenings also show there were alternatives to the westerns and serials of Saturday matinees. It is significant that attendances at the Library Theatre for its explicitly didactic programme remained stable at a time when cinema attendance was in freefall.

Films with a local angle appear to have been less of a draw than in Belfast, but there were intra-city variations and this altered significantly between venues. The success or failure of individual films also depended on a range of external factors such as the weather or the time and date of exhibition. The amorphous and unpredictable nature of audiences meant that cinemas often found it difficult to predict the success of any particular film. In 1962, journalist Anthony Tweedale cited the example of *King of Kings* (US, 1961), 'which arrived in the West End in the shadow of "Ben Hur," amid great ballyhoo, did fairly well there, flopped a bit in the provinces – but did wonders in Sheffield?'[90] But by bringing the records of several venues together it is possible for historians to provide reasons for film popularity in post-war Sheffield and perhaps to begin to enter the audience's mindscape.

[90] *Sheffield Telegraph*, 23 May 1962.

Conclusion

By assessing the people who visited the cinema and the places where they watched films, this book set out to examine and assess regional variations in cinema's decline across the United Kingdom from the end of the Second World War to the mid 1960s. One of its central aims has been to investigate the importance of place, alongside age, class and gender in shaping the cinema-going experience. In paying close attention to the detail provided by case studies of Belfast and Sheffield, it becomes clear that post-war patterns of cinema attendance were more heterogeneous than scholars such as Hanson, Harper and Porter have previously suggested. The methodological approach adopted in this research is a response to the spatial turn of new cinema history and the call for more empirical work that connects detailed regional findings of cinema-going to broader national developments. This investigation also contributes to the wider social and cultural history of post-war Britain, showing the connection between place, space and changing leisure habits over a period of twenty years.

Between 1945 and 1965, the nature of cinemas and the social function of cinema-going changed dramatically. Richard Farmer's study of wartime cinema-going showed the impact of the war on leisure habits in the immediate post-war years.[1] Restrictions on other leisure activities inflated cinema attendance and it continued to play a crucial role in the social lives of millions. Though admissions fell from 1948 onwards, they did not fall below their 1939 level until 1957. From 1957 to 1965 UK cinema admissions then fell dramatically from 915 million to 327 million. This decline did not occur uniformly. The fact that Northern Ireland had higher unemployment rates and lower average wages than other UK regions meant that cinema attendance remained buoyant for longer in Belfast than in Sheffield. This book confirms that the arrival of television was significant in cinema's decline, yet while the 1953 coronation certainly accelerated the growth of television ownership, it was also an important cinematic event that complemented and enhanced the television broadcast. The growth of television ownership should be viewed alongside a range of social and economic factors, all of

---

[1] R Farmer, *Cinemas and Cinema-Going in Wartime Britain: the Utility Dream Palace* (Manchester, 2016).

which were place specific and geographically diverse. In the 1950s, higher wages, greater amounts of disposable income and improved housing led people away from 'traditional' commercial leisure activities, such as the cinema, to home-centred activities, such as television viewing. The young urban working class were the most frequent cinema-goers, but the range of social spaces available to them expanded and there was a greater range of consumer goods for them to spend their money on. Simultaneously, greater amounts of disposable income, coupled with increased car ownership and a reduction in public transport services, meant that some citizens preferred to spend their leisure time further from home.

By 1965, cinema-going was more of an occasional activity than a habitual practice. People expected more from programmes and the content of a film became a greater determinant of attendance. As the regional controller for Star Cinemas stated in 1962: 'Everybody wanted films after the war, whatever they were like. It has never been the same since 1950'.[2] There were generational differences in cinema's decline and it became a more youth-oriented leisure activity. In the first chapter, an investigation of cinema's changing social role during the life cycle showed how its function and meaning changed from childhood to adolescence and into adulthood. Inner-city and suburban cinemas generally served their local communities and their closure made it difficult for those with family commitments and financial constraints to attend. Adolescents, meanwhile, spent greater amounts of their disposable income to travel to city centre cinemas as they provided social spaces for courtship free from the prying eyes of friends and relatives.

This book has shown that perhaps the most significant change of this period was to the place of cinemas in the built environment, a factor determined to a great extent by the actions of the large cinema chains. In 1945, cinemas were a visible presence in most parts of Belfast and Sheffield. By 1965, closures meant that there was a greater concentration of city centre cinemas and the pre-war cinemas that remained were often seen as uncomfortable and outdated relics. In the mid 1950s, the Rank Organisation increased its presence in Belfast by purchasing cinemas from local chains. In the early 1960s it closed many of its smaller inner-city and suburban cinemas, embarking on a programme of modernization and renovation of key sites. The fact that cinema attendance remained strong in Belfast encouraged independent exhibitors to construct cinemas to serve new housing estates on the outskirts of the city. Meanwhile, in Sheffield Rank adopted a different policy and, in 1956, constructed a large city centre cinema

---

[2] *Sheffield Telegraph*, 24 May 1962.

on a site it had purchased before the Second World War. Many of Sheffield's interwar housing estates were served by existing cinemas and exhibitors were unwilling to invest in new sites in suburban areas. ABC adopted a similar policy to Rank and constructed a new city-centre cinema in 1961. As cinema attendance declined, exhibitors had to do more to attract patrons and there was a greater focus on a more comfortable experience in better equipped buildings. In both cities, exhibitors emphasized the advantages of cinema over television through the introduction of new technologies such as CinemaScope. Reports of new cinemas highlighted the comfort, design and technological superiority over their pre-war counterparts. Though these reports were often promotional tools for the cinemas, they show the extent that citizens' expectations of leisure time had increased. Upmarket city-centre cinemas were the ones best placed to cope with these developments.

The use of oral testimony reveals that many aspects of the cinema-going experience were recalled in both Belfast and Sheffield, and residents no doubt shared similar experiences to cinema-goers in other industrial cities such as Birmingham, Cardiff, Dublin and Glasgow. In both cities a range of factors influenced cinema attendance, including accessibility, affordability, programming, relationships, publicity, travel, weather, work and domestic responsibilities. There was a clear hierarchy of cinemas and patrons made distinctions between local 'fleapits' and city centre 'picture palaces'. There were also intra-cinema distinctions as separate price categories and entrances meant that patrons remained segregated into the 1960s. In contrast, dance halls were more democratic spaces, with one admission price, one entrance and no delineation of patrons along socio-economic lines.[3] Patrons in both cities recalled everyday aspects of audience behaviour, such as smoking and queuing, and more conspicuous acts of rowdyism and misbehaviour. Cinemas were also recalled as sites of consumption and the purchase of ancillary items such as sweets, chocolate and ice cream was central to the cinema-going experience.

This research, however, has demonstrated that it is the variations in cinema-going customs between residents of Belfast and Sheffield that offer the greatest insight into the geographical diversity of leisure habits in the United Kingdom. Cinema-going was often determined at the local level by the range of cinemas available in communities and neighbourhoods. An examination of areas such as Heeley or the Holyland shows the importance of communal relationships and the close connection of people to their surrounding district. Decisions made by local governments, such as Belfast

---

[3] J. Nott, *Going to the Palais: a Social and Cultural History of Dancing and Dance Halls in Britain, 1918–1960* (Oxford, 2015), p. 306.

Corporation's refusal to permit Sunday opening, also affected cinema-going habits. There was no single cinema-going experience and patrons brought their own beliefs, values and experiences to each cinema trip. They were active consumers and displayed clear preferences for certain types of films. Though it was largely the same Hollywood fare that predominated in both cities, several films were disproportionately popular in either Belfast or Sheffield. The oral history testimony reveals the regionality of audience responses and it is apparent that Belfast cinema-goers had more distinct preferences than their Sheffield counterparts. Patrons reacted differently to British and American films and connected their memories to life experiences and the places where they lived. It is unsurprising therefore that Belfast cinema-goers displayed a preference for the small number of Irish-themed films that were shown during the period under review.

The most conspicuous difference between the two cities was the impact of Belfast's cultural conservatism and sectarian divide on the cinema-going habits of its citizens. This book shows that social and religious divisions manifested themselves in aspects of audience behaviour, such as reactions to *God Save the Queen* at the end of the evening's performance. Responses to the screening of *The Conquest of Everest* at the Strand showed the potential for divisions when mixed audiences were present. While social and geographical ties limited interaction between Catholics and Protestants, city centre cinemas were still largely shared leisure spaces. The segregated nature of many neighbourhoods meant that it was socioeconomic differences that were the most noticeable in local cinemas. While sectarian divisions meant that the exhibition of films such as *Martin Luther* were controversial, they did not prevent unionists from finding pleasure in *The Quiet Man*, or nationalists from enjoying the spectacle of the coronation in glorious Technicolor. These findings challenge dominant post-war narratives of Northern Ireland and provide a clearer picture of how wider social and economic changes impacted on leisure and social habits in Belfast.

The broad range of qualitative and quantitative sources used in this study have allowed for a detailed exploration of exhibition, programming and audience habits. Many business records and box-office figures of individual cinemas no longer remain, but those that do exist provide tangible evidence of programming strategies and film popularity in regional contexts. By combining these records with other sources it becomes clear that patterns of attendance were shaped by a range of factors other than the films themselves, such as the weather, the day of the week or the occurrence of public holidays. Cinema attendance was temperamental and responsive to local developments. An influenza epidemic could deter patrons or a rival attraction could quickly draw them away. The range of factors that drew patrons to the cinema were often interconnected and the example of

Captain Boycott shows the difficulty in disentangling the attraction of the cinema programme from the time and date of exhibition.

This book's use of existing sources in new ways, such as the works of post-war sociologists, offers new ways to link local patterns of cinema attendance to work, housing and leisure patterns. Local newspapers such as the *Belfast Telegraph* and the Sheffield *Star* help us to understand the spatial elements of cinema's decline as they offered different reasons for cinema closures and discussed these factors at different times. By drawing upon newspapers and trade journals in conjunction with 'bottom-up' testimony gathered from oral history interviews, this book has revealed the contrast between industry perspectives and the experiences of ordinary cinema-goers. This combination of sources also shows how the decline in attendance was understood, experienced and perceived in relation to space and place. The oral history testimony presented here shares characteristics with memories gathered by new cinema historians such as Matthew Jones and Annette Kuhn. Recollections of individual films were limited as interviewees emphasized the spatial and social elements of cinema-going and its connection to everyday life. This testimony does not provide a transparent view of the past and there were many aspects of audience behaviour that went unmentioned in the oral history interviews. Newspaper reports, for instance, frequently allude to sexual activity. In the work of Jancovich et al., the authors noted that memories of courtship were both 'positive and negative – both as a place of sexual awakening or as a place of sexual threat or harassment'.[4] While almost all the interviewees recalled the cinema as an important courtship venue, many did not expand beyond this. The fact that almost all the interviewees chose to identify themselves may have limited the amount of information they wished to reveal on the subject of sexual activity. There was also a reluctance, and perhaps timidity, on the part of the author to probe too far on the subject of sex in interviews with an older generation that were advertised as discussions of cinemas and cinema-going.

Many of the book's themes could be productively explored further. In his study of wartime cinema-going, Farmer dedicated a chapter to the men and women who worked in cinemas and 'who contributed to the production of an experience that was central to many millions of people every day'.[5] Where cinema employees have been considered in this book, the focus has been on how they provided a service to patrons and a thorough examination of cinema staff is an area for future research, especially as the number of

---

[4] M. Jancovich, L. Faire and S. Stubbings, *The Place of the Audience: Cultural Geographies of Film Consumption* (London, 2003), p. 173.

[5] Farmer, *Cinemas and Cinema-going in Wartime Britain*, p. 127.

staff employed fell from 78,981 in 1950 to 48,100 in 1961.[6] What happened to the managers, commissionaires, usherettes and projectionists who were also victims of cinema closures?[7] The records of Entertainments Duty are extant for many cinemas in Northern Ireland and there is scope for an economic history of cinemas that considers the contrast between cinemas in urban and rural locations, and which would build on current work on cinema-going in smaller towns.[8] These could also be compared to cinemas in the Republic of Ireland and further afield. In this book, council minutes have been deployed to show how local authorities regulated the cinema-going experience. They could, however, be used to explore regulation and censorship more extensively. Local newspaper reports reveal the high level of criminal activity in cinemas. These crimes include assault and petty theft by patrons, safe robberies during closed hours and exhibitors who were prosecuted for failure to comply with regulations. While examples of these crimes have been used in this book there is greater scope to assess the extent that cinema provided a locus for criminal activity, the role of exhibitors in preventing crime and the responses of the police and local authorities.

The downward curve in admissions continued from 1965 onwards. In Sheffield, cinema closures continued throughout the 1960s and from 1966 to 1969 a further four cinemas shut their doors. In the same period, UK cinema attendance fell from 289 million to 215 million and many venues were converted into dance halls, bowling alleys and bingo halls. The relative power of ABC and Rank increased and by 1965 they operated more than two-fifths of cinema seats. Many cinemas were subdivided and, in 1969, the Sheffield Gaumont became Rank's fifth two-screen cinema.[9] In Yorkshire and Humberside, cinema admissions fell from 20.6 million in 1966 to 7.5 million in 1975, and to 3.5 million in 1984.[10] The Odeon and the ABC closed in 1971 and 1988 respectively. In Belfast, the Apollo's closure in 1962 marked the end of the first wave of cinema closures, though five more cinemas closed from 1966 to 1967. The Troubles then hastened the decline of cinema-going as seventeen cinemas closed from 1969 to 1977. Civil disturbances led Rank to pull out of Northern Ireland in 1974 and in September 1977, the ABC

---

[6] *Kinematograph and Television Year Book* (London, 1963), p. 446.

[7] The subject of post-war female projectionists has received attention in R. Wallace, R. Harrison and C. Brunsdon, 'Women in the box: female projectionists in post-war British cinemas', *Journal of British Cinema and Television*, xv (2018), 46–65.

[8] M. Jones, 'Far from swinging London: memories of non-urban cinema-going in 1960s Britain', in *Cinema Beyond the City: Small-Town and Rural Film Culture in Europe*, ed. J. Thissen and C. Zimmerman (London, 2016), pp. 117–32.

[9] Cinema Theatre Association Archive, Clifford Shaw, The Regent.

[10] B. Doyle, 'The geography of cinemagoing in Great Britain, 1934–1994: a comment', *Historical Journal of Film, Radio and Television*, xxiii (2003), 59–71, at p. 63.

(Ritz), the New Vic (Royal Hippodrome/Odeon) and the Curzon were damaged by the IRA in a multiple firebomb attack.[11]

In many of the oral history interviews, participants reflected on their experiences in light of subsequent changes in the cities where they lived. While the majority of Sheffield interviewees understandably displayed nostalgia for former cinemas, there were many who viewed their demise as an inevitable part of post-war economic and social changes. David Ludlam, for instance, believed that cinemas:

> were an essential part of life in forty-five … it was an escapist spot when times were hard in the war. And gradually as other things took over, cinemas closed, tastes changed and I suppose you went along with that. I particularly didn't think, oh it's a shame that that's happened. It's just that something else came to take its place and the social scene changed.[12]

Local press reports also expressed similar sentiments. In May 1962, journalist Anthony Tweedale claimed that:

> [t]hree years ago there used to be 51 cinemas in Sheffield: now there are 19 in the suburbs, and seven in the city centre. But I doubt if this marks any great sociological upheaval. Many of the old cinemas would have had to go some time. Most would agree that nearly all the suburban houses that remain today are solid and reasonable, even if not the last word in luxury.[13]

These examples show that, for many people who lived during the period under review, the closure of outdated cinemas was simply a result of changing social habits. The evidence presented here, however, paints a more complicated picture linked to the broader social, cultural and economic developments of the United Kingdom.

By placing the leisure habits of Belfast residents in a broader geographical context, this book shows that the period under review was more than an antecedent to the Troubles. Although the interviews focused on the immediate post-war years, interviewees often discussed this period in relation to the later conflict. Noel Spence commented that cinemas:

> closed simply because people stopped going for a variety of reasons. One, TV, of course. But two, in Northern Ireland in particular, the Troubles. I mean people were too afraid to go out. Simple as that. I mean you weren't going to go out and risk getting blown up.[14]

---

[11]   M. Open, *Fading Lights, Silver Screen: a History of Belfast Cinemas* (Antrim, 1985), pp. 15–16.

[12]   Interview with David Ludlam, Sheffield, 25 June 2014.

[13]   *Sheffield Telegraph*, 24 May 1962.

[14]   Interview with Noel Spence, Comber, Co. Down, 26 March 2014.

Brian Hanna added that:

> it started to decline as television started to encroach and you've got to remember, by the time we got to 1969, groups of people gathering in cinemas and other places became riskier. I mean there was a vulnerability about the Troubles we had here. I think that wasn't the main reason it declined. I think maybe it had some impact. I think it was TV to a large extent and a more sophisticated public who had a wider range of things that they could do. But it was still popular.[15]

Belfast underwent many of the same social and economic changes as other industrial cities in the twenty years following the Second World War. This testimony, however, shows that cinema's decline is popularly understood as part of a broader chronology incorporating the Troubles.

In 1945, cinema was the UK's foremost commercial leisure activity, providing accessible and affordable entertainment to millions of citizens. As the nation moved from austerity to affluence, social habits changed and cinema was forced to compete with a range of other activities. By 1965, there were still over six million weekly cinema admissions, yet cinema was no longer *the* ubiquitous leisure activity. The closure of many cinemas meant that it was no longer a publicly visible part of communities, neighbourhoods and cities. As independent exhibitors fell by the wayside and large chains increased their share of the market, venues became increasingly uniform. By following the spatial turn in new cinema history to trace these developments, this research foregrounds the importance of place in shaping leisure habits and cinema cultures. The use of detailed case studies adopted here provides one way for new cinema history practitioners to connect local and national developments, and to investigate geographical variations in cinema habits.

[15] Interview with Brian Hanna, Belfast, 5 May 2015.

Appendices

Appendix 1. Belfast cinemas, 1945–65

Name	Location	Dates		Prices		Seating capacity
		Opening	Closing	1946	1962	
Alhambra	North Street	1872[1]	1959	6d to 2s		800
Alpha	Rathcoole	1957	1973			918
Ambassador	Cregagh Road	1936	1972	6d to 2s 3d		1,030
Apollo	Ormeau Road	1933	1962	7d to 1s	2s to 2s 6d	870
Arcadian	Albert Street	1912	1960	5d to 9d		600
Astoria	Newtownards Road	1934	1974	9d to 1s 9d	3s to 4s 6d	1,240
Broadway	Falls Road	1936	1972	9d to 1s 9d	2s to 3s 6d	1,380
Capitol	Antrim Road	1935	1975	9d to 1s 9d	2s to 3s 6d	1,000
Castle	Castlereagh Road	1934	1966	1s to 1s 9d	6d to 1s 6d	900
Central Picture Theatre	Smithfield	1913	1958	3d to 9d		440
Classic/Gaumont[2]	Castle Lane	1923	1961	1s to 3s 6d		1,807
Clonard Picture House	Falls Road	1913	1966	6d to 1s 6d		1,100
Coliseum	Grosvenor Road	1911	1959	6d to 1s		900
Crumlin Picture House	Crumlin Road	1914	1962	3d to 1s	6d to 2s	973
Curzon	Ormeau Road	1936	1999	7d to 1s 9d	2s to 3s 6d	1,478
Diamond Picture House	Falls Road	1920	1959	5d to 8d		600
Duncairn Picture Theatre	Duncairn Gardens	1916	1969	9d to 1s 6d	1s 6d to 2s 3d	826

Name	Location	Dates		Prices		Seating capacity
		Opening	Closing	1946	1962	
Forum	Crumlin Road	1937	1967		1s 9d to 2s 9d	1,250
Gaiety	North Street	1916	1956			900
Grand Opera House	Great Victoria Street	1895[3]	1972		3s 6d to 6s	
Imperial Picture House	Cornmarket	1914	1959	1s to 4s 6d		1,000
Lido	Shore Road	1955	1970		1s 6d to 2s 3d	1,025
Lyceum	New Lodge Road	1916	1961	9d to 1s 9d		950
Majestic	Lisburn Road	1936	1975			1,369
Mayfair[4]/News and Cartoon Cinema	College Square East	1910	1972	1s 9d to 3s 6d		500
Metro	Dundonald	1956	1961			1,000
New Princess Palace	Newtownards Road	1912	1960	9d to 1s		808
Park	Oldpark Road	1936	1972	9d to 1s 6d	1s to 1s 6d	960
Picture House/ Regent[5]	Royal Avenue	1911	1982	1s to 1s 3d	2s 4d	850
Picturedrome	Mountpottinger Road	1911	1970	9d to 2s	1s 9d to 3s	1,000
Popular Picture Theatre	Newtownards Road	1917	1962	3d to 1s	3d to 1s	700
Regal	Lisburn Road	1935	1967	9d to 1s 9d	3s to 4s 6d	1,380
Ritz/ABC[6]	Fisherwick Place	1936	1993			2,219
Royal	Arthur Square	1916	1961	1s to 2s		968
Royal Hippodrome/ Odeon[7]	Great Victoria Street	1907	1987	9d to 2s 3d	4s to 6s	1,800
Sandro	Sandy Row	1919	1961	3d to 9d		600
Savoy	Crumlin Road	1934	1967	6d to 1s 6d		1,050
Shankill Picturedrome	Shankill Road	1910	1958	3d to 6d		500
Stadium	Shankill Road	1937	1976		3s to 4s 6d	1,400

Name	Location	Dates		Prices		Seating capacity
		Opening	Closing	1946	1962	
Strand	Holywood Road	1935	Present			1,166
Tivoli	Finaghy	1955	1975		2s to 3s 6d	1,000
Troxy	Shore Road	1936	1977	9d to 2s	2s to 3s 6d	1,164
West End Picture House	Shankill Road	1913	1960	1d to 6d		800
Willowfield Picture House	Woodstock Road	1915	1973	9d to 1s		1,000
Windsor	Donegall Road	1935	1970	9d to 1s 9d	1s 6d to 2s 6d	1,250

Notes: [1] Film exhibition from 1953. [2] Renamed Gaumont in 1950. [3] Film exhibition from 1949. [4] Renamed News and Cartoon Cinema in 1958. [5] Renamed Regent in 1947. [6] Renamed ABC in 1963. [7] Renamed Odeon in 1960.

Sources: *Kinematograph Year Book 1947* (London, 1947), pp. 431–3; *Kinematograph and Television Year Book 1963* (London, 1963), pp. 353–6; M. Open, *Fading Lights, Silver Screens: a History of Belfast Cinemas* (Antrim, 1985).

Appendix 2. Sheffield cinemas, 1945–65

Name	Location	Dates		Prices		Seating capacity
		Opening	Closing	1946	1962	
Abbeydale Picture House	Abbeydale Road	1920	1975	6d to 1s 6d		1,512
ABC	Angel Street	1961	1988			1,327
Adelphi Picture Theatre	Vicarage Road	1920	1967	6d to 1s 6d	1s 9d to 2s 3d	1,238
Capitol/Essoldo[1]	Barnsley Road	1939	1975	10d to 2s 3d		1,716
Carlton	Eastern Avenue	1938	1959	10d to 1s 6d		1,222
Chantrey Picture House	Chesterfield Road	1920	1959	6d to 1s 6d		1,062
Cinema House	Barker's Pool	1913	1961	1s 9d to 2s 9d		763
Coliseum	Spital Hill	1913	1963	6d to 1s 6d		1,100

Name	Location	Dates		Prices		Seating capacity
		Opening	*Closing*	*1946*	*1962*	
Crookes Picture Palace	Crookes	1912	1960	10*d* to 1*s* 6*d*		647
Darnall Cinema	Catcliffe Road	1913	1957			483
Darnall Picture Palace	Staniforth Road	1913	1959	10*d* to 1*s* 6*d*		966
Don Picture Palace	West Bar	1912	1958	6*d* to 1*s* 6*d*		1,160
Electra Palace/ News Theatre/ Cartoon Cinema/ Classic Cinema[2]	Fitzalan Square	1911	1982	10*d* to 1*s* 6*d*		491
Forum/Essoldo[3]	Herries Road	1938	1969	10*d* to 2*s* 3*d*		1,814
Globe Picture Palace	Attercliffe Common	1913	1959	10*d* to 1*s* 6*d*		1,700
Greystones Picture Palace	Ecclesall Road	1914	1968	10*d* to 1*s* 9*d*	1*s* 3*d* to 3*s*	732
Heeley Coliseum	London Road	1913	1961	6*d* to 1*s* 6*d*		900
Heeley Green Picture House	Gleadless Road	1920	1959[4]	10*d* to 1*s* 6*d*		869
Heeley Palace	London Road	1911	1963[5]	6*d* to 1*s* 6*d*		1,044
High Green Cinema	Thompson Hill	1914	1957	9*d* to 1*s* 6*d*		320
Hillsborough Kinema House	Proctor Place	1912	1966	10*d* to 1*s* 6*d*		1,157
Hillsborough Park Cinema	Middlewood Road	1921	1967			1,300
Hippodrome	Cambridge Street	1907[6]	1963		1*s* 6*d* to 3*s* 6*d*	2,200
Lyric Picture House	Main Road	1920	1962	6*d* to 1*s* 6*d*		889
Manor	Manor Top	1927	1963[7]	6*d* to 1*s* 9*d*		1,537
Norfolk Picture Palace	Duke Street	1914	1959	6*d* to 1*s*		860
Odeon	Flat Street	1956	1971			2,300
Oxford Picture House	Addy Street	1913	1964	6*d* to 1*s* 6*d*		615

Name	Location	Dates		Prices		Seating capacity
		Opening	Closing	1946	1962	
Page Hall/Roxy[8]	Idsworth Road	1920	1959	6d to 1s 6d		1,000
Palace	Union Street	1910	1964	9d to 2s	2s 9d to 3s 9d	987
Paragon	Sicey Avenue	1934	1962	9d to 1s 9d	2s to 2s 6d	1,309
Park	South Street	1913	1962	5d to 10d		900
Pavilion	Attercliffe Common	1915	1960[9]	6d to 1s 9d		1,000
Phoenix	Langsett Road	1911	1960	10d to 1s 6d		613
Plaza	Richmond Road	1937	1963	10d to 1s 6d	2s to 2s 9d	1,100
Regal	Attercliffe	1935	1961	7d to 1s 9d		918
Regent/Gaumont[10]	Barker's Pool	1927	1985	1s 9d to 3s 6d		2,300
Rex	Mansfield Road	1939	1982	10d to 1s 9d		1,350
Ritz Picture House	Southey Green	1937	1962[11]	9d to 1s 9d		1,800
Roscoe Picture Palace	Infirmary Road	1922	1962	7d to 10d		950
Scala	Winter Street	1921	1952	9d to 1s 9d		983
Star	Ecclesall Road	1915	1962			957
Sunbeam Picture Palace	Barnsley Road	1922	1961	10d to 1s 6d		1,156
Tinsley Picture Palace	Sheffield Road	1912	1958	7d to 1s 6d		698
Unity Picture Palace	Langsett Road	1913	1959	6d to 1s 9d		855
Victory Picture Palace	Upwell Street	1921	1957	7d to 10d		900
Walkley Palladium	South Road	1914	1962	6d to 1s 6d	2s to 2s 9d	788
Weston Picture Palace	Upper St. Philips Road	1914	1957	7d to 10d		647
Wicker/Studio 7[12]	The Wicker	1920	1987			960

Name	Location	Dates		Prices		Seating capacity
		Opening	Closing	1946	1962	
Wincobank Picture Palace	Merton Lane	1914	1959	7d to 1s 6d		540
Woodhouse Picture Palace	Market Street	1914	1957			600
Woodseats Picture Palace	Chesterfield Road	1911	1961	6d to 1s 6d		640

Notes: [1] Renamed Essoldo in 1950. [2] Renamed News Theatre in 1945, Cartoon Cinema in 1959 and Classic Cinema in 1962. [3] Renamed Essoldo in 1956. [4] Reopened as the Tudor in 1961 and then closed in 1962. [5] Reopened in 1965. [6] Open as cinema from 1931. [7] Reopened and closed in 1969. [8] Renamed Roxy in 1946. [9] Reopened after closure. [10] Renamed Gaumont in 1946. [11] Reopened in 1965 and closed in 1966. [12] Reopened as Studio 7 in 1962.

Sources: *Kinematograph Year Book 1947* (London, 1947), pp. 356–8; *Kinematograph and Television Year Book 1963* (London, 1963), pp 306–7; C. Shaw and C. Stacey, 'A century of cinema', in *Aspects of Sheffield 2: Discovering Local History*, ed. M. Jones (Barnsley, 1999), pp. 182–200.

Appendix 3. Oral history interviewees

Name	Interview date	Year of birth	Place of birth
Allerton, Bill	27/07/15	1947	Sheffield
Ayton, Malcolm	24/07/15	1930	Sheffield
Bagshaw, Ted	16/07/15	1943	Sheffield
Brown, George	26/08/14	1943	Belfast
Bruton, Margaret	20/10/14	1941	Sheffield
Campbell, John	30/05/14	1936	Belfast
Campbell, Norman	04/06/14	1948	Belfast
Carroll, Helen	23/07/15	1925	Birmingham
Connolly, Anne	28/05/15	1946	Belfast
Davis, John T.	08/04/15	1947	Holywood
Dobson, Sylvia	02/07/14	1936	Sheffield
Dobson, Tony	02/07/14	1935	Huddersfield
Fearn, Sylvia	01/07/14	1937	Sheffield
Fielding, Jean	30/06/14	1939	Sheffield
Fielding, Pete	30/06/14	1937	Sheffield
Gatt, Bill	18/03/14	1944	Belfast

Appendices

Name	Interview date	Year of birth	Place of birth
Gorman, Ann	23/14/14	1948	Belfast
Hanna, Brian	05/05/15	1941	Belfast
Hargreaves, Betty	15/07/15	1930	Sheffield
Heathcote, Robert	30/07/15	1950	Sheffield
Higginbottom, Mike	20/08/15	1947	Sheffield
Lennox, Eric	02/05/14	1932	Belfast
Lockwood, Alan	24/07/15	1938	Sheffield
Ludlam, David	25/06/14	1930	Sheffield
Lowe, Pete	28/07/15	1931	Sheffield
Lowe, Valerie	28/07/15	1939	Sheffield
McConnell, David	24/09/14	1947	Belfast
McDonaugh, Margaret	18/05/15	1949	Belfast
McGivern, Sean (pseudonym)	22/09/15	1933	Belfast
McIlwaine, David	09/07/15	1929	Belfast
McVeigh, Jean	02/04/14	1943	Belfast
McVeigh, Terence	02/04/14	1927	Belfast
Mitchell, John	08/07/15	1943	Sheffield
Mitchell, Margaret	27/06/14	1953	Sheffield
Moseley, Eileen	27/08/15	1928	Devon
Murphy, Frank	23/07/15	1927	Sheffield
Palmer, Andrew (pseudonym)	07/08/15	1934	Sheffield
Palmer, Carol (pseudonym)	07/08/15		Sheffield
Riley, Jack	26/06/14	1926	Sheffield
Slater, Ann	28/08/15	1941	Sheffield
Slater, Bob	28/08/15	1939	Sheffield
Smyth, Elizabeth	27/08/14	1948	Belfast
Smyth, Ronnie	27/08/14	1949	Belfast
Spence, Noel	26/03/14	1944	Comber
Topham, Rosemary	17/08/15	1935	Sheffield
Walker, Ernest	26/11/15	1947	Sheffield
Walker, Lynda	26/11/14	1945	Sheffield
Weir, Wesley	19/03/15	1950	Belfast
Wilson, Jean	07/08/15	1929	Sheffield
Yeardley, Derek	25/06/14	1949	Sheffield

Bibliography

Archival sources

Belfast Central Library
Belfast cinema collection.
Belfast public libraries, Irish and local studies department, *Checklist of Belfast Cinemas* (Belfast, 1979).

Cinema Theatre Association Archive, Rochford
Sheffield Cartoon/Classic Cinema day book, April 1961–November 1964.
Gaumont, Sheffield, weekly return forms, 1948–58.

McClay Library, Queen's University Belfast
Belfast Corporation minutes, 1944–65.

Public Record Office of Northern Ireland (PRONI), Belfast
FIN/15/6/A/10, reduction in rates of Entertainments Duty, 1954.
FIN/15/6/A/12, reduction in rates of Entertainments Duty, 9 June 1958.
FIN/15/6/A/13, new arrangements for the payment of Entertainments Duty from 29 May 1960.
FIN/15/6/C/1/1–33, Entertainments Duty weekly summaries, Belfast cinemas, 1948–9.
FIN 15/6/C/1/34–74, Entertainments Duty weekly summaries, Belfast cinemas, 1952–3.
FIN 15/6/C/1/75–110, Entertainments Duty weekly summaries, Belfast cinemas, 1956–7.
FIN 15/6/C/1/111–143, Entertainments Duty weekly summaries, Belfast cinemas, 1960–1.

Sheffield City Archives

CA990/24a, Sheffield City Council, libraries, archives and information files, Library Theatre licences.

CA990/48, correspondence and papers regarding Library Theatre, 1948–70.

MD7325/1, Stanley Shirt (1920–89) of Sheffield, personal diaries, 1933–89.

MD7333/2/1–2, Rex Cinema (Sheffield) Limited, minute books, 1939–67.

MD7333/3/1, Rex Cinema (Sheffield) Limited, account ledger, 1938–86.

MD7333/4/1–2, Rex Cinema (Sheffield) Limited, payments ledgers, 1939–75.

MD7333/5/1–2, Rex Cinema (Sheffield) Limited, receipts ledgers, 1939–64.

MD7333/7/6–26, Rex Cinema (Sheffield) Limited, published accounts sheet, 1945–65.

MD7333/8/1–2, Rex Cinema (Sheffield) Limited, published accounts for shareholders, 1940–64.

Sheffield Local Studies Library

City of Sheffield, minutes of the council, 1944–65.

Kelly's Directory of Sheffield and Rotherham and Suburbs, 1945–65 (Sheffield).

Newspapers, periodicals and trade journals
ABC News
Belfast News-Letter
Belfast Telegraph
Billboard
Darts
The Economist
Financial Times
The Gown
Ideal Kinema
Ireland's Saturday Night
Irish Builder and Engineer
Irish Examiner
Irish Independent

Irish News
Irish Press
Irish Times
Irish Times Pictorial
Kinematograph Weekly
Kine Sales and Catering Review
Manchester Guardian
Monthly Film Bulletin
Motion Picture Herald
Northern Whig
Picture House
Picture Post
Sheffield Daily Telegraph
Sheffield Independent
Sheffield Telegraph
Sight and Sound
Sunday Independent (Ireland)
The Builder
The Star (Sheffield)
The Times

Parliamentary Papers
Distribution and Exhibition of Cinematograph Films, Report of the Committee of Enquiry Appointed by the President of the Board of Trade (*Parl. Papers* 1949 [C. 7837]).
Report of the Departmental Committee on Children and the Cinema (*Parl. Papers* 1950 [C. 7945]).

Publications
Abrams, L., *Oral History Theory* (London, 2010).
Abrams, M., 'The British cinema audience', *Hollywood Quarterly*, iii (1947), 155–8.
— 'The British cinema audience, 1949', *Hollywood Quarterly*, iv (1950), 251–5.

Allen, R. C., 'The place of space in film historiography', *Tijdschrift voor Mediageschiedenis*, ix (2006), 15–27.

Anderson, L., 'Postcards from the edge: the untidy realities of working with older cinema audiences, distant memories and newsreels', *Participations*, vi (2009), 180–98.

Atwell, D., *Cathedrals of the Movies: a History of British Cinemas and their Audiences* (London, 1980).

Ayres, J. D., 'The two screens: FIDO, RFDA and film vs. television in post-Second World War Britain', *Journal of British Cinema and Television*, xiv (2017), 504–21.

Barritt, D. and C. Carter, *The Northern Ireland Problem* (London, 1962).

Barton, B., *Northern Ireland in the Second World War* (Belfast, 1995).

Barton, R., *Irish National Cinema* (London, 2004).

BBC Handbook (London, 1955–66).

Bean, K., 'Roads not taken', in Belfast Exposed Photography, *Portraits from a 50's Archive* (Belfast, 2005), pp. 8–19.

Bebber, B. (ed.), *Leisure and Cultural Conflict in Twentieth-Century Britain* (Manchester, 2012).

Belfast Municipal Museum and Art Gallery, *The Museum in Pictures, Museum & Art Gallery, Stranmillis, Belfast, Souvenir (1929–1954): Illustrated Souvenir to Commemorate the Twenty-Fifth Anniversary of the Opening of the Museum and Art Gallery, Stranmillis, Belfast, in the Summer of 1929* (Belfast, 1954).

Bell, M., *Femininity in the Frame: Women and 1950s British Popular Cinema* (London, 2010).

Biltereyst, D. and P. Meers, 'Film, cinema and reception studies: revisiting research on audience's filmic and cinematic experiences', in *Reception Studies and Audiovisual Translation*, ed. E. Di Giovanni and Y. Gambier (Amsterdam, 2018), pp. 21–42.

Biltereyst, D., K. Lotze and P. Meers, 'Triangulation in historical audience research: reflections and experiences from a multi-methodological research project on cinema audiences in Flanders', *Participations*, ix (2012), 696–715.

Biltereyst, D., R. Maltby and P. Meers (eds.), *Cinema, Audiences and Modernity: New Perspectives on European Cinema History* (Abingdon, 2012).

— *The Routledge Companion to New Cinema History* (Abingdon 2019).

Binfield, C. (ed.), *The History of the City of Sheffield 1843–1993* (Sheffield, 1993).

Boal, F. W. and S. A. Royle (eds.), *Enduring City: Belfast in the Twentieth Century* (Belfast, 2006).

Brennan, E., 'Memories of television in Ireland: separating media history from nation state', *Media History*, xxiv (2018), 426–39.

British Association for the Advancement of Science, *Belfast in its Regional Setting: a Scientific Survey* (Belfast, 1952).

British Association for the Advancement of Science, *Sheffield and its Region: a Scientific and Historical Survey* (Sheffield, 1956).

Brodie, M., *The Tele: a History of the Belfast Telegraph* (Belfast, 1995).

Brooke, S., 'Review essay: screening the postwar world: British film in the fifties', *Jour. Brit. Stud.*, xliv (2005), 562–9.

Browning, H. E. and A. A. Sorrell, 'Cinemas and cinema-going in Great Britain', *Journal of the Royal Statistical Society*, cvxii (1954), 133–70.

Brownlow, G., 'Business and labour since 1945', in *Ulster Since 1600: Politics and Society*, ed. L. Kennedy and P. Ollerenshaw (Oxford, 2012), pp. 291–307.

Bryson, A., '"Whatever you say, say nothing": researching memory and identity in mid-Ulster, 1945–1969', *Oral History*, xxxv (2007), 45–56.

Bryson, A. and S. McConville, *The Routledge Guide to Interviewing: Oral History, Social Enquiry and Investigation* (London, 2013).

Burton, A. and S. Shibnall, 'Promotional activities and showmanship in British film exhibition', *Journal of Popular British Cinema*, ii (1999), 83–99.

Buscombe, E., 'All bark and no bite: the film industry's response to television', in *Popular Television in Britain*, ed. J. Corner (London, 1991), pp. 197–208.

Byrne, H., '"Going to the pictures": the female audience and the pleasure of cinema', in *Media Audiences in Ireland*, ed. M. Kelly and B. O'Connor (Dublin, 1997), pp. 88–106.

Caine, A., *Interpreting Rock Movies: the Pop Film and its Critics in Britain* (Manchester, 2004).

Campbell, J., 'Movie-house memories', *Causeway: Cultural Traditions Journal*, i (1994), 9–14.

Carter, M. P., *Home, School and Work: a Study of the Education and Employment of Young People in Britain* (Oxford, 1962).

Cathcart, R., *The Most Contrary Region: the BBC in Northern Ireland* (Belfast, 1984).

Central Statistical Office, *Annual Abstract of Statistics*, no. 84–103 (London, 1947–66).

Chapman, J., 'Cinema, monarchy and the making of heritage: *a Queen is Crowned* (1953)', in *British Historical Cinema*, ed. C. Monk and A. Sergeant (London, 2002), pp. 82–91.

Chapman, J., '"Sordidness, corruption and violence almost unrelieved": critics, censors and the post-war British crime film', *Contemporary British Hist.*, xxii (2008), 181–201.

— *Film and History* (Basingstoke, 2013).

Chapman, J., M. Glancy and S. Harper (eds.), *The New Film History: Sources, Methods, Approaches* (Basingstoke, 2007).

Chibnall, S., 'Banging the gong: the promotional strategies of Britain's J. Arthur Rank Organisation in the 1950s', *Historical Journal of Film, Radio and Television*, xxxvii (2017), 242–71.

Christie, I. (ed.), *Audiences: Defining and Researching Screen Entertainment Reception* (Amsterdam, 2012).

City and County Borough of Belfast, *Report of the Committee of Belfast Museum and Art Gallery*, 1946–52 (Belfast).

Crangle, J., '"Left to fend for themselves": immigration, race relations and the state in twentieth century Northern Ireland', *Immigrants and Minorities*, xxxvi (2018), 20–44.

Curran, J. and V. Porter, *British Cinema History* (London, 1983).

Dawn, N., A. Alexander, A. Bailey and G. Shaw, 'Investigating shopper narratives of the supermarket in early post-war England, 1945–1975', *Oral History*, xxxvii (2009), 61–73.

Dickinson, M. and S. Street, *Cinema and State: the Film Industry and the British Government 1927–84* (London, 1985).

Docherty, D., D. Morrison and M. Tracey, *The Last Picture Show? Britain's Changing Film Audiences* (London, 1987).

Doherty, J., *Standing Room Only: Memories of Belfast Cinemas* (Belfast, 1997).

Donaldson, S. N. et al., 'The 1957 epidemic of poliomyelitis in Belfast', *Ulster Medical Journal*, xxix (1960), pp. 14–21.

Donnelly, K. J., 'The policing of cinema: troubled film exhibition in Northern Ireland', *Historical Journal of Film, Radio and Television*, xx (2000), 385–96.

Doyle, B., 'The geography of cinemagoing in Great Britain, 1934–1994: a comment', *Historical Journal of Film, Radio and Television*, xxiii (2003), 59–71.

Dyja, E. (ed.), *BFI Film and Television Handbook* (London, 2004).

Eldridge, D., 'Britain finds Andy Hardy: British cinema audiences and the American way of life in the Second World War', *Historical Journal of Film, Radio and Television*, xxxi (2011), 499–521.

Eley, G., 'Finding the people's war: film, British collective memory, and World War II', *American Historical Review*, cvi (2001), 818–38.

Elliott, M., *Hearthlands: a Memoir of the White City Housing Estate in Belfast* (Belfast, 2017).

Ercole, P., D. Treveri Gennari and C. O'Rawe, 'Mapping cinema memories: emotional geographies of cinemagoing in Rome in the 1950s', *Memory Stud.*, x (2017), 63–77.

Eyles, A., *ABC: the First Name in Entertainment* (Burgess Hill, 1993).

— *Gaumont British Cinemas* (London, 1996).

— *Odeon Cinemas: Oscar Deutsch Entertains Our Nation* (London, 2001).

— *Odeon Cinemas 2: from J. Arthur Rank to the Multiplex* (London, 2005).

— 'Exhibition and the cinemagoing experience', in *The British Cinema Book*, ed. R. Murphy (3rd edn, London, 2013), pp. 67–77.

Farmer, R., '"A temporarily vanished civilisation": ice cream, confectionary and wartime cinema-going', *Historical Journal of Film, Radio and Television*, xxxi (2011), 479–97.

— *The Food Companions: Cinema and Consumption in Wartime Britain, 1939–45* (Manchester, 2011).

— *Cinemas and Cinema-going in Wartime Britain, 1939–45: the Utility Dream Palace* (Manchester, 2016).

Field, A., *Picture Palace: a Social History of the Cinema* (London, 1974).

Field, D. E. and D. G. Neill, *A Survey of New Housing Estates in Belfast: a Social and Economic Study of the Estates Built by the Northern Ireland Housing Trust in the Belfast Area 1945–1954* (Belfast, 1957).

Finlay, G., '"Celluloid menace", art or the "essential habit of the age"?', *History Ireland*, xv (2007), 34–40.

Fowler, D., *Youth Culture in Modern Britain, c. 1920–1970* (London, 2008).

Frazier, A., *Hollywood Irish: John Ford, Abbey Actors and the Irish Revival in Hollywood* (Dublin, 2011).

Geraghty, C., *British Cinema in the Fifties: Gender, Genre and the 'New Look'* (London, 2000).

Gibbons, L., *The Quiet Man* (Cork, 2002).

Gifford, D., *The British Film Catalogue 1895–1985: a Reference Guide* (Newton Abbot, 1986).

Gilbey, R. (ed.), *The Ultimate Film: the UK's 100 Most Popular Films* (London, 2005).

Gillett, P., *The British Working Class in Postwar Film* (Manchester, 2003).

Glancy, M., '*Picturegoer*: the fan magazine and popular film culture during the Second World War', *Historical Journal of Film, Radio and Television*, xxxi (2011), 453–78.

— *Hollywood and the Americanization of Britain: from the 1920s to the Present* (London, 2014).

Glen, P., '"Exploiting the daydreams of teenagers": press reports and memories of cinema-going by young people in 1960s Britain', *Media History*, xxv (2019), 355–470.

Government of Northern Ireland General Register Office, *Census of Population 1961: Belfast County Borough* (Belfast, 1963).

Government of Northern Ireland, *Juvenile Delinquency: Interim Report of the Northern Ireland Child Welfare Council* (Belfast, 1954).

Griffiths, T., *The Cinema and Cinema-Going in Scotland, 1896–1950* (Edinburgh, 2013).

Hall, S., 'Going to the Gaumont', *Picture House*, xlii (2018), 50–67.

Hampton, W., *Democracy and Community: a Study of Politics in Sheffield* (London, 1970).

Hansard (Northern Ireland), *Parliamentary Debates*.

Hanson, S., *From Silent Screen to Multi-Screen: a History of Cinema Exhibition since 1896* (Manchester, 2007).

Harman, R. and J. Minnis, *Pevsner Architectural Guides: Sheffield* (London, 2004).

Harper, S., 'A lower middle-class taste community in the 1930s: admissions figures at the Regent cinema, Portsmouth, UK', *Historical Journal of Film, Radio and Television*, xxiv (2004), 565–87.

— 'Fragmentation and crisis: 1940s admission figures at the Regent Cinema, Portsmouth, UK', *Historical Journal of Film, Radio and Television*, xxvi (2006), 361–94.

— '"It is time we went out to meet them": empathy and historical distance', *Participations*, xvi (2019), 687–97

Harper, S. and V. Porter, 'Moved to tears: weeping in the cinema in postwar Britain', *Screen*, xxxvii (1996), 152–73.

— 'Throbbing hearts and smart repartee: the reception of American films in 1950s Britain', *Media History*, iv (1998), 175–93.

— 'Cinema audience tastes in 1950s Britain', *Journal of Popular British Cinema*, ii (1999), 66–82.

— *British Cinema of the 1950s: the Decline of Deference* (Oxford, 2003).

Henderson, B., *Brum: a Life in Television* (Belfast, 2003).

Hennessey, P., *Never Again: Britain 1945–1951* (London, 1992).

— *Having it so Good: Britain in the Fifties* (London, 2006).

Hepburn, A. C., *A Past Apart: Studies in the History of Catholic Belfast, 1850–1950* (Belfast, 1996).

Hey, D., *A History of Sheffield* (Lancaster, 2011).

Hiley, N., '"Let's go to the pictures": the British cinema audience in the 1920s and 1930s', *Journal of Popular British Cinema*, ii (1999), 39–53.

Hill, J., *Sex, Class and Realism: British Cinema 1956–63* (London, 1986).

— *Cinema and Northern Ireland* (London, 2006).

Hilton, M., *Smoking in British Popular Culture 1800–2000* (Manchester, 2000).

Hodges, M. W. and C. S. Smith, 'The Sheffield estate', in *Neighbourhood and Community: an Enquiry into Social Relationships on Housing Estates in Liverpool and Sheffield*, ed. T. S. Simey (Liverpool, 1954), pp. 79–134.

Holmes, S., *British TV and Film Culture of the 1950s* (Bristol, 2005).

Holt, R. and T. Mason, *Sport in Britain 1945–2000* (Oxford, 2000).

Horn, A., *Juke Box Britain: Americanisation and Youth Culture 1945–60* (Manchester, 2009).

Hughes, T., *How Belfast Saw the Light: a Cinematic History* (Newtonards, 2014).

Hunter I. Q., L. Porter and J. Smith (eds.), *The Routledge Companion to Cinema History* (Abingdon, 2017)

Jackson, L. A. and A. Bartie, *Policing Youth: Britain 1945–70* (Manchester, 2014).

James, R., '"A very profitable enterprise": South Wales Miners' Institute cinemas in the 1930s', *Historical Journal of Film, Radio and Television*, xxvii (2007), 27–61.

— *Popular Culture and Working-Class Taste in Britain, 1930–39: a Round of Cheap Diversions?* (Manchester, 2010).

— 'Popular film-going in Britain in the 1930s', *Jour. Contemp. Hist.*, lxvii (2011), 271–87.

— 'Cinema-going in a port town, 1914–1951: film booking patterns at the Queens Cinema, Portsmouth', *Urban History*, xl (2013), 315–35.

Jancovich, M., L. Faire and S. Stubbings, *The Place of the Audience: Cultural Geographies of Film Consumption* (London, 2003).

Jarvie, I., 'International film trade: Hollywood and the British market', *Historical Journal of Film, Radio and Television*, iii (1983) 161–9.

— 'British trade policy versus Hollywood, 1947–1948: "food before flicks"?', *Historical Journal of Film, Radio and Television*, vi (1986), 19–41.

— '"These intimate little places": cinema-going and public emotion in Bolton, 1930–1954', *Cult. and Soc. History* (2019), doi.org/10.1080/14780 038.2019.1609801.

Jones, E., *A Social Geography of Belfast* (London, 1960).

Jones, M., 'Far from swinging London: memories of non-urban cinema-going in 1960s Britain', in *Cinema Beyond the City: Small-Town and Rural Film Culture in Europe*, ed. J. Thissen and C. Zimmerman (London, 2017), pp. 117–32.

Kinematograph Year Book, 1945–59 (London).

Kinematograph and Television Year Book, 1961–66 (London).

Kuhn, A., *An Everyday Magic: Cinema and Cultural Memory* (London, 2002).

Kuhn, A., D. Biltereyst and P. Meers, 'Memories of cinema-going and film experience: an introduction', *Memory Stud.*, x (2017), 3–16.

Kynaston, D., *Austerity Britain: 1945–51* (London, 2007).

— *Family Britain: 1951–57* (London, 2009).

— *Modernity Britain: Opening the Box, 1957–59* (London, 2013).

— *Modernity Britain: a Shake of the Dice, 1959–62* (London, 2014).

Lacey, J., 'Seeing through happiness: Hollywood musicals and the construction of the American dream in Liverpool in the 1950s', *Journal of Popular British Cinema*, ii (1999), 54–65.

Lamberti, E. (ed.), *Behind the Scenes at the BBFC: Film Classification from the Silver Screen to the Digital Age* (London, 2012).

Langhamer, C., *Women's Leisure in England: 1920–1960* (Manchester, 2000).

— *The English in Love: the Intimate Story of an Emotional Revolution* (Oxford, 2013).

Larmour, P., 'Cinema paradiso', *Perspective*, iv (1996), 23–7.

— 'The big feature', *Perspective*, v (1997), 29–36.

Lewis, A., 'Planning through conflict: the genesis of Sheffield's post-war reconstruction plan', *Planning Perspectives,* xxiv (2009), 381–3.

— 'Planning through conflict: competing approaches in the preparation of Sheffield's post-war reconstruction plan', *Planning Perspectives*, xxviii (2013), 27–49.

Lowell Macdonald, R., *The Appreciation of Film: the Postwar Film Society Movement and Film Culture in Britain* (Exeter, 2016).

Lynch, J., *A Tale of Three Cities: Comparative Studies in Working-Class Life* (Basingstoke, 1998).

Machale, D., *The Complete Guide to The Quiet Man* (Belfast, 2000).

Mcbride, S. and R. Flynn (eds.) *Here's Looking at You, Kid! Ireland Goes to the Pictures* (Dublin, 1996).

Mccormick, L., *Regulating Sexuality: Women in Twentieth-Century Northern Ireland* (Manchester, 2009).

McGuinness, D., 'Media consumption and Dublin working class cultural identity' (unpublished Dublin City University PhD thesis, 1999).

McKibbin, R., *Classes and Cultures: England 1918–1951* (London, 1998).

McKillop, I. and N. Sinyard (eds.), *British Cinema in the 1950s: a Celebration* (Manchester, 2003).

Macnab, G., *J. Arthur Rank and the British Film Industry* (London, 1994).

— *Delivering Dreams: a Century of British Film Distribution* (London, 2016).

Maguire, W., *Belfast: a History* (Lancaster, 2009).

Maltby, R. and M. Stokes (eds.), *American Movie Audiences: from the Turn of the Century to the Early Sound Era* (London, 1999).

— (eds.), *Identifying Hollywood's Audiences: Cultural Identity and the Movies* (London, 1999).

— (eds.), *Hollywood Spectatorship: Changing Perceptions of Cinema Audiences* (London, 2001).

— (eds.), *Hollywood Abroad: Audiences and Cultural Exchange* (London, 2004).

Maltby, R., D. Bitereyst and P. Meers (eds.), *Explorations in New Cinema History: Approaches and Case Studies* (Chichester, 2011).

Maltby, R., M. Stokes and R. C. Allen (eds.) *Going to the Movies: Hollywood and the Social Experience of Cinema* (Exeter, 2007).

Manning, S., 'Post-war cinema-going and working-class communities: a case study of the Holyland, Belfast, 1945–1962', *Cult. and Soc. History*, xiii (2016), 539–55.

— 'Television and the decline of cinema-going in Northern Ireland, 1953–63', *Media History*, xxiv (2018), 408–25.

Manvell, R., *The Film and the Public* (Harmondsworth, 1954).

Martin, A., *Going to the Pictures: Scottish Memories of Cinema* (Edinburgh, 2000).

Mayer, J. P., *British Cinemas and their Audiences* (London, 1948).

Middleton, R., *The British Economy since 1945* (Basingstoke, 2000).

Miskell, P., *A Social History of the Cinema in Wales, 1918–1951* (Cardiff, 2006).

Mitchell, G. A. M., 'Reassessing "the generation gap": Bill Haley's 1957 tour of Britain, inter-generational relations and attitudes to rock 'n' roll in the late 1950s', *Twentieth Century British Hist.*, xxiv (2013), 573–605.

Moran, J., *Armchair Nation: an Intimate History of Britain in Front of the TV* (London, 2013).

Northern Ireland Ministry of Finance, *Digest of Statistics Northern Ireland*, nos. 1–10, (Belfast, 1954–63).

Nott, J., *Going to the Palais: a Social and Cultural History of Dancing and Dance Halls in Britain, 1918–1960* (Oxford, 2015).

O'Brien, M. and A. Eyles (eds.) *Enter the Dream-House: Memories of South London Cinema from the Twenties to the Sixties* (London, 1993).

O'Connell, S. J., 'An age of conservative modernity, 1914–1968', in *Belfast 400: People, Place and History*, ed. S. J. Connolly (Liverpool, 2012), pp. 271–316.

— 'Violence and social memory in twentieth-century Belfast: stories of Buck Alec Robinson', *Jour. Brit. Stud.*, liii (2014), 734–56.

O'Leary, E., 'Teenagers, everyday life and popular culture in 1950s Ireland' (unpublished National University of Ireland, Maynooth PhD thesis, 2013).

Open, M., *Fading Lights, Silver Screens: a History of Belfast Cinemas* (Antrim, 1985).

Örnebring, H., 'Writing the history of television audiences: the coronation in the mass-observation archive', in *Re-viewing Television History: Critical Issues in Television Historiography*, ed. H. Wheatley (London, 2007), pp. 170–83.

Osgerby, B., *Youth in Britain since 1945* (Oxford, 1998).

Patton, M., *Central Belfast: a Historical Gazetteer* (Belfast, 1993).

Pevsner, N., *The Buildings of England: Yorkshire West Riding* (London, 1967).

Political and Economic Planning, *The British Film Industry* (London, 1952).

— *The British Film Industry 1958* (London, 1958).

Poole, J., 'British cinema attendance in wartime: audience preference at the Majestic, Macclesfield, 1939–1946', *Historical Journal of Film, Radio and Television*, vii (1987), 15–34.

Pybus, S. (ed.), *Damned Bad Place, Sheffield: an Anthology of Writing About Sheffield Through the Ages* (Sheffield, 1994).

Ramsden, J., 'Refocusing "the people's war": British war films of the 1950s', *Journal of Contemporary History*, xxxiii (1998), 35–63.

Richards, H. 'Memory reclamation of cinema going in Bridgend, South Wales, 1930–1960', *Historical Journal of Film, Radio and Television*, xxiii (2003), 341–55.

Richards, J., 'The coronation of Queen Elizabeth II in film', *The Court Historian*, ix (2004), 69–79.

— *The Age of the Dream Palace: Cinema and Society in 1930s Britain* (3rd edn, London, 2009).

— *Cinema and Radio in Britain and America: 1920–1960* (Manchester, 2010).

Ritchie, D. A., *Doing Oral History* (2nd edn, Oxford, 2003).

— (ed.), *The Oxford Handbook of Oral History* (Oxford, 2011).

Robertson, A., *The Bleak Midwinter 1947* (Manchester, 1987).

Rockett, K., *Irish Film Censorship: a Cultural Journey from Silent Cinema to Internet Pornography* (Dublin, 2004).

Rockett, K. and E. Rockett, *Film Exhibition and Distribution in Ireland: 1909–2011* (Dublin, 2011).

Roodhouse, M., '"In racket town": gangster chic in austerity Britain, 1939–1953', *Historical Journal of Film, Radio and Television*, xxxi (2011), 523–41.

Rowntree, B. S. and G. R. Lavers, *English Life and Leisure: a Social Study* (London, 1951).

Savage, R., *A Loss of Innocence? Television and Irish Society 1960–72* (Manchester, 2010).

Screen Advertising Association, *Spotlight on the Cinema Audience* (London, 1962).

Sedgwick, J., *Popular Filmgoing in 1930s Britain: a Choice of Pleasures* (Exeter, 2000).

— 'Product differentiation at the movies: Hollywood, 1946 to 1965', *Jour. Econ. Hist.*, lxii (2002), 676–705.

Sedgwick, J., P. Miskell and M. Nicoli, 'The market for films in postwar Italy: evidence for both national and regional patterns of taste', *Enterprise & Society*, xx (2019), 199–228.

Sedgwick, J. and M. Pokorny (eds.) *an Economic History of Film* (Abingdon, 2005).

Shail, R., *The Children's Film Foundation: History and Legacy* (London, 2016).

Shaw, C., *Images of England: Sheffield Cinemas* (Stroud, 2001).

Shaw, C. and S. Smith, *Sheffield Cinemas: Past and Present* (Sheffield, 1999).

Shaw, C. and C. Stacey, 'A century of cinema', in *Aspects of Sheffield 2: Discovering Local History*, ed. M. Jones (Barnsley, 1999), pp. 182–200.

Shaw, T., *British Cinema and the Cold War: the State, Propaganda and Consensus* (London, 2001).

Sheffield Cinema Society, *The A.B.C. of the Cinemas of Sheffield* (Sheffield, 1993).

Sheffield Transport Department, *The Tramway Era in Sheffield: Souvenir Brochure on the Closure of the Tramways, 8th October 1960* (Sheffield, 1960).

Smyth, P., *Changing Times: Life in 1950s Northern Ireland* (Newtonards, 2012).

Sorlin, P., *European Cinemas, European Societies 1939–1990* (London, 1991).

Spraos, J., *The Decline of the Cinema: an Economist's Report* (London, 1962).

Stacey, J., *Star Gazing: Hollywood Cinema and Female Spectatorship* (London, 1994).

Staples, T., *All Pals Together: the Story of Children's Cinema* (Edinburgh, 1997).

Stokes, M. and M. Jones, 'Windows on the world: memories of European cinema in 1960s Britain', *Memory Stud.*, x (2017), 78–90.

Street, S., *British Cinema in Documents* (London, 2000).

Stubbings, S., '"Look behind you!": memories of cinema-going in the "golden age" of Hollywood', in *Memory and Popular Film*, ed. P. Grainge (Manchester, 2003), pp. 65–80.

Study Group of the Public Health Department, 'Smoking habits of school children', in *British Journal of Preventative and Social Medicine*, xiii (1959), 1–4.

Summerfield, P., 'Public memory or public amnesia? British women of the Second World War in popular films of the 1950s and 1960s', *Jour. Brit. Stud.*, xlviii (2009), 935–57.

Swann, P., *The Hollywood Feature Film in Postwar Britain* (London, 1987).

The Motion Picture and Television Almanac (New York, 1952).

The Ulster Year Book: the Official Year Book of Northern Ireland (Belfast, 1953).

Thomas, N., 'Review essay: will the real 1950s please stand up? Views of a contradictory decade', *Cult. and Soc. History*, v (2008), 227–36.

Thumim, J., 'The "popular", cash and culture in the postwar British cinema industry', *Screen*, xxxii (1991), 245–71.

Todd, S., 'Phoenix rising: working-class life and urban reconstruction, *c.*1945–1967', *Jour. Brit. Stud.*, liv (2015), 679–702.

Treveri Gennari, D. '"If you have seen it, you cannot forget!": film consumption and memories of cinema-going in 1950s Rome', *Historical Journal of Film, Radio and Television*, xxxv (2015), 53–74.

Treveri Gennari, D. and J. Sedgwick, 'Memories in context: the social and economic function of cinema in 1950s Rome', *Film History*, xxvii (2015), 76–104.

Tuffrey, P., *South Yorkshire's Cinemas and Theatres* (Stroud, 2011).

UNESCO, *Basic Facts and Figures: Illiteracy, Education, Libraries, Museums, Books, Newspapers, Newsprints, Film and Radio* (Paris, 1952).

— *Basic Facts and Figures: International Statistics Relating to Education, Culture and Mass Communication* (Paris, 1960).

United States Census Bureau, *The Statistical History of the United States, from Colonial Times to the Present* (New York, 1986).

Van de Vivjer, L., D. Biltereyst and K. Velders, 'Crisis at the Capitole: a cultural economics analysis of a major first-run cinema in Ghent, 1953–1971', *Historical Journal of Film, Radio and Television*, xxxv (2015), 75–124.

Vinen, R., *National Service: a Generation in Uniform* (London, 2014).

Wallace, R., R. Harrison and C. Brunsdon, 'Women in the box: female projectionists in post-war British cinemas', *Journal of British Cinema and Television*, xv (2018), 46–65.

Walton, J., *The British Seaside: Holidays and Resorts in the Twentieth Century* (Manchester, 2000).

Ward, R., *In Memory of Sheffield's Cinemas* (Sheffield, 1988).

Watts, S., 'The future of film and TV in Britain', *The Quarterly of Film Radio and Television*, x (1956), 364–73.

Yorkshire Regional Association of the National Association of Youth Service Officers, *Adventuring with Youth in South Yorkshire* (1960).

Yow, V. R., *Recording Oral History: a Guide for the Humanities and Social Sciences* (2nd edn, Walnut Creek, 2005).

Zweig, F., *The Worker in an Affluent Society: Family Life and Industry* (London, 1961).

Index

Abbeydale Picture House, Sheffield, 20–1, 29, 30, 75, 109, 190

Abbott, Bud and Costello, Lou, 150

ABC, Belfast, 21, 86, 198–9; *see also* Ritz, Belfast

ABC, Sheffield, 45, 78, 84, 119–22, 124, 198

ABC News, 57, 82, 149

Abrams, Mark, 3, 64

Adelphi Picture Theatre, Sheffield, 23, 24

Adventure, 175

African Queen, The, 144, 148–9

Alhambra, Belfast, 39, 92, 103–4, 143, 146, 152

Alice in Wonderland, 150

Alpha, Belfast, 45, 98–100, 117, 134

Ambassador, Belfast, 152

Annie Get Your Gun, 149

Apartment, The, 125

Apollo, Belfast, 18–19, 24, 27, 28, 38, 95, 102, 108, 132, 134, 152, 198

Arcadian, Belfast, 131, 132, 148, 152

Assassin, The, 136

Associated British Cinemas (ABC), 11, 48, 57, 86–7, 92, 95, 109, 119–22, 124, 126, 134, 136, 138, 149, 151, 159, 160, 170–1, 195, 198

Astoria, Belfast, 95, 106, 132, 152

Astra, Christmas Island, 30

Avenue, Belfast, 102; *see also* Picture House, Belfast; Regent, Belfast

Ayres, John D., 87

Babette Goes to War, 170

Ballymena, 46

Bangor, 55, 79

Barber, Sian, 60

Barnsley, 23

Barritt, Denis, 75

Battle Inferno, 160

Bean, Kevin, 8

Beatles, the, 86

Beaver Valley, 150

Bebber, Brett, 5

Because You're Mine, 144

Belfast
armed forces in, 39–40, 103
cinema admissions in, 60, 62, 129–62
cinema licences granted in, 61
growth of cinema in, 10–12
historiography, 9–10
migrant communities in, 23–4
religious divisions in, 7–8, 19, 34–5, 46–9, 56, 75, 132, 196
social and economic conditions, 6–8, 156–7, 199–200
see also Northern Ireland

Belfast Corporation, 15, 39–40, 47, 56, 80, 92–3, 94, 150–1, 195–6

Belfast Institute Film Society, 140

Belfast Museum, 19

Belfast News-Letter, 96

Belfast Rural District Council, 45

Belfast Telegraph, 2–3, 15, 22–3, 25, 34, 35, 43, 44, 47, 53, 57, 59, 64, 67–8, 72, 73, 74, 79, 82, 93–4, 97, 100, 102, 103, 105, 107–9, 129, 131, 139, 140, 142–4, 148–9, 155, 156, 159, 161, 197

Ben-Hur, 159–60, 162, 191

Beret, Dawn, 121
Biltereyst, Daniel, 6, 18, 141–2
bingo, 1, 108, 117, 120, 123, 124, 198
Blackboard Jungle, 42–3
Black Shield of Falworth, 175
Blitz, the, 7, 92–3
Blue Angel, The, 189
Blue Lamp, The, 173, 175
Blue Skies, 175
Board of Trade, 12, 137, 174–6
Bogarde, Dirk, 177
Bond, James, 71
bowling, *see* ten-pin bowling
boxing, 142–3
Boys Town, 34
Bridge on the River Kwai, 159
British Board of Film Censors (BBFC), 150, 190
British Broadcasting Corporation (BBC), 33, 37, 52–4, 60, 61, 62, 64, 68, 70, 71, 76, 87, 135, 143, 150, 159
British Film Institute, 177, 190
British Film Production Fund, 67, 148, 167, 170
Broadcasting Research Unit, 4
Broadway, Belfast, 95, 129–62
Broadway Melody of 1940, 139
Browning, H. E., 135, 147, 149, 163, 170, 171
Brownlow, Graham, 7
Bryson, Anna, 47
Burton, Alan, 157

cafés, 1, 9, 70, 76
    in cinemas, 59, 96, 100, 132
Cage of Nightingales, A, 139
Caine, Andrew, 78
Caine Mutiny, The, 98
Capital and Provincial News Theatres, 100–1, 179
Capitol, Belfast, 95, 107, 132, 152
Capitol, Sheffield, 21, 112

Captain Boycott, 142–3, 147, 162, 197
Carlton, Sheffield, 109, 116
Carlton Browne of the F.O., 184
car ownership, 69, 79–80, 106, 194
Carson, Frank, 161
Carter, M. P., 9, 27–8, 75, 172–3
Cartoon Cinema, Sheffield, 15, 124, 163, 179–83, 185, 191; *see also* Electra Palace, Sheffield; News Theatre, Sheffield; Classic Cinema, Sheffield
Case of Charles Peace, The, 178
Castle, Belfast, 152
Central Picture Theatre, Belfast, 92, 102
Chantrey Picture House, Sheffield, 20, 116
Chapman, James, 55
Chesterfield, 23, 123
Chibnall, Steve, 83, 151, 157
cinema attendance
    and affluence, 4–5, 51, 69–80, 89, 102–3, 151, 194, 200
    audience demographics, 3–4, 29–32, 59, 70–1, 84–5, 88–9, 106, 118, 172–3, 194
    and the life cycle, 24–32, 33–4, 194
    and population shifts, 1, 4–5, 51, 61, 64, 91, 95–100, 109–11, 115, 117–18, 126, 151, 164, 194
    regional variations in, 2–4, 6, 17, 49–50, 51–2, 89, 162, 195–6
    and television, 1, 4–5, 12, 22, 26–7, 31, 51–2, 59, 60–9, 70–1, 97, 101, 102–3, 105, 106, 108, 114, 115–17, 121, 193–4
    UK admissions, 1, 4, 10–12, 17, 51, 119, 135, 151–2, 164–6, 193, 200
Cinema House, Sheffield, 59, 81, 109, 122–3

cinemas
 advertising and promotion of, 3,
  31, 69, 84–5, 86, 106, 117,
  124, 157–8, 159, 169, 172,
  178, 195
 children's matinees in, 3, 25–6, 28,
  56, 124, 149–50, 186, 191
 closure of, 1, 4, 12, 32, 60, 91,
  102–9, 115–19, 122–5, 194,
  198–200
 courtship in, 3, 20, 21, 27–30, 69,
  71, 75, 84, 101, 194, 197
 crime in, 39, 41, 43, 198
 employees, 25, 116–17, 171, 197–8
 film hire, 3, 117, 135, 167, 170–1,
  188
 food and drink in, 31, 114–15,
  135, 168–9, 195
 misbehaviour in, 25, 28, 31, 37–8,
  40–3, 195
 national anthem in, 3, 46–8, 49,
  58, 196
 opening of, 91–102, 112–15, 119–
  122, 152, 194–5
 profitability of, 2–3, 103, 115, 123,
  129, 166, 167, 182–3
 programming in, 21–2, 31, 33, 85,
  101–2, 105–6, 106–7, 117,
  124, 135–40, 155, 158–161,
  169–70, 173–4, 179–83,
  185–90
 queues, 3, 31, 37, 39, 40, 106, 112,
  123, 156, 157, 159, 195
 renovation of, 83, 100–2, 103, 106,
  111–12, 117–19, 124–6, 179
 smoking in, 14–15, 43–6, 168–9,
  195
 social and economic distinctions
  between, 18–24, 102, 131–4,
  194–5
 technology in, 80–3, 96–7, 112–14,
  121–2, 195

Sunday opening of, 23, 39–41, 103,
  141, 195–6
CinemaScope, 80, 81–3, 97, 107, 112,
  171, 172, 195
Cinematograph Exhibitors' Association
  (CEA), 16, 38, 42, 43, 45, 58, 81,
  87, 93, 103, 108, 110, 120, 131,
  140, 166, 170, 171, 174–6
Cinematograph Trade Benevolent
  Fund, 148
Circuits Management Association, 112
City Films Kine Society, 183
City for Conquest, 139
Classic, Belfast, 92, 95, 142, 146, 149;
  see also Gaumont, Belfast
Classic Cinema, Sheffield, 15, 124–5,
  163, 179–83, 184, 185, 190; *see
  also* Electra Palace, Sheffield; News
  Theatre, Sheffield; Classic Cinema,
  Sheffield
Clonard Picture House, Belfast, 43,
  132, 146, 152
Coliseum, Belfast, 46–7, 103–4, 146,
  152
Coliseum, Sheffield, 41
Columbia Pictures, 142
Comber, 100, 137
Conquest of Everest, The, 47, 196
Coronation Day, 57
coronation of Queen Elizabeth II, 52,
  54–9, 193, 196
Court Jester, The, 156
Courtneys of Curzon Street, The, 137
Crimson Pirate, The, 144
Crookes Picture Palace, Sheffield, 29,
  32, 42, 118
Cruel Sea, The, 36
Crumlin Picture House, Belfast, 55–6,
  118, 152, 159
Curran Theatres, 92, 93–4, 95, 98,
  108, 132, 136, 143
Curtis, Tony, 35

Curzon, Belfast, 18–19, 21, 25, 38, 44, 134, 146, 152, 199

Dam Busters, The, 174, 175, 183, 184
dancing/dance halls, 1, 27, 31, 42, 70, 71–5, 76, 79, 98, 104, 105, 195, 198
Darby O'Gill and the Little People, 160
Dark Victory, 175
Darnall Cinema, Sheffield, 115
Darnall Picture Palace, Sheffield, 116
Darts, 21, 22, 184–5
Davis, John, 114
Day, Doris, 35–6
Day in the Country, A, 80
Denison, Michael, 148
Desert Hawk, The, 173
Desert Rats, The, 33–4
Diamond Picture House, Belfast, 103, 132
Dickinson, Margaret, 126
Docherty, David, 71, 80
Doctor at Large, 175, 177, 183, 184
Doctor at Sea, 177
Doctor in the House, 175, 177
Doherty, James, 40, 132, 134
Donat, Robert, 142
Doncaster, 23
Donegan, Lonnie, 77
Don Picture Palace, 116
Don't Bother to Knock, 121
Doyle, Barry, 2, 51–2
Diamond, Harry, 45
drive-in cinema, 84
Dublin, 57–8, 143, 195
Duchin, Eddy, 158
Duncairn Picture Theatre, Belfast, 102, 134, 146, 152
Dundonald, 96–7
Dunkirk, 175

Ealing Studios, 36

Ecclesfield Cinema House, Ecclesfield, 112
Economist, The, 9, 11–12, 22, 81, 115, 168, 179, 180
Eddy Duchin Story, The, 158
Electra Palace, Sheffield, 179; *see also* News Theatre, Sheffield; Cartoon Cinema, Sheffield and Classic Cinema, Sheffield
Elizabeth is Queen, 57, 174, 175
Elizabeth II, Queen, *see* coronation of Queen Elizabeth II
Elliott, Marianne, 49
Entertainments Duty/Entertainment Tax, 3, 15, 16, 62, 67, 68, 97, 103, 104, 106, 115–16, 117, 129–62, 166, 169–70, 198
Ercole, Pierluigi, 49–50
Essoldo Circuit, 112
Eveleigh, R. V. C., 83–4, 101, 104, 107, 108, 160

Faire, Lucy, 17, 55, 59, 67, 79, 197
Fancy Pants, 183, 184
Farmer, Richard, 2, 4, 15–16, 134–5, 193, 197
fashion, 35–6, 73, 78–9, 103, 144
Father of the Bride, 174
Father's Little Dividend, 172, 174, 175
Favell, Arnold, 38, 42, 110, 115, 118
Federation of British Film Makers, 135
Field, Dorita, 32, 54, 64, 98
Film Industry Defence Organisation (FIDO), 87–8
films
  behaviour and dress, impact on, 25–6, 35–6, 78–9
  British films, reception of, 36–7, 137–8, 174, 177–8, 183
  foreign language films, exhibition of, 22–3, 125, 139–40, 160, 183–90

Hollywood films, reception of, 8, 33–6, 137, 162, 174, 183, 196
Irish-themed films, popularity of, 141–7, 160
on television, 67, 86–8
Flame of Araby, The, 184
Ford, John, 144, 146
Forum, Belfast, 43, 92, 146, 152
Forum, Sheffield, 21, 112
Fowler, David, 10, 43
France, cinema admissions in, 12
Freaks, 184
Furneaux, Yvonne, 82

Gaiety, Belfast, 46, 92, 102
Gallaher's Tobacco, 46, 65
Garbo, Greta, 125
Gaumont, 11, 56, 92, 94, 104, 149, 170–1
Gaumont, Belfast, 25, 55–6, 84, 95, 105, 107, 147, 148, 152, 159; *see also* Classic, Belfast
Gaumont, Sheffield, 21, 36, 39, 41, 58–9, 69, 84, 85, 114, 163, 177, 178, 183, 198; *see also* Regent, Sheffield
Gent, Harold, 45, 88, 171
Germany, cinema admissions in, 12
G.I. Blues, 184
Gigi, 159
Glancy, Mark, 35, 138
Glen, Patrick, 41
Globe Picture Palace, Sheffield, 24, 109, 117
Going My Way, 34
Gone with the Wind, 144
Gown, The, 22, 84
Granada television, 52
Grand Opera House, Belfast, 28, 101, 105
Grandsen, Sir Robert, 97
Granger, Stewart, 142
Great Expectations, 189

Green Mare's Nest, The, 184
greyhound racing, 67
Griffiths, Trevor, 6
Grosvenor Hall, Belfast, 34
Guns of Navarone, The, 106
Guys and Dolls, 157–8

Hall, Sheldon, 114, 163, 178
Hallamshire Cinemas Ltd., 115
Hamlet, 189
Hans Christian Anderson, 173, 174, 175
Hanson, Stuart, 4–5, 32, 36, 80, 84, 193
Harper, Sue, 3–4, 5, 14–15, 17, 78, 105–6, 137, 151, 160, 162, 164, 176, 177, 178, 193
Hayes, Richard, 151
Healy, Cahir, 45
Heeley Coliseum, 20, 26–7
Heeley Green Picture House, Sheffield, 20, 117
Heeley Palace, 20, 84–5, 109
Helzapoppin, 138
Henderson, Brum, 65, 68
Henry V, 188
Hercules, 184
Hercules Unchained, 86
Hey, David, 10
Hill, Jeffrey, 5
Hill, John, 10
Hillsborough Kinema House, Sheffield, 116
Hippodrome, Sheffield, 31, 109, 119, 123
Hiroshima Mon Amour, 185
Hodges, Mark, 29, 32, 66, 110
Holiday Camp, 174, 175
Hollywood Canteen, 173
Holmes, Su, 86
Horn, Adrian, 5, 8, 30, 35, 70, 72, 73, 76
House of Wax, 80, 171

ice skating, 31, 72–3
Ideal Husband, An, 138
Ideal Kinema, 84, 100, 121–2, 126
Il Tetto, 125
Imperial Picture House, Belfast, 39–40, 56, 92, 103, 152, 156, 157
Independent Television (ITV), 52–3, 61, 71, 83, 115
Intimate Stranger, The, 69
Ireland, Republic of, 198
    censorship in, 151
    cinema admissions in, 12
    coronation of Queen Elizabeth II in, 57–8
    television in, 52 n. 9
Irish Builder and Engineer, 96, 97
Irish Examiner, 57–8
Irish Independent, 102, 108, 138, 146
Irish Theatres, 92, 95, 103, 106
Italy, cinema admissions in, 12–13
Ivanhoe, 144

Jack and the Beanstalk, 144, 149–50
Jacqueline, 147, 178
James, Robert, 6, 14–15, 17, 131
Jancovich, Mark, 17, 55, 59, 67, 79, 197
Johnny Belinda, 136, 175
Jones, Matthew, 14, 33, 197
Jones, Tom, 86
Jour de fête, 140
Journey to the Center of the Earth, 184
Just for Fun, 190
Just my Luck, 178

Kane, Eden, 86
Kelly's Directory of Sheffield and Rotherham, 185
Kelvin,Belfast, 39, 93; *see also* Mayfair, Belfast; News and Cartoon Cinema, Belfast
Kermesse Heroique, 140
Kinematograph Renters' Society, 117

Kinematograph Weekly, 7, 16, 22, 38, 43, 46, 67, 68, 83, 85, 86, 93, 94, 95, 96–7, 98, 100, 104, 107, 113, 120, 125, 132, 134, 139, 145, 147, 156–8, 159, 160, 161, 168, 177
Kinematograph Year Book, 11
Kine Sales and Catering Review, 114–15
King of Kings, 191
King Solomon's Mines, 183, 184
Knife in the Water, 190
Korda, Alexander, 87
Kuhn, Annette, 6, 14, 18, 33, 197
Kynaston, David, 54

Langhamer, Claire, 5, 28, 71, 118
Laughter in Paradise, 184
Lavers, G. R., 74, 179
Les Enfants du Paradis, 140
Library Theatre, Sheffield, 15, 183–90, 191
Lido, Belfast, 85, 96, 97, 107, 134, 152, 153, 161
Lion is in the Streets, A, 157
Lodge, George, 34–5, 95, 103, 157
Lovely To Look At, 144
Lucan, Arthur, 149
Lyceum, Belfast, 95, 102, 107, 153
Lyric, Belfast, 92
Lyric Picture House, Sheffield, 109

Macbeth, 150
Majestic, Belfast, 56, 92, 134, 136, 146, 149, 151, 153, 157, 160
Maltby, Richard, 6, 13, 49, 141–2
Manchester Guardian, 56
Man of the Moment, 177, 178
Manor, Sheffield, 124, 166
Man with the Golden Arm, The, 156
March Hare, The, 147
Martin Luther, 34–5, 196
Mason, James, 146
Master of Ballantrae, The, 82
Maurey, Nicole, 121

Mayfair, Belfast, 22–3, 42–3, 92, 93, 100–1, 140, 153; *see also* Kelvin, Belfast; News and Cartoon Cinema, Belfast
McBride Neill, John, 96, 100, 134
McCallum, John, 149
Meers, Philippe, 6, 18, 141–2
Metro, Dundonald, 96–7, 107
Metro-Goldwyn-Mayer (MGM), 134, 155, 157, 159
Midgley, Harry, 47–8
Midland Picture House, Belfast, 92
Misadventures of Buster Keaton, The, 184
Miskell, Peter, 6, 13
Monaghan, Rinty, 142–3
Monsieur Vincent, 187
Monthly Film Bulletin, 85 n. 201, 140
Moran, Joe, 51, 52 n. 9, 54, 63–4
Morgan the Pirate, 184
Morrison, David, 71, 80
Motion Picture Herald, 178
Movietone, 57
Mrs. Miniver, 139
Murder Incorporated, 151
music, popular, 71, 73, 76–8
    in cinemas, 85–6
    in films, 42–3, 78
My Brother Jonathan, 138
My Wild Irish Rose, 136, 140

National Association of Theatrical and Kinema Employees (NATKE), 82, 116
National Service, 30
Neagle, Anna, 138
Neill, Desmond, 32, 54, 64, 98
new cinema history, 1–2, 6, 13, 17, 49, 51, 89, 91, 190, 193, 197, 200
New Princess Palace, Belfast, 153
News and Cartoon Cinema, Belfast, 22–3, 100–1; *see also* Kelvin, Belfast; Mayfair, Belfast

newsreels, 33, 55–6, 58–9, 100, 135, 170
News Theatre, Sheffield, 23, 42, 58, 81, 124, 179; *see also* Electra Palace, Sheffield; Cartoon Cinema, Sheffield; Classic Cinema, Sheffield
New Vic cinema, Belfast, 199; *see also* Royal Hippodrome, Belfast; Odeon, Belfast
Nicoli, Marina, 12–13
Night to Remember, A, 147, 178

Norfolk Picture House, Sheffield, 117
Northern Ireland
    cinema admissions in, 62, 135, 151–2
    cinemas in, 11, 91
    juvenile delinquency in, 27
    Ministry of Commerce, 93
    Ministry of Home Affairs, 150–1
    Ministry of Finance, 93, 129–31, 161
    Parliament of (Stormont), 45–6, 47–8, 94, 137
    social and cultural history of, 8, 35, 70
    unemployment in, 7, 94, 193
    see also Belfast
Northern Ireland Child Welfare Council, 27
Northern Ireland Council for the Encouragement of the Music and the Arts (CEMA), 104
Northern Ireland Housing Trust, 54, 98
Northern Whig, 39, 57, 81, 137–8, 140, 144, 157
Northwest Passage, 139
Nott, James, 72, 74
Nudist Story, The, 161
Nugent, Sir Roland, 137
Nun's Story, The, 159

O'Connell, Sean, 7
O'Dea, Jimmy, 149
O'Hara, Maureen, 143, 145
O'Neill, Terence, 130, 158, 161
O'Rawe, Catherine, 50
Odd Man Out, 146, 178
Odeon, 11, 56, 69, 93, 94, 95, 104, 108, 112–15, 160, 170–1
Odeon (NI) Ltd., 83–4, 95, 101–2, 103–4, 106, 107, 132, 160
Odeon, Belfast, 102, 106, 108, 198–9; *see also* Royal Hippodrome; Belfast; New Vic, Belfast
Odeon, Sheffield, 45, 68, 83, 84, 109, 112–15, 120, 122, 198
Old Mother Riley, 149
On Moonlight Bay, 144
oral history methodology, 13–14, 17–18, 25, 30, 33–4, 47, 49–50, 54–5, 131, 197
Orbison, Roy, 86
Oxford Picture House, Sheffield, 109

Paragon, Sheffield, 123, 124
Paramount, 33, 82, 155
Paris, Palace Hotel, 160
Park, Belfast, 146, 153
Park, Sheffield, 118
Parker, Cecil, 142
Pavilion, Sheffield, 24, 109
Pelicans, The, 190
Phoenix, Sheffield, 42, 118
Picnic, 154, 156
Picturedrome, Belfast, 134, 146, 153
Picture House, Belfast, 92, 93–4, 132; *see also* Avenue, Belfast; Regent, Belfast
Picture Parade, 86
Picture Post, 7–8
Plaza, Sheffield, 41, 124
Political and Economic Planning, 81
Pollyanna, 119

Popular Picture Theatre, Belfast 92–3, 108, 153
Porter, Vincent, 3–4, 5, 78, 105–6, 137, 151, 160, 162, 176, 177, 178, 193
Powell, Victor, 104
Presley, Elvis, 4, 77
Prisoner of Zenda, The, 149
Psycho, 27
public transport, 4, 20, 27, 28, 32, 46, 58, 79–80, 98, 101, 110–11, 179, 194

Queen is Crowned, A, 56–7, 59
Queen's Cinema, Belfast, 92
Queen's University Film Society, 19, 140
Quiet Man, The, 142, 143–6, 162, 196
quotas, 7, 137–9, 174–7
Quo Vadis, 171, 175

radio, 55, 63, 65, 73, 76, 116
Ramsden, John, 36
Randle, Frank, 178
Rank, J. Arthur, 94
Rank Organisation, 11 n. 49, 22, 43, 68–9, 83–4, 93–5, 103–4, 105, 106, 108, 109, 112–15, 126, 132, 147, 194–5, 198
Reach for the Sky, 114
Regal, Belfast, 95, 106, 132, 153
Regal, Sheffield, 24, 122
Regent, Belfast, 58, 94, 95, 102, 105, 129–62; *see also* Avenue, Belfast; Picture House, Belfast
Regent, Sheffield, 109, 188; *see also* Gaumont, Sheffield
Reo, Ballyclare, 96
Rex, Sheffield, 15, 59, 61, 88, 163, 164–78, 183, 185, 190–1
Rhodes, Eric, 100
Richard, Cliff, 78

Richards, Jeffrey, 55
Rio Bravo, 175
Rio Grande, 146
Ritchie, Donald, 14
Ritz, Belfast, 21, 31, 56, 57, 78, 80–2, 83, 85–6, 92, 108, 129–62, 199; *see also* ABC, Belfast
Ritz, Sheffield, 21
River of No Return, 172
RKO Pictures, 87
Road to Utopia, 173
Robe, The, 125
Rob Roy, 173, 175
Rock-a-Bye Baby, 159
Rockett, Kevin, 10, 129, 132
Rogers, Roy, 25, 149–50
roller skating, 74
Rolling Stones, the, 86
Roman Holiday, 125
Romantici a Venezia, 140
Rooney, 147
Roscoe Picture Palace, Sheffield, 81, 124
Rotherham, 23, 52, 123, 171
Rowntree, Seebohm, 74, 179
Rowson, Simon, 163
Royal, Belfast, 92, 105, 153, 157
Royal Hippodrome, Belfast, 56, 80, 82, 83, 85 n. 201, 92, 101–2, 105, 107, 132, 146, 147, 148, 152, 153, 156, 198–9; *see also* Odeon, Belfast; New Vic, Belfast
RTÉ, 52

Sabrina, 98
Safari, 154
Sanders of the River, 137
Sandro, Belfast, 108
Saturday Night and Sunday Morning, 119
Savoy, Belfast, 146, 153
Scala, Sheffield, 115
Scala Cinemas, 38

Screen Advertising Association, 30, 88–9
Second World War, 1, 2, 11, 35, 36–7, 48, 91, 109, 112, 138, 160, 168, 193, 197
Sedgwick, John, 12–13, 14–15, 162
Sergeants 3, 184
Seventh Veil, The, 138
Shail, Robert, 25
Shankill Picturedrome, 102, 106
Shapiro, Helen, 86
Shaw, Clifford, 186
Sheffield
    cinema admissions in, 163
    cinema licences granted in, 61
    growth of cinema in, 10–12
    social and economic conditions, 6–7, 9, 199
    historiography, 10
    migrant communities in, 23
    see also Yorkshire
Sheffield and District Cinematograph Theatres, 109
Sheffield City Council, 15, 40 n. 147, 42, 44, 45, 110, 117, 123, 185
Sheffield Film Society, 183–4, 190
Sheffield Telegraph, 69, 84, 113–14, 121
Sheffield University Film Unit, 184–5
Sheridan, Dinah, 114
Singing Fool, The, 132
Singin' in the Rain, 173
Slack, Harold, 121
Smith, Cyril, 29, 32, 66, 110
Solid Gold Cadillac, The, 158
Song of Bernadette, 34
Sorrell, A. A., 135, 147, 149, 163, 170, 171
South Pacific, 83, 159
Spraos, John, 4, 32, 62, 64, 88, 112
Spring in Park Lane, 136, 138
Square Peg, The, 175, 178
Stacey, Jackie, 36
Stadium, Belfast, 106, 146, 153

Star, Sheffield, 23, 109

Star, The, Sheffield, 15, 27, 31, 38, 48, 52, 59, 66, 68, 75, 76, 77–9, 111, 112–13, 115–17, 118–19, 120, 123, 124–5, 126, 164, 169–70, 182, 183, 188, 197

Star Cinemas, 85, 109, 112, 122, 125, 166, 194

Steele, Tommy, 78

Steel Town, 178

Stokes, Melvyn, 13

Story of Esther Costello, The, 147

Strand, Belfast, 47, 56, 92, 129–62, 196

Street, Sarah, 126

Streetcar Named Desire, A, 144, 151

Stubbings, Sarah, 17, 55, 59, 67, 79, 197

Student Prince, The, 34

Studio 7 cinema, Sheffield, 125–6; *see also* Wicker, Sheffield

Summer Holiday, 78

Sunbeam Picture Palace, Sheffield, 123

Swordsman, The, 136

Sylvie et la Fantome, 140

Tall Men, The, 184

Tamango, 160

Tarzan, the Ape Man, 184

Technicolor, 56, 142, 171, 196

Teddy Boys, 41–3, 49, 125

television
    and cinema attendance, 1, 4–5, 12, 22, 26–7, 31, 51–2, 59, 60–9, 70–1, 97, 101, 102–3, 105, 106, 108, 114, 115–17, 121, 193–4
    and the coronation of Queen Elizabeth II, 54–7, 59, 193
    hire purchase of, 63–7
    introduction of, 52–3
    licences, 53–4, 62–3, 68
    ownership, 1, 54–5, 62–8
    promotion of cinemas on, 86
    rentals, 64–6
    see also BBC, ITV and UTV

Ten Commandments, The, 119

ten-pin bowling, 1, 101, 119–20, 124, 126, 198

This is the Army, 160

This Modern Age, 188

Thissen, Judith, 51, 89

Thomas, Nick, 5

Thorburn, June, 121

3D films, 80–1, 171

Tinsley Picture Palace, Sheffield, 116

Tivoli, Belfast, 95, 96, 107, 153

Todd, Richard, 121

Todd-AO, 80, 83

Top Hat, 173

Town Like Alice, A, 172

Tracey, Michael, 4, 71, 80

Tread Softly Stranger, 178

Treasure Island, 188

Treveri Gennari, Daniela, 49–50

Trigger Junior, 149–50

Trouble in Store, 177

Troxy, Belfast, 85, 129–62

Tudor, Sheffield, 117; *see also* Heeley Green Picture House, Sheffield

20th Century Fox, 83

Two Way Stretch, 184

Ulster Television (UTV), 52 n. 9, 53, 65, 68, 70, 86, 105

Une Femme Disparaît, 186

Union Cinemas, 92, 134

Union Street Picture Palace, Sheffield, 10, 123

United States of America (USA)
    army in Northern Ireland, 7, 35
    cinema admissions in, 12–13, 80, 89, 105–6, 155
    distribution companies, 155

drive-in cinemas, 84
Hollywood films, reception of, 8,
      33–6, 137, 162, 174, 183, 196
Unity Picture Palace, Sheffield, 48, 117
Universal, 33, 59
Up in the World, 178
Victory Picture Palace, Sheffield, 115
VistaVision, 80, 82, 83

Walking My Baby Back Home, 84
War and Peace, 155, 162
Warner Brothers, 134, 151
Warter, Philip, Sir, 119
Wayne, John, 143, 145
Welles, Orson, 150
West End Jungle, 161
West End Picture House, Belfast, 106
Weston Picture Palace, Sheffield, 115
Wicker cinema, Sheffield, 22, 23, 42,
      109, 125; *see also* Studio 7, Sheffield
When You Come Home, 178
Whispering Smith, 38
White Christmas, 82
Wicked Lady, The, 138
Willowfield Picture House, Belfast, 153

Wilson, Harold, 176
Wincobank Picture Palace, Sheffield, 116
Windsor, Belfast, 146, 153
Wisdom, Norman, 177–8
Woodhouse Picture Palace, Sheffield,
      38, 115
Woodseats Picture Palace, Sheffield, 20,
      85, 123
World War II, *see* Second World War
Wuthering Heights, 125, 182, 184

X certificate, 38, 119, 150–1, 161

Yorkshire, 9, 83, 85 n. 101, 112, 169,
      178, 182
   cinema admissions in, 163, 198
   television in, 52–3
   see also Sheffield
Young Ones, The, 78, 160
Young Lions, The, 157

Zarak, 157–8
Zorro, 26
Zweig, Ferdynand, 66, 79–80

Recent and forthcoming titles

The Family Firm: Monarchy, Mass Media and the British Public, 1932–53 (2019)
Edward Owens

Cinemas and Cinema-Going in the United Kingdom: Decades of Decline, 1945–65 (2020)
Sam Manning

Civilian Specialists at War: Britain's Transport Experts and the First World War (2020)
Christopher Phillips

Individuals and Institutions in Medieval Scholasticism (2020)
edited by Antonia Fitzpatrick and John Sabapathy

Unite, Proletarian Brothers! Radicalism and Revolution in the Spanish Second Republic (2020)
Matthew Kerry

Masculinity and Danger on the Eighteenth-Century Grand Tour (2020)
Sarah Goldsmith

The Memory and Meaning of Coalfields: Deindustrialization and Scottish Nationhood (2021)
Ewan Gibbs

Lightning Source UK Ltd.
Milton Keynes UK
UKHW020121170320
360465UK00001B/1